D0062786

# *Walk in* ANCIENT PATHS

## The Good Way of Wisdom

*To Sharon*

*May this be a great blessing in your life*

*Ruth Sears*

Ruth Sears

ISBN 978-1-64471-235-1 (Paperback)
ISBN 978-1-64471-236-8 (Digital)

Copyright © 2019 Ruth Sears
All rights reserved
First Edition

All rights reserved. No part of this publication may be reproduced, distributed, or transmitted in any form or by any means, including photocopying, recording, or other electronic or mechanical methods without the prior written permission of the publisher. For permission requests, solicit the publisher via the address below.

Covenant Books, Inc.
11661 Hwy 707
Murrells Inlet, SC 29576
www.covenantbooks.com

# INTRODUCTION

We only live once in life and thinking persons desire to learn how best to live our lives. We are fascinated by timeless wisdom derived from King Solomon whom God blessed with wisdom above all other men and that of the sages of his court collected from cultures far and wide. Human nature has not changed in three thousand years, so observations about how life works better if we follow biblical principles can move us along life's path of improvement and ease our relationships with people. Most of our life, as we know, consists of dealings with others and adjustments as to how we correctly view ourselves as we mature. If we are extremely prideful or abrasive, others will be repelled. If we are encouraging and joyful, others will be attracted.

Reading and understanding the wisdom of the ages, grouped by topic each month, gets us thinking of areas of our lives in which we lack understanding—areas where we can increase our awareness and ability to effectively deal with our work, our families, and the marketplace. Grasping how God desires to bless us when we act righteously and disfavor us when we act treacherously or unjustly inspires us to study, think deeply, and apply these principles to our daily living.

# Contents

January: Benefits of Wisdom

| | | |
|---|---|---|
| 1 | Long Life | 19 |
| 2 | Health | 20 |
| 3 | Blessings | 21 |
| 4 | Attractiveness | 22 |
| 5 | Honor | 23 |
| 6 | Joy | 24 |
| 7 | Provision | 25 |
| 8 | Stability | 26 |
| 9 | Confidence | 27 |
| 10 | Peace | 28 |
| 11 | Direction | 29 |
| 12 | Deliverance | 30 |
| 13 | Discernment | 31 |
| 14 | Delight of God | 32 |
| 15 | Victory | 33 |
| 16 | Facilitates Prayers | 34 |
| 17 | Protection | 35 |
| 18 | Long Life | 36 |
| 19 | Contentment | 37 |
| 20 | Purpose | 38 |

21  Mercy.................................................................39

22  Eases Learning.................................................40

23  Legacy.............................................................41

24  Smooth Path ..................................................42

25  Favor...............................................................43

26  Generosity.......................................................44

27  Resilience ........................................................45

28  Wealth.............................................................46

29  Humility ..........................................................47

30  Honesty...........................................................48

31  Common Sense ...............................................49

February: Wise Speech

1   Power of Words ..............................................50

2   Few Words .....................................................51

3   Honesty...........................................................52

4   Gossip.............................................................53

5   Encouragement ..............................................54

6   Treachery........................................................55

7   Avoidance of Angry Words ..............................56

8   Source of Truth ..............................................57

9   Counsel...........................................................58

10  Criticism ........................................................59

11  Envy...............................................................60

12  Quarreling.......................................................61

13  Humility .........................................................62

14  Self-Control ...................................................63

15  Nagging ..........................................................64

16  Patience...........................................................65

17  Mercy..............................................................66

18  Counsel ...............................................................67

19  Discretion .........................................................68

20  Healthful ..........................................................69

21  Honesty ............................................................70

22  Fools ................................................................71

23  Righteous .........................................................72

24  Appropriateness ...............................................73

25  Peace ...............................................................74

26  Wisdom ...........................................................75

27  Gratitude ..........................................................76

28  Refreshing ........................................................77

March: Proverbs on Relationships

1   Wise Children ...................................................78

2   Foolish Children ...............................................79

3   Correction of Children ......................................80

4   Grandchildren ..................................................81

5   Friendship ........................................................82

6   Siblings ............................................................83

7   Authorities .......................................................84

8   Humility before Authorities .............................85

9   Righteous Rulers ...............................................86

10  The Poor ..........................................................87

11  Wise Wife .........................................................88

12  Fools ................................................................89

13  Neighbors .........................................................90

14  The Jones ..........................................................91

15  Meddlers ...........................................................92

16  Friends ..............................................................93

17  Peers .................................................................94

18  Harlots ...................................................................95

19  Counselors ............................................................96

20  The Fool ...............................................................97

21  Deceiver ................................................................98

22  Faithfulness ..........................................................99

23  Enemies ..............................................................100

24  The Proud ...........................................................101

25  Pets/Animals ......................................................102

26  Parents ................................................................103

27  The Righteous ....................................................104

28  The Generous Person ..........................................105

29  The Angry Person ...............................................106

30  The Proud ...........................................................107

April: Proverbs on Attitudes

1   Rebellion .............................................................108

2   Complaining ........................................................109

3   Pride ....................................................................110

4   Quarrelsome ........................................................111

5   Simplicity ............................................................112

6   Gratitude .............................................................113

7   Humility ..............................................................114

8   Joy .......................................................................115

9   Greed ...................................................................116

10  Peace Loving .......................................................117

11  Compassion to Poor ............................................118

12  Hope ....................................................................119

13  Teachable .............................................................120

14  Watchful ..............................................................121

15  Confidence ...........................................................122

16 Covetous ........................................................123

17 Critical ..........................................................124

18 Hard-Hearted..................................................125

19 Contented .....................................................126

20 Touchy ..........................................................127

21 Faithful .........................................................128

22 Foolish ..........................................................129

23 Friendly.........................................................130

24 Envious .........................................................131

25 Cheerful ........................................................132

26 Industriousness..............................................133

27 Perverse .........................................................134

28 Helpful...........................................................135

29 Seeking...........................................................136

30 Reverence ......................................................137

## May: Proverbs on Living Well

1 Carpe Diem ...................................................138

2 Diligence........................................................139

3 Health ...........................................................140

4 Living Humbly...............................................141

5 Honesty .........................................................142

6 Abundance .....................................................143

7 Joy..................................................................144

8 Strength .........................................................145

9 Pursuit of Wisdom .........................................146

10 Transparency..................................................147

11 Self-Control ...................................................148

12 Soul Keeping..................................................149

13 Peaceful Rest ..................................................150

14   Confidence..................................................151

15   Resilience ..................................................152

16   Beloved ....................................................153

17   Vitality......................................................154

18   Stability....................................................155

19   Safety ......................................................156

20   Tactful......................................................157

21   Marriage....................................................158

22   Softness....................................................159

23   Wealth......................................................160

24   Faithful ....................................................161

25   Peace .......................................................162

26   Optimism ..................................................163

27   Guidance...................................................164

28   Well-Spoken..............................................165

29   Blessedness ...............................................166

30   Fearlessness...............................................167

31   Priorities...................................................168

June: Proverbs on Direction

1    Eyes.........................................................169

2    Ears .........................................................170

3    Feet .........................................................171

4    Thoughts ..................................................172

5    Parental Advice..........................................173

6    Blockages ..................................................174

7    Acknowledgment .......................................175

8    Illumination...............................................176

9    Openness ..................................................177

10   Made Plain................................................178

11  Integrity .................................................179

12  Straightness .............................................180

13  Commandments ......................................181

14  Righteousness...........................................182

15  Pondering................................................183

16  Acceptability of Prayers ...........................184

17  Guardrails ...............................................185

18  Steps.......................................................186

19  Priorities.................................................187

20  Good Hearts ...........................................188

21  The Way .................................................189

22  Away from Evil.........................................190

23  Established ..............................................191

24  Leading ..................................................192

25  Prosperity................................................193

26  Answer to Prayer .....................................194

27  God's Will...............................................195

28  Head Butting ..........................................196

29  Lots.........................................................197

30  Soul Maintenance....................................198

July: Proverbs on Authority

1   Good Government.....................................199

2   Humility ..................................................200

3   Punishment..............................................201

4   Truthfulness .............................................202

5   Wisdom ...................................................203

6   Topsy-Turvy..............................................204

7   Intimidation.............................................205

8   Wise Servants...........................................206

9    Justice.................................................................207

10   Multitude...........................................................208

11   Criticism of Employees ....................................209

12   Parents ...............................................................210

13   Wicked Ruler.....................................................211

14   Great Leaders ....................................................212

15   Close to the Vest................................................213

16   Prudence ............................................................214

17   God-Ordained ...................................................215

18   Just Rule.............................................................216

19   King Pleaser .......................................................217

20   Favor...................................................................218

21   That Look...........................................................219

22   Sovereignty.........................................................220

23   Diplomacy .........................................................221

24   Fickleness...........................................................222

25   Diligence............................................................223

26   Bribery ...............................................................224

27   Counsel...............................................................225

28   Teachable ...........................................................226

29   Merit...................................................................227

30   Cover-Ups ..........................................................228

31   Disunity..............................................................229

## August: Proverbs Parallels

1    Speech................................................................230

2   Powerful Tongue.................................................231

3   Life-Preserving Speech........................................232

4   Poison Tongues...................................................233

5   Lips of Knowledge..............................................234

| | | |
|---|---|---|
| 6 | Soft Words | 235 |
| 7 | Idle Words | 236 |
| 8 | Muzzling | 237 |
| 9 | Humility before Honor | 238 |
| 10 | Long Life | 239 |
| 11 | Peace | 240 |
| 12 | Guidance | 241 |
| 13 | Edification | 242 |
| 14 | Truth | 243 |
| 15 | Humility | 244 |
| 16 | Prosperity | 245 |
| 17 | Rewards | 246 |
| 18 | Stability | 247 |
| 19 | Optimism | 248 |
| 20 | Poor | 249 |
| 21 | Happiness | 250 |
| 22 | Resilience | 251 |
| 23 | Perfect Peace | 252 |
| 24 | Smooth Road | 253 |
| 25 | Direction | 254 |
| 26 | Generosity | 255 |
| 27 | Sowing/Reaping | 256 |
| 28 | Multiplication | 257 |
| 29 | Appearance | 258 |
| 30 | Long Life | 259 |
| 31 | Foolish Speech | 260 |

September: Proverbs Parallels

| | | |
|---|---|---|
| 1 | Anger | 261 |
| 2 | Good Children | 262 |

3    Disciplining Children......................................263

4    Confidence....................................................264

5    Counsel.........................................................265

6    Covetousness.................................................266

7    Criticism .......................................................267

8    Daily Communion..........................................268

9    Self-Improvement..........................................269

10   Devising Evil .................................................270

11   Double Dealing..............................................271

12   Envy..............................................................272

13   Faithfulness ..................................................273

14   Friendship .....................................................274

15   Rewards of Generosity....................................275

16   Guarantor .....................................................276

17   Advice for a Fool ...........................................277

18   Healing .........................................................278

19   Dishonesty ....................................................279

20   Humility .......................................................280

21   Greed ............................................................281

22   Reward of Peace ............................................282

23   Compassion for the Poor................................283

24   Pride..............................................................284

25   Boasting about Tomorrow ..............................285

26   Example of Punishment .................................286

27   Promises to the Righteous ..............................287

28   Good Self-Interest .........................................288

29   Deliverance/Escape........................................289

30   Multiplication ...............................................290

# October: Proverbs on Self-Governance

| | | |
|---|---|---|
| 1 | Self-Control | 291 |
| 2 | Loose Lips | 292 |
| 3 | Financial | 293 |
| 4 | Self-Correcting | 294 |
| 5 | Hardening | 295 |
| 6 | Watched | 296 |
| 7 | Preparation | 297 |
| 8 | Honesty | 298 |
| 9 | Commitment | 299 |
| 10 | Plans | 300 |
| 11 | The Path | 301 |
| 12 | Wide Road | 302 |
| 13 | Hunger | 303 |
| 14 | Pursuit | 304 |
| 15 | Vengeance | 305 |
| 16 | Selfishness | 306 |
| 17 | Mouthiness | 307 |
| 18 | Forgetting | 308 |
| 19 | Lazybones | 309 |
| 20 | Alcohol | 310 |
| 21 | Commandments | 311 |
| 22 | Reverence | 312 |
| 23 | Reproofs | 313 |
| 24 | Good Sense | 314 |
| 25 | Planning Ahead | 315 |
| 26 | Fear of the Lord | 316 |
| 27 | Daily Communion | 317 |
| 28 | Covetousness | 318 |

29   Redirection ..................................................319

30   Diligence ....................................................320

31   Our Thoughts .............................................321

November: Proverbs on Fools

1    Know-It-All .................................................322

2    Criticism .....................................................323

3    Parents ........................................................324

4    Unreliable ...................................................325

5    Pitiless ........................................................326

6    Self-Destructive ...........................................327

7    Dangerous ...................................................328

8    Wandering ...................................................329

9    Disgraced ....................................................330

10   Heedless ......................................................331

11   Futility of Wisdom .......................................332

12   Thoughts .....................................................333

13   Imprudence .................................................334

14   Pride ...........................................................335

15   Sacrifices .....................................................336

16   God's Scorn .................................................337

17   Transparency ...............................................338

18   Calamitous Future ........................................339

19   Speech .........................................................340

20   Acquisition of Wisdom .................................341

21   Comparison with Self ...................................342

22   Peers ...........................................................343

23   Polar Opposites ...........................................344

24   See-Through Folly ........................................345

25   Banishment .................................................346

26  Dishonorable.................................................347

27  Definition ....................................................348

28  Laughter......................................................349

29  Subordinate .................................................350

30  Dense .........................................................351

December: Proverbs on Finishing Well

1   Aging ..........................................................352

2   Long Life .....................................................353

3   Gratitude .....................................................354

4   Parenting......................................................355

5   Governance ..................................................356

6   Legacy.........................................................357

7   Humility ......................................................358

8   Integrity ......................................................359

9   Health .........................................................360

10  Wealth ........................................................361

11  Punishment..................................................362

12  Boasting ......................................................363

13  Peace ..........................................................364

14  Abundance ..................................................365

15  Transparency................................................366

16  Simplicity....................................................367

17  Fat Soul.......................................................368

18  Gaining in Altitude ......................................369

19  Straight On ..................................................370

20  Right Speaking.............................................371

21  Accumulation...............................................372

22  Greed ..........................................................373

23  Humility .....................................................374

24  Obedience .........................................................375
25  Generosity ........................................................376
26  Vitality ............................................................377
27  Honesty ...........................................................378
28  Exalted ............................................................379
29  Flourishing .......................................................380
30  Beloved ...........................................................381
31  Examples .........................................................382

# January 1

## Proverbs on Benefits of Wisdom—Long Life

"Forget not God's law and keep his commandments for they shall add to you length of days" (3:2).

A number of verses in Proverbs explicitly state that obedience to God's laws as a general rule extends one's life. Logically, this makes sense since God's precepts were established by our Creator for *our* benefit. So if we strive to live our life in accord with those precepts, designed with *our* God-created bodies and souls in mind, the wheels of life naturally run more smoothly. However, if we rebel and go our own way, we reap negative consequences, and wrenches are thrown into the wheels of life. Just like engines slow down and grind to a halt when grit enters the pistons or crankshaft, so do our lives seize up and run with difficulty when we deviate from God's path.

Let's look at some of these verses. They are so many that the principle is reinforced many times over. Here are seven other verses reflecting this key benefit of living God's way. "Length of days is in wisdom's right hand" (3:16). "Wisdom is a tree of life to those who lay hold of her" (3:18). "Keep my commandments and you shall live and let your heart receive my words" (4:4). "Hear my child and receive my instruction that years of life may be multiplied to thee" (4:10). "The fear of the Lord shall prolong days" (10:27).

The reverse is also pointed out: "The years of the wicked shall be shortened" (10:27).

While these Proverbs do not rise to the level of promises from God, they reflect long experience and God's truth. Therefore, if we desire to live a long, full, abundant life, we should spend time studying God's Word and thinking deeply about how best to apply it and implement it in our lives.

# January 2

## Proverbs on Benefits of Wisdom—Health

"Do not be conceited; fear God, depart from evil, for it shall be health to you" (3:7).

Just as Proverbs observes that obedience to God's law extends life, a logical subset of that principle is that improved health results from living according to God's wisdom. This makes common sense, since our guilt level surely drops when we *know* we are doing our best to learn and walk God's path. Psychiatrists and medical professionals have known for years based on observation and are documenting in scientific studies that mind and body or soul and body are intricately related. Our fears and stress naturally lessen when we are following the path of least resistance—the smooth way designed by God for our optimum benefit. Conversely, bitterness, unforgiveness, and grudge holding take a serious toll on our "insides," as we nurse past hurts, causing our stomachs and jaws to clinch and multiplying negative emotions.

The flip side of this theme is that Christlike abundant living boosts our good feelings, greases the wheels of our "internal operations," and eases tensions, resentments, and negative effects on our bodies. If one is looking for a good reason to "let go and let God," improved health is a major one!

Here are some supporting verses reflecting this theme:

"Hearken to my words and incline your ear to my sayings; let them not depart from your eyes, keep them in your heart, for they are life to those who find them and health to all flesh" (4:20). "The law of the wise is a fountain of life" (13:14). "The fear of the Lord is a fountain of life to decline from the ruin of death" (14:27). "Soundness of heart is the life of flesh" (14:30). "He that trusts in the Lord shall be healed" (28:26). "Your body shall rejoice when your lips speak aright" (23:16).

# JANUARY 3

## Benefits of Wisdom—Blessings

"Blessed is the man who finds wisdom and is rich in prudence" (3:13).

*Blessed* carries many varied meanings, as can be shown from the diverse biblical translations of the word. *Happy, prosperous, favored,* and *abundance* capture the primary gist. Of course, this is the introductory word to the beatitudes from the Sermon on the Mount, the sayings of Jesus. However one translates the word, who would not desire blessings? The promise of blessings is a strong incentive to pursue wisdom and God's knowledge as a high priority.

Similar Proverbs are: "He that hears my Word shall rest without terror and enjoy abundance without fear of evils" (1:33). "The learned in word shall find good things" (16:20). "He that keeps prudence shall find good things" (16:20). "The pursuit of wisdom is better than of silver and wisdom's fruit is pure gold" (3:13). "The wise servant shall prosper in his dealings and his way shall be made straight" (14:15). "Get wisdom because it is better than gold" (16:16).

The analogy to gold implicates preciousness, supreme value. While most secular thinking values money above all things, Proverbs clearly states that wisdom gets number 1 ranking since so many advantages flow from learning God's principles of wisdom and applying them consistently and diligently in one's life.

Psalms has many echoes of this promise as well. King David and other psalmists revel in the knowledge that they are and will continue to be blessed of God. Numerous Psalms verses begin with "Blessed is the man..." However, one pictures blessings, God is a personal God who surely designs, arranges, and brings them about to our individual best advantage.

# January 4

## Benefits of Wisdom–Attractiveness

"Wisdom shines in the face of the wise" (17:24).

If you're a people watcher and aware, you can spot major differences in the emotions and attitudes displayed on people's faces. Some people appear utterly hopeless with deep scowls; others virtually beam with life and graciousness.

Wise people gain a discernment about the state of others' souls by close observation: "The hearts of men are laid open to the wise like a reflection in water" (27:19). I have heard one pastor comment that "the Christ in me is drawn to the Christ in you," as one explanation for the ability of a spiritual person to see reflections of holiness or spirituality in another.

Similar verses are: "Good instruction shall give grace" (13:15). "Knowledge is a fountain of life to him that possesses it" (16:22). "The life of the wise is a fountain of life" (13:14). "The fear of the Lord is a fountain of life to decline from the ruin of death" (14:27). This image of a fountain of life, of course, appears in Revelation with the source being the throne of God. Fountains renew, refresh, cleanse, and are attractive, so all these characteristics flow (pun intended) from a soul of wisdom. Since the body and soul are so inexorably intertwined, it makes logical sense that a healthy soul flows over to benefit and beautify one's body and face.

"Soundness of heart is the life of flesh" (14:30). This is how Proverbs summarizes this mind/body connection. Even old age cannot mar such inner beauty: "A joyful mind makes age flourishing" (17:22). "Your body shall rejoice when your lips speak aright" (23:16).

# January 5

## Benefits of Wisdom—Honor

"The wise shall possess governments" (3:13).

Fools may not like people of wise character because they may feel guilt at not measuring up, but they cannot help but respect them. And other people of wise character are highly inclined to respect those with evident wise character. This leads to placement in positions of responsibility, calls for leadership and recognition when jobs are well done. Both in secular and church-related positions of responsibility, wise persons inevitably are honored by others.

Similar verses are: "He that yields to reproof shall be glorified" (13:18). Yielding to reproof means remaining teachable, able to accept criticism, suggestions for improvement without hardening one's back and rebuffing others' suggestions out of pride and intractability. This is a chief characteristic of the wise: ability to remain humble, teachable, and amenable to others' suggestions.

"A wise servant shall rule over foolish sons and shall share in the inheritance" (17:2). That is, merit, not family relationship, takes priority. A long faithful worker is noticed; similarly an irresponsible family member, even among the inner circle of immediate family, is recognized, but for the wrong reasons. Faithfulness is rewarded on earth as well as in heaven.

"The path of life is above for the wise that he may decline from the lowest hell" (15:24). Character and right conduct naturally lead to an upward spiral of increasing responsibility, rewards, recognition, and advancement. Conversely, poor conduct and irresponsibility disgust others counting on them, naturally leading to a downward spiral of errors, demotions, "passing over" for open positions, and disrespect. "The wise in heart shall be called prudent" (16:21). When others notice prudence and faithfulness, respect rises. Our consciences teach us what sort of conduct to respect.

# January 6

## Benefits of Wisdom—Joy

"Your body shall rejoice when your lips speak aright" (23:16). Since the Creator of the universe as part of creation prepared principles of right conduct, our conscience and inner promptings of the Holy Spirit let us know when we are following the smooth path of good behavior and obedience. Our bodies and souls glide along secure in the knowledge that the skids are greased for us to prosper. This brings inner joy! And examining further the reason for joy, I believe it naturally arises from having hope in eternal life and hope in salvation for the end of our days. "Fear the Lord all day so you'll have hope in the end" (23:17).

But not only ourselves but also others rejoice with us! "When just men increase, the people shall rejoice" (29:2). When a wise and amiable leader of good will is in place, the governed breathe a sigh of relief and relax that they can go about their personal business without unjust interference in their lives. Conversely, when a mean, arrogant, and intolerant dictator is in place, people are perpetually uneasy, glancing over their shoulder, keeping their heads down to avoid notice. "When it goes well with the just, the city shall rejoice" (11:10).

Not only our colleagues or subordinates will have joy, but also perhaps, more importantly, our parents and family members! "Study wisdom to make your parents' heart joyful and to give an answer to a criticizer" (27:11). We nearly all have a story of a family member in trouble, addicted perhaps, estranged from the family. That is a situation that brings misery and dread to our hearts every time we think of them. On the other hand, when a young family member is raising children in the joy of the Lord with wise parenting skills, we smile at every remembrance of them and look forward to visits.

# January 7
## Benefits of Wisdom—Provision

"The Lord shall not afflict the soul of the just with famine" (10:3).

There are many assurances of provision for the wise, righteous, or just person. God and his ministering angels watch from above and provide for their needs and often their just wants. "To the just their desire shall be given" (10:24). Thus, not only necessities but also if one is living obediently, God delights in showering them with abundant blessings. Sure, subsistence is our first concern. "The just is delivered out of distress" (11:8).

"To him that sows justice, there is a faithful reward" (11:18). "The tabernacles of the just shall flourish" (14:11). This level of provision far exceeds mere subsistence. God has many ways of bringing about provision including through the natural laws of reaping and sowing. "To the just good shall be repaid" (13:21). That is, if we bring meals to the sick and visit the afflicted in their distress, the natural response of others is to do the same for us in our time of need. That is not to say we treat others well simply so that reciprocation will occur, but it is the natural effect.

"The fear of the Lord is unto life and he shall abide in abundance without being visited by evil" (19:23). "The crown of the wise is their riches" (14:24).

The major principle is assurance of necessities and even abundance, but there is an underlying assurance of contentment in any circumstance. "One is as it were rich when he has nothing and another as it were poor, when he has great riches" (13:7). The import of this promise or even observation is that the wise grateful heart counts his/her blessings and optimistically looks at the bright side while the ungrateful holder of immense assets is rarely ever able to enjoy his/her assets.

# January 8

## Benefits of Wisdom—Stability

"By wisdom the house shall be built and by prudence strengthened" (24:3).

Many of the analogies in Proverbs concerning the stability of the wise, just, or righteous person deal with houses, buildings, structures, or foundations. This brings to mind the gospel parable about building one's house upon the rock, not the shifting sand. "The just is as an everlasting foundation" (10:25). "The root of the just shall not be moved" (12:3). "The house of the just shall deliver them" (12:6). "The house of the just is very much strength" (15:6).

What is the source of that strength? "He that is good draws grace from the Lord" (12:2).

In addition to stability in our lives, extended family legacies are strengthened by goodness. "The good man leaves heirs, sons and grandsons" (13:22). This is to be contrasted with the house of the fool, in which early deaths are predicted, fragmentation and estrangement are common, and grudge holding and unforgiveness lead to bitterness, divorce, quarrels, and infighting.

But even when bad things happen to good persons or families, resiliency is a saving characteristic of the wise: they recover more quickly. "The just shall spring up as a green leaf" (11:28). Picture a young tender plant or branch that is stepped on, battered, or injured: it quickly repairs itself and becomes good as new. Child psychologists have reported recently that resiliency is a primary indicator of success in school and more generally in life. Parents and teachers must hold out hope of quick recovery after hard knocks so children will come to have assurance that the worst thing is not the last thing—that better times are around the corner. Children suffering hard knocks need encouragement just as do adults—reminders that God is with us, cares for us, and is ultimately a good and loving God who will be with us during dark times.

# January 9
## Benefits of Wisdom—Confidence

"Keep the law and counsel and you shall walk confidently and your foot shall not stumble" (3:23).

If we know we are striving to understand God's wisdom and apply it in our lives, this naturally gives us confidence that we are living well—in accordance with the principles set in place by our Creator who understands and made us. Further, "He that walks sincerely walks confidently" (10:9). *Sincerely* in this context means honestly, transparently, with integrity. If we tell the truth, we do not have to rack our brains to recall which "version of the truth" we previously told to remain consistent.

"In the fear of the Lord is confidence of strength and there shall be hope for his children" (14:26). We will be better parents when we're not wishy-washy and unsure of right and wrong. We can with confidence instill correct truth in our children or others for whom we are daily setting an example. Stability at home arises from consistent discipline and confident parents.

"There shall be safety where there are many counsels" (24:6). "Plans are strengthened by counsel" (20:18). This is another advantage of wise people: they are not too arrogant to seek the wisdom of others further along in the faith than them. Knowing that they can bounce issues off other wise persons, especially two or three, and getting consistent feedback vastly bolsters one's own sense of correctness. Confirmation of tough decisions by others is encouraged and the sign of a wise person.

"Blessed is the man that hears many and that watches daily at my gates" (8:34). Daily Bible reading, study, and striving to understand God's best principles for good living uplifts our confidence levels and lessens nagging doubts and fears.

"The wicked man flees when no one is chasing him but the just, bold as a lion, shall be without dread" (18:1).

# January 10

## Benefits of Wisdom—Peace

"All the paths of wisdom are peaceable" (3:17).

"He that fears the commandment dwells in peace" (13:13).

The wise person who understands God's principles for living and works hard at applying them in his/her life does not frequently fret about determining God's will. Therefore, it is easier to live in peace knowing we are "in the flow" of God's will for our lives. Peace leads to contentment which leads to joy. "Joy follows those who take counsels of peace" (12:20).

When trials assail us, one ultimate question we can ask ourself is, "What is the worst thing that can happen?" We die and go to heaven to be with our Lord and loved ones forever. Even death itself becomes not a thing to be acutely feared.

Following the commandments places responsibility on ourself not to nitpick or dredge up quarrels with others—this is surely contrary to God's will. "Strive not against a man without cause when he has done you no evil" (3:30). As mature individuals, we must recognize that we cannot change others; this relieves much stress, anxiety, and quarreling. We can set a good example and, if asked, give Godly advice, but it is not our duty to judge and correct others.

What about the unlovable? The irritating persons in our lives that we feel no one can peaceably live with? There is hope. "When the ways of man shall please the Lord, he will convert even his enemies to peace" (16:7). I believe this is hearty assurance that our job is to perfect ourselves with the help of the Holy Spirit. First, our mature Christian lives will be a beacon to others, but based on this verse, God will see from above and aid in reconciliation or at least peaceful coexistence.

# JANUARY 11

## Benefits of Wisdom—Direction

"In all your ways think on God and He will direct your steps" (3:6).

What comfort it is to be assured that a loving God cares for us and cares enough to observe our paths and provide direction. He has a God's eye view, better than even a bird's-eye view, of our future, surrounding circumstances. One analogy is that we are pedestrians on the ground walking with 360° horizontal dimensional vision. God, however, from on high has multidimensional vision plus a view of the future, so his perspective is many times improved over our one-dimensional view. Psalms says that a thousand years is as a day to God. I envision life to God much like our TV recording functionality. He can fast-forward to see the future, so of course, his knowledge and perspective is exponentially superior.

"Keep the law and counsel and the Lord will be at your side and will keep your foot that you won't be taken" (3:26). "I will show you the way of wisdom and lead you by the paths of equity" (4:11). "The path of the just as a shining light goes forward and increases to perfect day" (4:18).

"Make straight the path of your feet and let your eyes look straight on and all your ways shall be established" (4:26). "The wise servant shall prosper in his dealings and his way shall be made straight" (14:15).

"The steps of men are guided by the Lord" (20:24). This more general observation, note, covers not just wise persons but all persons. God is omniscient and omnipresent so he has the information and power to direct paths. "The heart of man disposes his way but the Lord must direct his steps" (16:3). Again, this shows the sovereignty of God, but wicked persons have no knowledge or assurance of this, so it brings no comfort.

# January 12
## Benefits of Wisdom—Deliverance

"The just shall be delivered by knowledge" (11:9).

Throughout Proverbs, the "just" seems to be used as a synonym for the "righteous" or the "wise person" since justice is an overriding characteristic of the person following God's path for wise living. Those who study God's laws, the commandments, and strive to determine his will are, by virtue of that knowledge alone, able to steer clear from many pitfalls. "He that keeps the commandment keeps his own soul" (19:16). There is a direct cause-and-effect relationship between our understanding of God's laws and our ability to walk the correct path. "The mouth of the just shall deliver them" (12:6). "He that keeps the commandment keeps his own soul" (19:16). "He that walks uprightly shall be saved" (18:18).

Conversely, we bring upon ourselves much negativity if we ignore those laws and go our own way. But God and his ministering angels watch over us. Even when our knowledge does not save us, he gives us many assurances of his watch care. "The just is delivered out of distress" (11:8). "The just shall be delivered from death" (10:2).

Also we can be of benefit to others if they are wise enough to listen to our advice: "The just considers seriously the house of the wicked that he may withdraw the wicked from evil" (21:12). We can be a light and beacon to others if they are humble enough and teachable enough to be open to the advice of wise persons.

Finally, our own families benefit from our righteousness. "The seed of the just shall be saved" (11:21). God's blessings extend down through generations of godly families. Psalms states this over and over.

Evil people may be even substituted in our place to save us from disaster. "The wicked is delivered up for the just—the unjust for the righteous" (21:18).

# JANUARY 13

## Benefits of Wisdom—Discernment

"If you shall seek wisdom and incline your heart to know prudence, you shall understand the fear of the Lord and find the knowledge of God" (2:5).

Knowledge may be considered bits and pieces, building blocks of wisdom, while wisdom is more all-encompassing. Perhaps we undertake a study of God's principles concerning speech: gossip, lying, criticism, backbiting. This would make us knowledgeable about what the Bible has to say about speech. But having the motivation to apply that knowledge in every area of our life would reflect wisdom. "The righteous heart seeks after knowledge" (27:11). "The prudent shall look for knowledge" (14:18). "The heart of the wise seeks instructions" (15:14). "The mind of the just studies wisdom" (15:28).

Proverbs contemplates that we must also learn from experience, from our mistakes, and from the mistakes of others. "He that is righteous corrects his way" (21:29). The wise person is observant of the world we live in and avoids pitfalls by observing ill effects that redound to others. "When the wicked perish, the just shall be multiplied" (18:28). In other words, we can benefit by carefully paying attention to the trials of others to avoid them ourselves.

We also must remain teachable to knowledge, to advice from other wise persons. Sometimes, the more we know about God's ways, the more we are tempted to become self-righteous, a negative prideful form of righteousness. "The wise of heart receives precepts" (10:8). "A wise man shall hear and be wiser" (1:5). We must keep our ears attuned and our eyes observant to what is going on around us to benefit from life's experiences. "He that regards reproofs shall become prudent" (15:5). Being open to advice and counsel is the height of wisdom.

# January 14

## Benefits of Wisdom—Delight of God

"He that follows justice is beloved by the Lord" (15:9).

How wonderful that we can bless God's own heart based on our conduct. This is a tiny bit of reciprocation going back to God, in comparison to all his great blessings to us: life being the first. Much like the delight we receive from observing our own children and grandchildren, especially when darling toddlers, God has his eye on us and delights in our right doing.

"The Lord's communion is with the simple" (3:32). This refers to those with childlike faith who take at face value his commandments and precepts. God, of course, observes both our conduct and the depth of our hearts. "Every way of a man seems right to himself, but the Lord weighs hearts" (21:2). "He that is good draws grace from the Lord" (12:2). This carries the flavor of an upward spiral of our faith walk up to the heavens. Grace upon grace is a heavenly phrase. Grace is its own reward but other rewards abound. God rewards those who obediently follow his ways; the delight of God naturally results in such rewards.

"To him that sows justice there is a faithful reward" (11:18). "To the just good shall be repaid" (13:21). "The just runs to the name of the Lord and shall be exalted" (18:10). This reflects the honor that will accrue to the faithful saints who live a Godlike existence, bringing them nearer and nearer to the throne of God for eternity.

# January 15

## Benefits of Wisdom—Victory

"An obedient man shall speak of victory" (21:28).

Victory has many aspects when applied to life. It brings images of triumph, abundant living, prevailing over one's enemies and success. It is okay to be pleased with oneself when that pleasure arises from the knowledge that one is following God's wisdom to the best of one's ability.

Abundance flows from the promise of victory: "To the just their desire shall be given" (10:24). Each of us was designed uniquely to love different things, to be delighted by different things. God delights in showering us with the unique things that make us happy. Are you passionate about horses? Theater? Travel? Cooking? What thrills you may not thrill me, but God created us so he understands what delights our souls. I love books and learning and have been blessed with "pass ons" from friends, family, and library donations.

Even though in some dark valleys in life, we think that right will never prevail, Proverbs shows otherwise. "The good man shall be above the fool" (14:14). Surely, this illustrates that respect and honor will come, in the end, to the wise person, both on earth and in heaven. "The just shall see the downfall of the wicked" (29:16). Revelation makes clear that good will ultimately prevail in the whole world.

A flavor of honor (already discussed in another devotion) is intertwined with victory in addition to hope at death and after death. "The just has hope in his death" (14:32). "He that walks uprightly shall be saved" (28:18). End of life does not have to be a dreaded time but a comforting thought. It is also comforting to know we leave our living legacy in the form of family. "The good man leaves heirs, sons and grandsons" (13:22).

And the final victory is promised to the wise. "Justice shall deliver from death" (10:2).

# January 16

## Benefits of Wisdom—Facilitates Prayers

"He will hear the prayers of the just" (15:29).

If we believe in the power of prayer, the thought that God attends to the prayers of the righteous, just, wise person is very reassuring. There are passages in Psalms and 1 Peter that warn about the reverse scenario: sin blocks our prayers, or God stops his ears to the cries of the wicked. Thus, here is one more very convincing reason to strive for holiness, perfection, and obedience to God's commandments.

The delightful Mitford series religious novels refer often to the "prayer that never fails"—"Thy will be done." When we do not know what to pray for, we can begin by praying for knowledge and wisdom about what to pray for. "The Lord gives wisdom, prudence and knowledge" (2:6). "The wise of heart receives precepts" (10:8). God is the source of inspiration: "I give you thoughts, knowledge and words of truth" (22:21).

The most specific answers to prayers can be dropped into our thoughts even at night while we are sleeping. "Lay out your works to the Lord and your thoughts shall be directed" (16:3). Have you had the experience of laying out your worries, concerns, anxieties, unsolved problems to God on your pillow just before dropping off to sleep and, in the morning upon arising, a solution is just there in your brain? Perhaps our brain cells are processing, sorting, and searching for a solution using "fresh information" given them just before sleep, but who do we think created our brains in that fashion?

We must acknowledge God, bring him into our difficulties if we want his help. Notice the "condition" which precedes the following promise. "In all your ways think on God and He will direct your steps" (3:6).

# JANUARY 17

## Benefits of Wisdom—Protection

"The name of the Lord is a strong tower" (18:10).

While Psalms is replete with assertions that God is our strength, refuge, fortress, strong tower, bulwark against evil and the like, Proverbs has a few similar assurances. In thinking particularly of the medieval age, nobles in Northern Italy, Tuscany, and thereabouts built small square but very tall stone thick-walled towers in which they would hole up for protection when neighboring nobles would mass up for attack. For example, in the single small hill town of San Gimignano, Italy, the skyline still has nearly twenty of these narrow but strong high towers powerfully declaring "safety inside."

This verse encourages us, when facing the slings and arrows of life, to train ourselves to think first of calling on the Lord for help. In his name, many have been saved. Newspapers and magazines recount stories of those home alone facing an intruder who strongly called on the name of the Lord, and the attacker was intimidated and left without doing harm.

"The horse is prepared for the day of battle, but the Lord gives safety" (21:31). In biblical times, the horse and chariot were the ultimate in battle technology, the most powerful defense "machinery" of the day. In our time, battleships, nuclear arsenals, and airpower may be the equivalent. I believe this verse encourages us to be prepared with all the technology our era affords, but the better solution would be to also call on the Lord for safety and protection when under attack. His power is ultimate. He also knows best the weaknesses of our enemies and can act accordingly in our defense.

# January 18

## Benefits of Wisdom—Long Life

"Forget not God's law and keep his commandments, for they shall add to you length of days" (3:2).

Earlier devotions have discussed the benefits of health and happiness, but a longer span of life is associated with wisdom as well in several specific verses. "Length of days is in wisdom's right hand" (3:16). In other words, it is a natural consequence of living correctly. "Wisdom is a tree of life to those who lay hold of her" (3:18). A tree of life is an image appearing in several books of the Bible, but it carries with it the sense of sturdiness, heartiness, well rootedness, renewal, flourishing. Trees have long life and are a good metaphor for a long life. "Keep my commandments and you shall live and let your heart receive my words" (4:4).

"Love and keep wisdom and it shall preserve thee" (4:6). "Hear my child and receive my instruction that years of life may be multiplied to thee" (4:10). Put more directly, "The fear of the Lord shall prolong days" (10:27). In contrast, the "years of the wicked shall be shortened" (10:27).

Although some people do not look forward to old age, the wise person as a general rule finds benefits even in old age. "Old age is a crown of dignity when it is found in the ways of justice" (16:31). "The joy of young men is their strength; the dignity of old men is their gray hairs" (20:38). As a practical matter, the wise person understands the passing of the torch and does not struggle against it: "You shall not always have power; a crown shall be given to generation to generation" (27:24).

# January 19

## Benefits of Wisdom—Contentment

"Count your blessings to be satisfied with what you produce" (27:27).

This verse calls to mind Howard Hughes, one of the wealthiest billionaires in the United States, who could never be satisfied with his accumulated wealth or possessions. He became utterly paranoid about others taking them, about germs and illness or potential assassins. His focus was totally on *losing* what he had instead of enjoying what he had. That single example makes clear that the amount of one's wealth is not the key to happiness or contentment. Rather, it is one's attitude toward wealth that gives happiness.

Generosity and mercy benefit the giver in addition to the receiver. "The soul that blesses shall be made fat" (11:25). Have you heard of helper's high? Some child psychologists are writing out prescriptions to troubled teens who are miserable because of their total narcissism: e.g. "Spend ten hours this week helping X." Reports of success with this tactic have been amazing, as self-esteem is generated by their ability to positively affect others' lives. Having a purpose in life and gratitude for one's possessions, however big or small, is the key to contentment.

"He that is greedy of gain troubles his own house" (15:27). "Labor not to be rich; set bounds to your prudence" (23:4). If all our energy is focused on getting more, we are stabbing ourselves in the foot. Cultivating an attitude of gratitude smoothes the way to true contentment. "Don't lift up eyes to riches you can't have; those riches will fly away" (23:5).

"One is as it were rich when he has nothing and another as it were poor, when he has great riches" (13:7). Missionary team members returning from a medical mission to the Tarahumara Indians in the Copper Canyon of Mexico reported that they were shocked to observe that the poorest of the poor, mothers doing handweaving in dirt-floored hovels, sang, laughed, treated their children sweetly and were more content overall than team members' affluent teens back home. An inspiration to us!

# January 20

## Benefits of Wisdom—Purpose

"The wise man makes straight his steps" (15:21).

Wisdom and understanding of God's commandments and directions for correct living give one an underlying sense of purpose in life. Our steps can be aimed toward a particular goal, not aimlessly wandering from one "ism" to another "fad" in life. "There are many thoughts in the heart of a man but the wise of the Lord shall stand firm" (19:21). Have you had occasion at high school reunions to engage with classmates you haven't seen for a long time, only to find out they are pursuing a path in life 180 degrees opposite of what they were pursuing five years ago at the last reunion? Some folks ricochet from one pursuit—New Age spirituality, for example, to yoga, to marathons, to communal living. They "burn out" on a chosen path and hop to another in an ungrounded manner. While there is nothing wrong with trying out different hobbies and pursuits, the philosophical or religious basis of our lives does not lend itself nicely to such major shifts.

"He that is pure, his work is right" (21:8). We can feel assurance that our course is blessed and approved of by God if we are following his commandments as the bedrock of our lives. "He that follows justice is beloved by the Lord" (15:9). "Evil men have no hope of things to come" (24:20). On the other hand, wise persons have hope of victory in life and beyond. The wise do not suffer from guilt anxiety late at night when insomnia stalks but can use that "awake" time to pray for those needing intercessory prayer.

"The wise servant shall prosper in his dealings and his way shall be made straight" (14:15A). Straight way is superior to an unpredictable, searching, wandering path of indecision.

# January 21

## Benefits of Wisdom—Mercy

"He that gives to the poor shall not want." (28:27)

"The just are merciful and show mercy" (13:13). "The just takes notice of the cause of the poor" (29:7). But this principle boomerangs to the benefit of the mercy giver since the law of reaping and sowing applies to the virtue of mercy, making good redound to the enhancement of our own soul. "To the just, good shall be repaid" (13:21). "He that shows mercy to the poor shall be blessed" (14:21).

Being merciful or generous brings its own reward of honor. "A man's gift enlarges his way and makes room before princes" (18:16). "Many honor and are friends of him who gives gifts" (19:6). "He that makes presents shall purchase victory and honor" (22:9). Thus, blessings and honor are natural consequences of the generous, merciful person; whether in areas of finance, like charity to the underprivileged or in areas of personal relationships, such as extending forgiveness before the other party does so.

The contrary is also true: if we are stingy and unmerciful, this characteristic harms our own soul. "He that despises the entreaty of the poor shall suffer indigence" (28:27). That is, the law of reaping and sowing works both ways. Much like Scrooge, our souls shrivel and become self-focused, to our detriment, if we have the means to help someone and choose not to.

# January 22

## Benefits of Wisdom—Eases Learning

"The learning of the wise is easy" (14:6).

The getting of wisdom is an upward spiral. Once a person understands one concept, integration between and among branches of knowledge eases. "Give an occasion to a wise man and wisdom shall be added to him" (9:9). If a fool were in a teachable moment, he or she might not have their antenna up to grasp the significance of a concept. However, a wise person is observant and notices all things.

Knowledge leads to prudence and wisdom. One thing leads to another. "Blessed is the man who finds wisdom and is rich in prudence" (3:13). They are interrelated. "The prudent shall look for knowledge" (14:18). "The mind of the just studies wisdom" (15:28). "A wise heart shall acquire knowledge" (18:15).

"They that seek the Lord take notice of all things" (18:5). This calls out the important characteristic of being observant to glean knowledge from all our activities. We are engaged and pay attention. This trait is to be contrasted with the fool who cares nothing about learning but only about letting everyone know his opinion, his views, and his own situation.

There are a great many verses about speech, which we will examine in another month, but one caution to wise persons is to limit their words, considering carefully anything that proceeds from their mouth. This is because we learn more, we become wiser, when we are listening and observing as opposed to flapping our mouths. We should strive to learn from others and from circumstances. We are put on earth to become wise and increase in holiness and obedience to God's laws.

# January 23

## Benefits of Wisdom—Legacy

"The seed of the just shall be saved" (11:21).

"The good man leaves heirs, sons and grandsons" (13:22). "The memory of the just is with praises" (10:7).

Proverbs shows us that the benefits of a life of wisdom are multigenerational. Not only do the benefits of righteous living return to our own lives, but also blessings flow down from generation to generation. What a wonderful power to realize that wise living helps not only us but also those of our loved ones following after us. "The house of the just shall stand firm" (12:7). "House" in this sense does not refer to a building but to the institution of our extended family as illustrated in many biblical passages.

"In the fear of the Lord there shall be hope for his children" (14:26). If we set an excellent example of wise, prudent living by our conduct, our children and grandchildren cannot fail to notice this pattern. "Grandchildren are the crown of old men." One of the joys of old age is reveling in the knowledge that our "houses" are established in wisdom and that our lives will have a legacy of goodness multiplied exponentially. "Instruct your children and they shall give delight to your soul" (29:17). In contrast, how miserable we can be to realize that our missteps in life, our rebelliousness, our disregard for God's way has made a mess of those following after us. Those regrets are doubly painful since we share some responsibility for those affected lives.

God understands how powerful family ties and legacies are and cautions us to think not only of ourselves in choosing our instructions for life but also those coming after us.

# January 24

## Benefits of Wisdom—Smooth Path

"The road of the godly leads upward, leaving hell behind" (15:24).

Many verses in Proverbs provide that obstacles shall be removed, the pathway straightened and smoothed and, in general, our way in life shall be improved if we are wise, righteous, obedient, and humble. This is to be contrasted with the way of the rebel, evil, wicked one which shall have thorns.

"A lazy fellow has trouble all through life; the good man's path is easy!" (15:19). "The path of the godly leads away from evil; he who follows that path is safe" (16:17). I believe path smoothing is part of God's provision for the righteous person. "I would have you learn this great fact: that a life of doing right is the wisest life there is. If you live that kind of life, you'll not limp or stumble as you run" (4:11–12). "The good man walks along in the ever-brightening light of God's favor; the dawn gives way to morning splendor, while the evil man gropes and stumbles in the dark" (4:18–19).

There are several aspects involved in this benefit. The first verses quoted seem to deal with removal of obstacles from the path. The later verses describe the benefit as illumination of the path, perhaps to see and avoid obstacles that remain in the path. Either way, the end result is the avoidance of many pitfalls, difficulties, and obstructions that threaten to trip one up.

"Watch your step. Stick to the path and be safe. Don't sidetrack; pull back your foot from danger" (4:26–27). This and other verses clarify that a knowledge of God's principles for life—sticking to the righteous path laid out by God is overall the best way to experience a smoother life.

# JANUARY 25

## Benefits of Wisdom—Favor

"If you want favor with both God and man, and a reputation for good judgment and common sense, then trust the Lord completely; don't ever trust yourself. In everything you do, put God first, and he will direct you and crown your efforts with success" (3:4–6).

Wise persons following God's principles for living enjoy special favor from God and other men! "For whoever finds me (wisdom) finds life and wins favor from the Lord" (8:35). "If you search for good, you will find God's favor; if you search for evil, you will find his curse" (11:27). "Curses chase sinners, while blessings chase the righteous!" (13:21). "The good man is covered with blessings from head to foot, but an evil man inwardly curses his luck" (10:6). "A good man obtains favor from the Lord, but the man of wicked devices he condemns" (12:2). "Good understanding gives favor, but the way of transgressors is hard" (13:5).

Enterprises undertaken by the good man will generally enjoy success. "The work of the wicked will perish; the work of the godly will flourish" (14:11). "The Lord despises the deeds of the wicked, but loves those who try to be good" (15:9). "Have two goals: wisdom—that is, knowing and doing right—and common sense. Don't let them slip away, for they fill you with living energy and bring you honor and respect" (3:21–22).

The honor and respect of fellowmen in life is invaluable. Folks like to conduct business with businessman and women they hold as honorable. Success multiplies when one satisfied customer mentions that fact to his or her neighbors, friends, and in this online world, on Facebook or other social media sites. Integrity is pure gold in the world of personal relationships and business. Favor is easy to obtain for the wise person, but once lost, it is nearly impossible to regain.

# January 26
## Benefits of Wisdom—Generosity

"He that is just will give and not cease" (21:26).

When one is infused with the Holy Spirit in the pursuit of God's wisdom, one's heart naturally softens toward others, especially those of the household of God and the poor. "The just takes notice of the cause of the poor" (29:7). This benefit overlaps with mercy and compassion; the softened heart naturally observes those in the world around him or her and the heartstrings are tugged: how can I help? What can I do to ease the suffering of this fellow child of God? The character of Ebenezer Scrooge comes to mind as the penny pinching "all mine" mentality gave way to the joyous privilege of being able to make another's life easier.

Mercy and generosity to the poor rebounds to the benefit of the giver. "He that gives to the poor shall not want. He that despises the entreaty of the poor shall suffer indigence" (28:27). "He that shows mercy to the poor shall be blessed. He that believes in the Lord loves mercy" (14:21). Unlike some prosperity doctrine preaching, we do not give to receive; nevertheless, it is a God ordained consequence. It is the time honored reaping and sowing principle at work.

A generous person also has a side benefit in that generosity brings one to the attention of those in authority and brings honor. "A man's gift enlarges his way and makes room before princes" (18:16). "Many honor and are friends of him that gives gifts" (19:6). "He that makes presents shall purchase victory and honor" (22:9). While some philanthropists give in order to be "made much of," wise godly persons give because their heart inclines them to do so. If the natural consequence is to be honored, then this displays the biblical principle of letting our light shine before others so that God will receive glory.

# January 27

## Benefits of Wisdom—Resilience

"The just shall spring up as a green leaf" (11:28).

Resilience is an extremely important benefit of wisdom. The Bible tells us that bad things will happen to us at some point in our life. So how we deal with those potholes in the road determines the course of life after tragedy. Will we lose our faith? Will we become embittered and cynical? Or will we use the terrible event to learn, become more compassionate so that we may help others, and become more aware and sensitive to suffering in the lives of others around us?

Modern psychology is placing more and more importance upon the skill of "recovering" from bad things in our lives. Knowing that negative circumstances will arise at some point can inoculate us from a Pollyanna attitude and help us maintain an even keel when the valley of the shadow of evil approaches. Keeping our eye on God, our faith and trust in his power to deliver us, soften the blow, and console us in our grief. This is the key to overcoming obstacles and living a life of success.

What the good man has that the ungodly does not is hope. "The just has hope in his death" (14:32). Even if this life disappoints us and our circumstances do not meet expectations, we have hope in eternal life after death. Revelation assures us that in heaven, there are no more tears, death, or sorrow. Focusing our attention on this assurance, our hope of salvation in Christ, goes a long way to maintaining a stable perspective, no matter our current dilemma. "The root of the just shall not be moved" (12:3). That is, a bad event will not knock us from the path of righteousness. "The just is as an everlasting foundation" (10:25).

# January 28
## Benefits of Wisdom—Wealth

"By instruction, the storerooms shall be filled with wealth" (23:4).

While we have previously looked at Proverbs showing a correlation between wisdom and blessings, favor, abundance generally, this verse hones in on material goods. If a person is righteous, their priorities are in line with God's rules for living. That means their priorities are correct: they are not squandering hard earned salary on wine, women, and entertainment but are planning ahead as prudence dictates. Taking a long view enables a wise person to work diligently as commanded by God in all we undertake, realistically assess needs for the future, store up excess for a rainy day and rationally, not impulsively, spend to cover our needs, but not our every want.

Proverbs 30:24 holds up ants as an example of unusual wisdom, for although "they aren't strong, they store up food for the winter." In comparison, wise persons should be looking ahead, living beneath their means at all times to store up for inevitable hard times. Like the wise woman in Proverbs 31, she does not fear the coming winter because she has prepared warm garments ahead of time to wear. "She has no fear of winter for her household, for she has made warm clothes for all of them" (31:21).

Staying out of debt is a sign of wisdom. "The rich rule over the poor; the borrower serves the lender" (22:7). Since in our times credit card debt can rapidly eat up a consumer, we see that the bill collector has the power to terrify our dreams, to garnish our wages, and to torpedo our future plans. Therefore, avoidance of debt should be the goal of a righteous person.

We are also cautioned to not strive after wealth: "Don't lift your eyes up to riches you can't have; those riches will fly away" (23:5). Hankering after expensive "status" catalog items is not profitable; throw them away!

# January 29
## Benefits of Wisdom—Humility

"Where humility is, there also is wisdom" (11:2).

Wisdom and humility go hand in hand. While this chapter touts the benefits of wisdom, the benefits of humility are nearly the same. "The fruit of humility is the fear of the Lord, riches, glory and life" (22:4). The same advantages we have been examining accruing to the righteous also accrue to the humble. In the biblical upside-down economy, "Humility goes before glory" (15:33). "Glory shall uphold the humble of spirit" (29:23). "Before a man be glorified, his heart is humbled" (18:12).

Other benefits of humility and meekness ensue. "To the meek, the Lord will give grace" (3:34). It seems that in this sense, grace implies attractiveness, acceptance, and pleasantness.

So while at first blush, it seems counterintuitive in our competitive arrogant culture that humility ends up "on top," God assures us that this is so, both on earth and in heaven.

We recall other verses about how much God despises pride and arrogance, so by implication, God must delight in the humble of heart. The saintliest of persons always wears a mantle of humility. Mother Teresa comes to mind. Not just faith-filled persons but nearly everyone universally admired her good works and humility. The very antithesis of a "success" in popular culture gained the respect and admiration of people from all walks of life. Perhaps it was the shock of her simple nonmaterial lifestyle that endeared her to our world— her humility, mercy, and grace attracted all of us to a great admiration of her way of life.

Have you known others like her of utmost humility who wanted no admiration but inherently drew admiration? It is clear that the more we study not only Proverbs but also the New Testament, humility naturally flows from the wisdom gained.

# January 30
## Benefits of Wisdom—Honesty

"He that hates bribes shall live" (15:27).

Most of the Proverbs concerning honesty are of the negative variety. They recount all the negative consequences of the dishonest person: the liar, fraud, briber, robber, thief, deceiver, and unjust person.

It is clear that Proverbs wants us to learn what *not* to do so that we shall "live" and not only live but also prosper, sleep well at night, and remain content, without a guilty conscience. "A deceitful balance is an abomination before the Lord; a just weight is his will" (11:1). Justice is such a strong theme in Isaiah, Micah, and other Old Testament prophets' writings that we can be assured it is God's will.

Dishonesty is self-destructive. "The deceitfulness of the wicked shall destroy them" (11:3). "No good shall come to the deceitful son" (14:15). "The robberies of the wicked shall be their downfall because they would not do justice" (21:7). "He that deceives the just in a wicked way shall fall in his own destruction" (28:10).

Furthermore, deceit is nonproductive. While cheating others is done to get ahead, it is simply not effective. "The deceitful man shall not find gain" (12:27). Of course, let us recall that not stealing is one of the Ten Commandments, so it is on God's top ten disapproval list.

Crime indicates lack of self-respect. "He that partakes with a thief hates his own soul" (29:24). Lack of self-respect leads to a downward spiral of other sins. "Deceitful souls go astray in sin" (13:13). "The crafty man is hateful" (14:17).

But the good man who avoids crime and dishonesty shall live. "The lip of truth shall be steadfast forever" (12:19). Justice is counted in God's scorebook, so anything that smacks of lying, cheating, or stealing must be avoided by the wise person.

# January 31

## Benefits of Wisdom—Common Sense

"He that is righteous corrects his way" (21:29).

One of the chief attributes of a wise person is to benefit from experience, to learn from errors so as to avoid a similar fate the second time around. The saddest sight is a person who blithely repeats an error by ignoring the outcomes of prior poor decisions. This is sad because the mess was entirely avoidable had he or she heeded the earlier disasters—either in his/her own life or by observing those around him/her.

"The righteous heart seeks after knowledge" (27:11). We are never too old to increase in knowledge and experience, both of which put us in good stead to take the smooth godly path. "They that seek after the Lord take notice of all things" (18:5). We do not have our heads in the sand but, like an ostrich whose head is continually swiveling on its long neck, are looking ahead for obstacles and dangers to avoid.

"A wise man shall hear and be wiser; he that understands shall possess governments" (1:5). This indicates that wise persons stand out in a crowd—their character, their wisdom are evident. Persons in high places want to benefit from that wisdom. Wisdom is an upward cycle trending to places of honor. "Possess governments" refers to holding positions of authority or being advisors to those in highest places. "Give an occasion to a wise man and wisdom shall be added to him" (9:9). A wise person is always listening, watching, heeding the words and actions of those in the world, and attempting to benefit from what he/she sees. In contrast, fools stroll along with their eyes on themselves, believing they have no need of advice/counsel from anyone.

Furthermore, "The learning of the wise is easy" (14:6). This is a blessing given to those aware of and who diligently follow God's principles of living.

# FEBRUARY 1

## Wise Speech—Power of Words

"The power of life and death are in the tongue" (18:21).

Have you ever considered how much of our lives is "lived through our mouths?" And how quickly non-Christians judge us based on what proceeds out of our mouths? Proverbs and Psalms, the wisdom books, and James have much to say about godly speaking—words of caution and positive advice. Boiled down, scripture encourages our words to be few, gracious, truthful, deliberate, considered, guarded, and encouraging.

As a beginning point, we are impressed with the ultimate power arising from our mouths: "The power of life and death are in the tongue" (Prov. 18:21). "The tongue is a little member, but it can kindle a forest fire!" (Jas. 3:5). Wow, that's serious! It's easy to observe others digging their hole deeper—back talking to teachers, police officers, even judges! But have we examined our own words and their consequences?

The tongue has power "to defile the whole body" (Jas. 3:6). "It is an unruly evil, full of deadly poison" (Jas. 3:8). We are cautioned about the severe consequences of failing to properly govern our tongue: "If any one among you thinks he is religious, and does not bridle his tongue...this one's religion is useless" (Jas. 1:26). In other words, our Christian example can be undermined in the blink of an eye with a blip of the tongue. We all recognize how quickly relationships can crash and burn after angry ill-considered words and how accusations of hypocrisy directly follow.

On the other hand, it's fascinating watching excellent parents, teachers, or mentors bring to life burned-out kids with the power of life-giving affirmations. "A word fitly spoken is like apples of gold in settings of silver" (Prov. 25:10). "The mouth of the righteous is a well of life" (Prov. 10:11).

# FEBRUARY 2

## Wise Speech—Few Words

"Be not rash with your mouth and let not your heart be hasty to utter anything before God; for God is in heaven, and you are upon earth: therefore, let your words be few" (Eccles. 5:2).

"He that refrains his lips is most wise" (10:10). The fewer words that proceed out of our mouths, the less chance we will have to beg forgiveness, spend much time in regretting damage to relationships, or make amends. "A wise man defers speaking and keeps his thoughts until afterwards" (29:11). It is better to think through the consequences of a comment before making it than mull over the "bullets" one has let slip out of his or her mouth without thought.

"Don't tell all in a quarrel, it's too difficult to make amends when you have dishonored your friend" (25:8). The main currency of personal relationships is words. A years long relationship can be quickly undermined by loose lips. Loose lips sink ships for sure, as the famous World War II slogan cautioned, but loose lips can torpedo relationships just as surely. "He that keeps his mouth and tongue, keeps his soul from distress" (21:23). Since our mouths often work faster than our brains, it is wise policy to consider well the effect of our words before they sail out of our lips.

"The discreet man considers his steps" (14:15). "Even a fool if he will hold his peace shall be counted wise, and if he closes his lips a man of understanding" (17:28). In other words, it is better our peers, bosses, and subordinates think we are reticent, deliberate, and reluctant to speak than to make known our ill-considered thoughts and be demonstrated to be foolish. In a similar vein is: "A cautious man conceals knowledge but the heart of fools publishes folly" (12:23).

# FEBRUARY 3

## Wise Speech—Honesty

"The just shall hate a lying word" (13:5).

Verses cautioning against lying are numerous in Proverbs and let us not forget that one of the Ten Commandments prohibits bearing false witness against our neighbor. If a godly principle makes the "top ten," it surely must be important in God's economy. "Lying lips are an abomination to the Lord" (12:22).

First off, dishonest speech does not pay; we will be found out. "He that perverts his ways shall be found out" (10:9). Regrets will surely follow. "The bread of lying is sweet to a man but afterwards his mouth shall be filled with gravel" (20:17).

Secondly, we will be punished for lies, and they will boomerang to harm us. "A false witness shall not be unpunished and he that speaks lies shall not escape" (19:5). "He that gathers treasures by a lying tongue is vain and foolish and shall stumble upon the snares of death" (21:6). More directly, "A lying witness shall perish" (21:28).

Thirdly, lying is unbecoming to anyone but especially to those in authority and will undermine public opinion of our character. "Lying lips do not become a prince" (17:7) (or CEO, congressman, pastor, leader of any type). "A deceitful tongue loves not truth. A slippery mouth works ruin" (26:28).

Fourth, when we are called upon to support justice by testifying to our knowledge, false testimony can lead to a serious miscarriage of justice. "A man that bears false witness against his neighbor is like a dangerous weapon" (25:18). Our entire system of due process is founded upon the duty of witnesses to testify truthfully. Our legal system and our society in general suffer when witnesses are untruthful. "An unjust witness scorns judgment" (19:28). Ignoring the miscarriage of justice is a dangerous path leading to the disintegration of the foundations of our government.

# February 4

## Wise Speech—Gossip

"When the talebearer is taken away, contentions shall cease" (26:26).

"Practice not evil against your friend when he has confidence in you" (3:29). Gossip or backbiting can damage relationships faster than nearly anything due to the strong power in negative words. Lying is the heart of the sin of gossip. "The double dealer utters lies" (14:25). Gossip then is a particular form of lying that involves casting negative light on a person either through direct words or implication. Sometimes, what is not said or the raising of an eyebrow or the rolling of one's eyes can accomplish as much smearing of character as a juicy tale.

Gossips will be found out. "He that covers hatred deceitfully, his malice shall be laid open publicly" (26:26). The gossip will eventually be traced to the offending lips with the resultant relationship damage.

"Better are the wounds of a friend than deceitful kisses of an enemy" (27:6). In other words, even if a true friends hurts our feelings by constructive criticism, that is better than a mean gossip talking behind our backs in a manner designed to destroy our credibility or respect. Both are hard to take, but the intentions of a friend are for our benefit while the intentions of our enemy who gossips is pure hatred.

Whether or not the purpose of a gossiper is to make themselves look better at our expense, i.e. to bring someone on a pedestal down to their level or merely to pay back a perceived wrong done to them, the damage done is the same.

Later trying to make amends is rarely effective. "It is ruin to a man to destroy good men and thereafter to retract" (20:25). Explanations always come too late, just as newspaper retractions of errors are always in tiny print in an obscure location. The original readers/hearers rarely are convinced to change their minds.

# February 5

## Wise Speech—Encouragement

"The good counsels of a friend are sweet to the soul" (27:9).

The power of the tongue can be used to bless and encourage those around us. "A word fitly spoken is like apples of gold in a frame of silver" (25:11). Recall how thrilling it is to be praised, especially in front of others! We could nearly bust our buttons. One of our duties in raising children or being a friend is to let fly, without hesitation, praises when praises are due. We all hunger for a good word. When encouragement is lacking, children grow up to have stunted egos who are continually striving, sometimes in the wrong places and in the wrong ways, to regain the approval of a negative parent or parent figure. A hole is left in the self-esteem of a young person when no one can find a good thing to say about them.

We all value friends who tell us how much we mean to them. "A man amiable in society shall be more friendly than a brother" (18:24). "Like iron sharpening iron, so a man sharpens a friend" (27:17). While this verse is often applied in situations of constructive criticism, I believe that praising a friend can give a boost and encouragement to improve in the future. Management 101, Parenting 101 principle: "Catch them doing something right" since we all know that incents future good behavior of the same ilk.

Have you ever considered praising your boss or superior? When sincere praise is delivered, not just "buttering up" kind of praise, then honor redounds to the praiser. "He that is the keeper of his master shall be glorified" (27:18). When we look out for the best interests of our superior, such that he or she receives positive recognition, that will return to us in promotions, recognition, or raises as well.

# February 6

## Wise Speech—Treachery

"He that deceives the just in a wicked way shall fall in his own destruction" (28:10).

"Strive not against a man without cause when he has done you no evil" (3:30). There are many flat prohibitions against turning on another person. "The soul of the wicked desires evil; he will not have pity on his neighbor" (21:10).

One cannot gain in the long term by treachery. It will bring about the ruin of the wrongdoer. Backstabbing our colleague, friend, or family member has no payoff. We will suffer for our wrong deeds. The wise person understands this relationship and therefore is never tempted to gain a short term advantage by casting negative reflections on others. "Judgments are prepared for scorners and striking hammers for the bodies of fools" (19:29). "The devices of the wicked shall be rooted out" (15:5). "He that is perverse in his ways shall fall at once" (28:18). "A snare shall entangle the wicked man when he sins" (29:6).

Furthermore, not the mere ineffectiveness of treachery but the judgment of God is a deterrent for such conduct. "In the path of justice is life but the byway leads to death" (12:28).

The disapproval of wise men will fall upon those dealing treacherously with others. "He that walks in the right way and fears God is despised by him that goes by an infamous way" (14:2). "He that devises evils shall be called a fool" (24:8). Painting another with a black brush will necessarily splash some of the blackness on the painter. Whether in the midst of a high profile political campaign or a group of junior high "mean girls," betrayal in all forms is despised. Once one has gained a reputation of being unfaithful or disloyal friends, it is nearly impossible to resuscitate one's reputation.

# February 7

## Wise Speech—Avoidance of Angry Words

"He that is easily stirred up to wrath shall be more prone to sin" (29:22).

Sometimes, anger is displayed in fistfights, rude gestures, pushing, or shoving, but more often, anger is evidenced by imprudent words that one later regrets. "A spirit that is easily angered: who can bear?" (18:14). It is extremely difficult to live, work with or have a long-term relationship with a hothead. "The anger of a fool is heavier than stones or sand" (27:3). This tells us that a display of anger weighs on us, gets us down, and keeps us awake at night. It is difficult to ignore or brush under the rug. An outpouring of angry words has a large negative impact, and we will surely regret saying them.

"Anger has no mercy when it breaks forth. Who can bear the violence of one provoked?" In other words, once the first angry word breaks out of our mouths, a torrent is likely to follow. "He that provokes wrath brings strife" (30:33). Most often, such provocation comes in the form of imprudent or even intentionally aggressive comment.

Confrontations can be avoided in many instances when wise persons understand that it does little good to correct a fool. "Do not instruct a fool because he will despise you" (23:9). "Wisdom is too high for a fool" (24:7). "The instruction of fools is foolishness" (16:22). Why waste your breath and get yourself a black eye along with it? "A parable is unseemly in the mouth of fools" (26:7). Our attempts to instruct a fool will likely backfire, compounding the original dispute and causing hard feelings of a long-term nature. Warning a fool about his/her intemperate angry words is simply ineffective. "A reproof avails more with a wise man than a hundred stripes with a fool" (17:12).

# February 8

## Proverbs on Speech—Source of Truth

"I give you thoughts, knowledge and words of truth" (22:21).

God is the source of all wisdom and truth, so our speech can reflect godly virtues if we open ourselves as channels of God's truth. Practically, how do we facilitate this? First, we hear, read, and reflect on God's Word daily, seeking devotions and scriptural resources. Second, we intentionally align our wills with God's, submitting our efforts to his direction. Third, we pray for inspiration to solve our pending problem, dilemma, or issue. Fourth, we take time to create silence to courteously listen for God's leading. We keep our ears and hearts tuned to his frequency, our radar on, and our antenna adjusted to God's channels. We remain expectant and patient. We get ourselves out of the way to make room for an inflow of thoughts and words from God. The Holy Spirit is the facilitator; we are merely the receiving vessel.

If we regularly absorb God's precepts, it is easier to detect falsehoods and imposters. Misleading guidance just doesn't "go down smoothly"; we have serious reservations about the integrity of the speaker. Something "grates on" our souls and we do not feel at peace about the wrong advice.

If we are floundering, at loose ends in a sea of doubts, God can be our touchstone of truth. We can pull ourselves near that rock of truth to take a time out to reconsider our course. We can sort through our biblical knowledge and see if our plans reflect the actions of righteous examples over time. If we laid our proposal at the feet of Jesus, would he approve?

Sometimes, we try to force an answer to our liking, but in the short and long run, we would be wiser to directly seek words of truth from God.

# February 9

## Wise Speech—Counsel

"Hear counsel and receive instruction that you may be wise at your end" (19:20).

The wise person remains teachable and anxious to receive God's wisdom and the wisdom of the more spiritually mature or his/her elders. "Plans are strengthened by counsel" (20:18). If you are about to embark on a new enterprise or a direction you know little about, the best plan is to seek and be open to the counsel of godly persons with more experience in the area. "There shall be safety where there are many counsels" (24:6). If we do not know where to go to seek counsel, we should ask the Holy Spirit to guide us to a source of applicable wisdom. "Keep the law and counsel and you shall walk confidently and your foot shall not stumble" (3:23).

In contrast, the fool deems himself too wise for counsel and goes it on his or her own. "It is better to meet a bear robbed of her cubs than a fool trusting in his own folly" (17:12). A fool has no use for advice or counsel from others—wise or not. A fool's perspective is that no one knows more than he or she does. "Wisdom is too high for a fool" (24:7).

A fool rebels against advice even from his own parents! "A fool laughs at the instruction of his father" (15:5). "The fool despises his mother" (15:20). Therefore, he surely will refuse to listen to her counsel. We are all familiar with the stereotype of the teenager who believes his parents are the dumbest people on earth but, in a few short years of maturity, returns to seek their counsel on the important decisions of early life. Perhaps this is nature's way of causing necessary separation from a dependent child to an independent adult, but a knowledge of what Proverbs has to say about parents' counsel will ease the transition.

# FEBRUARY 10

## Wise Speech—Criticism

"Remove from you a negative mouth and let detracting lips be far from you" (4:24).

When we take it upon ourselves to criticize someone, we are setting ourselves up as judge and jury, believing that we are wiser or more experienced than them. When we are a parent, we are placed in a position of offering constructive criticism for the benefit of our children. In nearly every other situation, however, it is not our job to criticize, especially when not asked for advice. No one likes to associate with a person who frequently badmouths them; it is instinctive to steer clear of them. The popular childhood book about Thumper the rabbit instilled in generations of people the expression, "If you can't say something nice, don't say anything at all."

"All fools are meddling with reproaches" (20:3). This verse calls a spade a spade: criticism is generally meddling unless we are a parent or perhaps an employer.

We must put ourselves in the opposite position and think how we would be affected if the criticism were directed to us. "A sorrowful spirit dries up the bones" (17:22). Continual criticism shrivels the souls of children whose egos are fragile, but it has the same effect, albeit hopefully not as powerfully, on adults. The golden rule should be the measure of our consideration of whether to express some criticism.

If we must criticize, we must ensure that the criticism is honest and constructive. "He that rebukes a man shall afterward find favor with him, more than he who deceitfully flatters" (28:23). "Open rebuke is better than hidden love" (27:5).

Oftentimes, ill-considered criticism operates to harden another's position. "The wicked man impudently hardens his face" (21:29). Criticism can entrench a fool's conduct since a rebellious spirit is a chief characteristic of a fool. Think carefully about the willingness of the recipient to hear criticism before it is loosed.

# February 11

## Wise Speech—Envy

"Don't envy sinners" (23:17).

If we open our mouths and express envy for another, we are reflecting sin in our own soul. "Envy is the rottenness of the bones" (14:30). Comparisons of most sorts are deadly, nonproductive and generally harmful. When in the gospels, Peter asked Jesus, "What about him? (John, the beloved disciple)," Jesus answered Peter roughly, "Mind your own business—what is that to you?" We are cautioned to avoid thinking and thereafter speaking words of envy. We have enough work to do improving ourselves without concerning ourselves with how we compare with another of God's children. Since each person is created with different strengths, weaknesses, gifts, and graces, we should avoid constantly comparing ourselves, leading to envious thoughts and words.

We are cautioned to avoid close associations with envious persons. "Eat not with an envious man, because he has false imaginings and his mind is not with you" (23:6–7). Eating in the scriptures often is indicative of close companionship, as fellowship in the breaking of bread represents community and intimacy.

We can help the self-esteem of our children by reminding them often that they are their own person and that while their friend may be a sports natural, their gifts may lie in another area. Refocusing their envy to self-improvement is the better course. Envy is poisonous and, if obsessed over, will have a toxic effect on self-image. Our task should be to do our utmost to improve ourselves, asking for God's help and guidance as necessary. A healthy life view is first between us and God, us as God's uniquely created child and God as the sovereign who fashioned us and saw us within the womb before we were even born. Envy skews that viewpoint in an unhealthy way.

# February 12

## Proverbs on Speech—Quarreling

"An evil man always seeks quarrels" (17:11).

There are many verses in Proverbs showing that this is a salient trait of an ungodly person—frequent tendency to quarrel. "Hatred stirs up strifes" (10:12). "A passionate man provokes quarrels" (29:22).

So the opposite of a godly heart filled with love is an angry, evil heart filled with the desire to quarrel. We should examine ourselves: do we have a quick temper? Are we irritable and easily offended? If so, that is a telltale sign that we need a dose of God's spirit to calm our hearts and bring peace.

We should avoid keeping company with those with quarreling mouths. "Be not a friend to an angry man. Do not walk with a furious man lest you learn his ways and take scandal to your soul" (22:24). Actions can become habits and observing another frequently quarreling cannot help but rub off on our conduct. Beware!

What are the consequences of a quarreling mouth? "He that troubles his own house shall inherit the winds" (11:29). Perhaps this comes about through estrangement and alienation due to giving offense once too often. Perhaps parents lose patience and evict a teen or older parents harden their hearts against grown children who disrupt harmonious family relations. Hotheads are often estranged from their families with consequent loss of not only familial affections but of proceeds of estates as well.

Proverbs actually encourages communities or families to cast out perpetual quarrelers to restore peace. "Cast out the scoffer and contention shall go out with him and quarrels and contention shall cease" (22:10). It is also pure folly and risky to insert our noses into a quarrel that does not concern us. "Don't interfere with another man's quarrel—it'll backfire" (26:17). Let us mind our own business.

# FEBRUARY 13

## Proverbs on Speech—Humility

"Among the proud there are always contentions" (13:10). Close examination of quarrelling usually finds pride at the root of the quarrel. Someone has been offended due to another's not giving him/her their due. Lowering our pride threshold allows many quarrels to die before they are born. Once we humbly place in perspective our place in the universe and begin to remind ourselves that the world does not revolve around us, many potential harsh comments are swallowed, thus avoiding a quarrel.

"He that boasts and puffs himself up stirs up quarrels" (28:26). The antidote to a prideful explosion of hurt feelings is a humble re-examination of the true reason behind our offense-likely being puffed up.

"To the meek the Lord will give grace" (3:34). I believe this promise encompasses grace of speech.

The proud person must have the last word in an argument, but the humble is magnanimous to "just let it go." The humble person is able to disinterestedly seek the root of the complaint and modulate his/her speech in the manner least likely to escalate the issue. It takes two to tango and two to quarrel, and if the humble person will simply zip the lip and not worry about winning the argument, the hateful words sink below the horizon and disappear. Whether or not the scoffer continues poking at the issue like a man with a fire poker roiling up a simmering blaze, the humble man can simply let the fire die out without adding more coals of contention.

The humble person is okay with the other being entitled to keep his/her "wrong" opinion without feeling a duty to correct or impose a retraction of their opinion. The humble person cares more about how the Lord views his heart than about how others view his/her "loss" of the argument.

# February 14

## Proverbs on Speech—Self-Control

"A man who can't mind his speech is like a city without walls" (25:28).

How much of our lives is lived through our mouths! Yes, we walk, sit, drive, and work. But most of the transactions in our culture are accomplished through speech, whether talking face-to-face, typing with our fingers on our various devices, speaking into a phone, or reading the written word. The danger for sin is daily, hourly, by the minute. Committing adultery, murder, or others of the Ten Commandments is rare and isolated, but we have opportunity nearly perpetually to harm others with our tongues.

Perhaps "self-control" is the last of the Galatians fruit of the spirit listings because it is hardest to develop. "He that rules his spirit is better than he that conquers cities" (16:32). A soldier trains all his career to conquer a city; it may take a lifetime of prayer, study, and wisdom to develop self-control. We can save ourselves a myriad of apologies, take backs, amends and makeup conversations to just "put a sock in it" in the first place. Just like the old saw about the difficulty of putting toothpaste back into the tube or the horse back into the barn, controlling our impulses to criticize, interfere, or bad mouth another is a higher order skill to be learned.

When we realize that one inappropriate remark can get us fired from a job, kill tender love in a marriage, or damage the precious ego of a child, much is at stake. Since the "power of life and death" is in the tongue, we must treat its use as a dangerous weapon. Visualizing our ability to put a lock on our speech, to carefully monitor each word preparing to emerge from our mouth—in short, control our mouths—is a good start to keeping our "city" secure.

# FEBRUARY 15

## Proverbs on Speech—Nagging

"It is better to sit in a corner of the housetop than with a nagging spouse" (21:9).

The problem with marriage is its everydayness. Rain, shine, sickness, health—we are in the relationship for the long haul. Therefore, small gnats are magnified into eagles, so tolerance is necessary. After one or two politely-worded requests, we must recognize that continued mention of the verboten topic will be perceived as nagging and the listener will instinctively start to "tune out." Similarly, "It is better to dwell in a wilderness than with a quarrelsome spouse" (21:19). "A contentious spouse is like a leaky roof" (17:15). To examine the root of this simile, we must ask, "How is a leaky roof?" It is irritating! So will we be to our spouse if we continue to repeat the same request! If our spouse does not indicate that she/he will comply with our request, we must either make plans to accomplish the request without his/her help or "give it up" and determine to live without it.

It is especially risky to nag a fool, scorner, or unrighteous person. "He that teaches a scorner does an injury to himself" (9:7). "Teaches" in case likely refers to a correction, criticism, or request for change. In short, it is nearly futile to waste one's breath in such correction, for the pride of the listener will be pricked, causing the temperature to rise in the relationship. "He that rebukes a wicked man gets himself a blot" (9:7). The request will boomerang, and the requester will regret bringing the matter up. "Rebuke not a scorner lest he hate you" (9:7). It seems pretty clear that the listener will brush off the request, turn it around, and use it as a weapon against the requester. Nagging, in short, is rarely effective and likely destructive.

# February 16

## Proverbs on Speech—Patience

"He that answers before he hears shows himself to be a fool and worthy of confusion" (18:13).

How often we are tempted to cut to the chase and respond to an inquiry even before it is fully stated. This is not only the height of rudeness but also can lead to severe embarrassment if the issue is not at all what we surmised. "The impatient man shall work folly" (14:17). Patience in speech is common courtesy—not to interrupt, showing respect for our slow talking elders or southern relatives is by far the wiser course. "The learning of a man is known by patience; his glory is to pass over wrongs" (19:11). Just as Thomas Jefferson counseled to silently count to ten before responding with a hasty rebuttal, giving a little planning to our reply might save us serious regrets.

"By patience a prince (boss) shall be appeased" (25:15). By not blurting out the first thing on our tongue, we can show wisdom and maturity. No matter how skilled we are or how smart about accomplishing our employment, we can blow our reputation in a jiffy by impatiently jumping to a conclusion. "He that is impatient shall suffer damage and when he takes away, shall add another thing" (19:19). Perhaps the "takeaway" is referring to crossing a to do item off our list. Instead of accomplishing one thing, we have regressed and now must make it up to the listener by performing two tasks. "The patient man is better than the valiant" (16:32). Even young teens just entering the world of college oral exams or the workforce should take heed of this. The younger and more inexperienced we are, the longer should be the passage of time to allow thorough evaluation before letting loose our response.

# February 17

## Proverbs on Speech—Mercy

"Open your mouth for the disabled for children's causes" (31:8). Christians are expected to advocate for the disadvantaged and weak ones of society. We are not to stand idly by and let things flow without positive influence on our part. We have a duty to, with our words and mouths, speak up to bring to bear our merciful perspective to bring social justice.

"Charity covers all sins" (10:12). Charity is not limited to giving monies but encompasses charitable conversation, acknowledgment that others aren't perfect just as we aren't and giving someone a "pass" instead of unloading double barreled criticism. "He that is a friend loves at all times" (17:17). Yes, we may love by bringing a casserole following a hospitalization, offering to run errands for a person stuck at home, but many times, the friend desires a compassionate listener with a mouth that limits its comments to sympathetic acknowledgment.

Job's three friends showed laudable mercy for the first few days of his distress by merely sitting quietly at his side lending support. Any other speech would likely have backfired, bringing more pain to Job as it did later in their vigil. Especially in the raising of children, imperfectly half-formed persons, permitting a do-over instead of unleashing negativity is often the most merciful thing we can do.

Can you recall when you fell and skinned your knee as a child? Yes, the hug of a concerned parent was healing, but more so was the merciful murmurings of "there, there—it'll be better in a minute." Mercy in speech, mercy in gracious notes of sympathy, and mercy in calling a week after the burial are good deeds long remembered by the tenderhearted grieving one. When our hearts are broken and bruised, a few merciful comments go a long way toward healing.

# February 18

## Proverbs on Speech—Counsel

"There shall be safety where there are many counsels" (24:6).

If we are asked to give advice on a subject known to us, it is a kindness for us to render our best opinion in the furtherance of a project. One opportunity to use our speech in a positive manner is to not hesitate when asked to help another with pending plans. If our motives are pure, our advice might be the make it or break it "straw" that decided the course of action forevermore. "Plans are strengthened by counsel" (10:18). Thus, any aid we can contribute to crystallize a group consensus or clarify the thinking of the decision maker can be invaluable.

On the other hand, if we are not asked for our opinion, we should not offer it without first inquiring whether it is wanted. Arrogance and pride might tempt us to offer unsolicited opinions, but our thoughts may be tossed aside without consideration if they are unsought.

The verses on control of speech likewise apply here. The door of our mouth should be regulated by wise perception about whether counsel is applicable, needed, and wanted. If it is unwanted, we are wasting our breath even if the listener should be asking for it. Counselors must be sensitive to the who, what, when, and why of fluid situations to know when to offer advice and when to remain silent.

Rebellious spirits are rarely receptive to advice of any kind, thinking they know it all. Attempts to give even wonderful advice will be in vain. Rebels harden their hearts and minds against counsel in most forms, for they cannot admit to themselves that they lack in good sense.

Our prayer should be to sensitize our hearts to the appropriateness of giving and receiving counsel.

# FEBRUARY 19

## Proverbs on Speech—Discretion

"Even a fool if he will hold his peace shall be counted wise, and if he closes his lips a man of understanding" (17:28).

"He that refrains his lips is most wise" (10:10). "A cautious man conceals knowledge but the heart of fools publishes folly" (12:23). Before we simply blurt out information known to us, like a good reporter, we must analyze who it concerns, whether it will be helpful or hurtful, whether the timing of such disclosure is ideal. There are many angles to revealing sensitive information, for everyone's interests differ. Even if it is in your best interest to disclose the fact, is it in the best interest of others it concerns? "The discreet man considers his steps" (14:15). "The wisdom of a discreet man is to understand his way" (14:8).

"Tell secrets only to friends, not strangers, lest a friend overhear and be insulted" (15:9). The unknown listener in the corner may be the sworn enemy of the person about whom the juicy tidbit concerns.

Even in a quarrel when no holds are barred, we are thinking least clearly so more discretion is advisable. "Don't tell all in a quarrel; it's too difficult to make amends when you have dishonored your friend" (15:8). If the news is bad, the better course is to hush it up. "He that conceals a transgression seeks friendships; he that repeats it separates friends" (17:9). We should steer clear of those anxious to repeat harmful intelligence. "Meddle not with he who reveals secrets or walks deceitfully with wide lips" (20:19). The more we keep company with those lacking discretion, the more apt we are to adopt their ways and ignore the advice of Proverbs.

"He that keeps his mouth keeps his soul, but he that is without guard on his speech shall meet with evils."

# February 20

## Proverbs on Speech—Healthful

"The mouth of the just is a vein of life" (10:11).

Since our thought, speech, and physical bodies are closely related, it is thrilling to note how positive of an influence we can have on ourselves and those around us when our speech is correct, obedient to God's law, and true. Whether as a teacher, parent, loyal friend, or casual encourager, little will we realize how much of an impact our words have. Once let "loose in the air," a word may be firmly ensconced in the hearer's memory long after we've forgotten it.

I recall the Ann Landers column describing an elementary teacher's assignment to write one good thing down about every student in their class. Stories later emerged about how more than one student had tenderly folded and secreted the positive comment in a tiny corner of their wallet, dresser drawer, or precious box. Later in life, some students with negative parents recalled how that was the *first* positive comment about themselves they had ever heard and it strongly shaped their self-perception. In an honor college class, this exercised was performed, and I can recall nearly every word about me. We are hungry for good news about ourselves from our fellow man. Especially on the tender egos of growing children, a single compliment, an effusive acknowledgment of their special talent or a comment about a gift they may have overlooked may set them on the pathway to an entire career.

Not only does Proverbs speak about comments about us, but also comments we give others redound to our benefit. "Your body shall rejoice when your lips speak aright" (23:16). Often, we are nudged by the Holy Spirit to encourage another, and when we are obedient, our spirits rightly soar, and our health improves!

# FEBRUARY 21

## Proverbs on Speech—Honesty

"The lips of truth shall be steadfast forever" (12:19).

When our speech is truthful, we have so much less to worry about. No long nights tossing and turning worrying about our guilt or chance of discovery, no agonizing trying to recall which version of the "truth" we told so we may remain consistent. Life is simple when we tell the truth. I have always found it interesting that the Ten Commandments do not contain a blanket commandment to always tell the truth. Rather, the commandment prohibits bearing false witness against our neighbor, a very specific kind of testimony that could land another in jail or serious harm.

Perhaps, but this is just my idea, we are not obligated to tell the whole truth if that would cause harm or even pain to another. Maybe little white lies are a kindness if they smooth over hurt feelings and their purpose is to avoid causing more pain than necessary. "Does this dress look good on me?" Husbands, beware of full disclosure!

"Deceitful souls go astray in sin" (13:13). If our purpose in lying is to cheat another out of a fair transaction, clearly, that is prohibited by Proverbs and is sin. For what purpose are we telling a lie? To hurt or harm? Or to overlook a fault or cover over a meanness? Our motive is always the issue, not the piece of information being told.

"Deceit is in the heart of them that think evil things" (12:20). The evil heart's motive is generally self-interest, self-promotion, avoidance of penalty. The pure heart's motive in speaking is to do a kindness, encourage, or give beneficial counsel. Let us examine our motives when a statement is being made that involves shades of gray, shades of truth.

# FEBRUARY 22

## Proverbs on Speech—Fools

"Eloquent words do not become a fool nor lying lips a prince" (17:7).

"A fool receives not the words of prudence unless you say those things which are in his heart" (18:2).

Words are of little consequence to the fool, for he/she does not care whether they harm others. Fools are self-focused and believe themselves not needing of advice, whether from God or man. A fool—also known as wicked, evil, unrighteous, or the rebel—has certain characteristics that bear on his/her speech. He spends little time thinking about the impact of his/her words and less time considering whether they are truthful. "A fool laughs at the instruction of his father" (15:5). Thus, a fool has little regard even for the advice of someone who loves him. "In the mouth of a fool is the rod of pride" (14:32).

Pride, arrogance, and self-focus were the root of original sin leading to the ousting of Lucifer from the portals of heaven. Such sin is still the primary motivator behind all the types of evil speech proceeding from his/her mouth. Refusal to bow to the wisdom of Proverbs, the wisdom of our parents or elders or even the wisdom of godly objective counselors leads to carelessness in the speech passing from the lips of a fool. "Sudden calamity shall fall upon those who hate instruction" (1:27). Obedience to godly wisdom is a guide to the words proceeding from the mouth of righteous men, but fools pay no heed leading to negative consequences. "A man that wanders out of the way of doctrine shall abide with corpses" (21:16). "The foolish pulls down with his own hands (words?) that which is built" (14:1). One negative comment can undo months of truce building or attempts of reconciliation. Foolish words can be as destructive as a hammer to a house.

# February 23

## Proverbs on Speech—Righteous

"The mouth of the just shall deliver them" (12:6).

In contrast to the speech of the fool, the "just" is a synonym for the obedient one, the righteous one, or the favored one of God. Speech is one of the key ways to distinguish between the fool and the righteous.

Prayer is a blessed form of speech of the righteous, and they have a special advantage. "He will hear the prayers of the just" (15:29). The prayers of the righteous are not blocked by sin, unreconciled relationships, or guilt. (See 1 Peter.) "He that is pure, his work [including his speech] is right" (21:8).

"To him that sows justice there is a faithful reward" (11:18). Speaking in a considerate, thoughtful, just manner promotes social justice and leads to positive benefits. "The just are merciful and show mercy" (13:13). "The habitations of the just shall be blessed" (3:33). Since most of our family relationships flow from conversations, righteous speech is the bedrock of a peaceful, blessed home.

"The tongue of the just is as choice silver" (10:20). Silver is valuable, and silver is desired by others. Both characteristics apply to exemplary speech. Further, silver is precious and sought after. Much like the passages in Proverbs comparing wisdom to precious metal and jewels, pure positive speech should be desired and sought after.

"The just shall be delivered by knowledge" (11:9). Knowledge and wisdom instruct one's lips. For example, when stopped by an officer, replying with respect, truthfulness, and moderation goes a long way to deliver the driver from ill consequences. It is very important in our current climate of distrust to instruct our children thoroughly in proper deference and tone of voice when challenged by law enforcement. Delivery from other negative consequences in life goes much smoother when mature, thoughtful answers are given to government agencies, employers, and family members.

# February 24

## Proverbs on Speech—Appropriateness

"To speak a word in due time is like apples of gold on beds of silver" (25:11).

Timing is as important as content in speech. A word spoken too soon gives away a coveted secret. A word spoken too late fails to save someone from the penitentiary. Again, precious jewels is an apt metaphor for precious words. The ultimate compliment refers to two types of precious metals: silver and gold. This double metaphor implies special emphasis on the benefit of a word spoken in due time.

"A soft tongue breaks hardness" (25:15). An argument can be immediately de-escalated by the gentle word, avoiding dangerous risk of escalation into a physical brawl. Although we are cautioned against nagging, the harshness of nagging can be avoided but still accomplish the repeated request if the tone is deliberately soft. Some teachers employ a device to defuse tempers in the schoolroom. The louder a student shouts, the softer the teacher replies in an attempt to calm the student and entice them to be quiet and listen intently for the teacher's soft answer.

The effect of cursing is addressed in Proverbs. "A curse without cause shall boomerang" (26:2). The import of this verse is that although delivered with venom, it will be ineffective if there is no basis to it. It is easily deflected and ignored. One way to identify an enemy is to notice carefully the manner in which a comment is made. "Don't trust an enemy when he speaks low" (26:25). If he is whispering over in the corner and his eyes are darting to and fro, a conspiracy may be afoot.

Finally, "He that follows after words only shall have nothing" (19:7). Some exclaimers are full of big promises and hearty assurances, but they disappear like smoke without effect. Take heed.

# FEBRUARY 25

## Proverbs on Speech—Peace

"Joy follows those who take counsels of peace" (12:20).

Peace is good for our souls and good for our bodies if the result is joy. We were created to experience joy, so the words that issue from our mouths can be shaped to either further that goal or undercut it.

Words of reconciliation, words of forgiveness, and words of blessing make for peace and resulting joy. "There is living truth in what a good man says, but the mouth of the evil man is filled with curses" (10:11).

The peaceful response may entail giving someone a "bye," a "do over," or permitting an excuse. Wisdom comes in discerning whether a person would benefit or would become "enabled" to sink deeper and achieve less. "Some people like to make cutting remarks, but the words of the wise soothe and heal" (12:18). If we made our mission in life to use our words to bring peace to all we meet, how much better would our world be. If teachers strove to bring peace to the classroom, parents to the dinner table, and pastors to a hurting congregation, God would surely smile on our efforts.

"All the paths of wisdom are peaceable" (3:17). Whatever we say in the midst of work, play, family business, it all redounds to peace when our words are spoken in wisdom with a view to peace.

Obedience to God's way puts to bed any enmity with God and smoothes our way among our fellowmen.

"He that fears the commandments dwells in peace" (13:13). Men particularly are endowed with a competitive spirit that sometimes leads to highway competition and road rage. Our response to someone passing us should not be affront but peace: what does it harm us when he gets ahead? We can maintain perfect equanimity when our mind is stayed on him.

# FEBRUARY 26
## Proverbs on Speech—Wisdom

"The lips of knowledge are a precious vessel" (21:11).

Many verses speak of gaining words of knowledge and words of wisdom to keep in our "vessel," our mind and heart. "Apply yourself to instruction and your ears to words of knowledge" (23:12). The purpose of applying ourselves is to educate ourselves and understand God's wisdom to improve our actions and our speech. "Wisdom shall be beautiful for you, if you keep it in your heart, it will flow in your lips that you may trust in the Lord" (22:18–19). Thus, knowledge and wisdom gained should be reflected in more prudent speech, spoken in accordance with God's principles for living.

"Study wisdom to make your parents' heart joyful and to give an answer to a criticizer" (27:11). This sounds like Paul's admonition to always be ready to give a testimony when questioned about the reason for our faith. If we lose a perfect opportunity to explain the basis for our faith to an inquirer, it may never come again.

"Knowledge is a fountain of life to him that possesses it" (16:22). Fountains are refreshing, cleansing, and renewing. Likewise, if we study wisdom, this will affect our words to make them refreshing, cleansing, and renewing to ourselves and others. "Be wise and guide your mind in the way" (23:19). Biblical phrases and biblical principles will reside in our minds and be ready on our tongue when needed if we systematically pursue wisdom for the purpose of right living. "Cease not to hear instruction and be not ignorant of the words of knowledge" (19:27). Gaining knowledge is a lifelong pursuit; we have never arrived to a place where no further study is needed. We can only improve our life and the beauty of our speech if we apply ourselves to wisdom.

# February 27

## Proverbs on Speech—Gratitude

"Count your blessings and be satisfied with what you produce" (27:27).

Gratitude is the premiere attitude we should cultivate, which leads to worship. Someone said primitive man first conceived of God so he'd have someone to thank for our beautiful world. Even native peoples who have never heard of Christianity nearly all have rituals of thanksgiving for harvest, for beauty in nature and for our very lives.

The fastest way to work ourselves out of a self-pity party funk is to literally take a moment to either write down or systematically recall all the blessings we have and their source. It is difficult to remain "down" when we look up. Cultivating a morning habit of thanking God for another gift of a day is one way to set our day off on the right foot. Gratitude journals are the rage in many Bible study courses these days since they force us to think through all of life's blessings and how life would be in their absence. The Lord's Prayer was given by Christ as a daily example of thankfulness.

Psalms are full of gratitude by King David and others and can be used as our pattern of prayer. This characteristic of thankfulness is one of the chief reasons David is known as a man after God's own heart. When we cannot create our own prayers, we can easily reach for Psalms as a way of "counting our blessings and being satisfied with what we produce."

The happiest people in the world are the most grateful. This correlation is strong and can be observed by the astute. Conversely, the unhappiest people in the world take all the credit for their blessings and have a feeling of entitlement that undercuts a proper attitude of gratitude.

# February 28

## Proverbs on Speech—Refreshing

"Good news from afar is refreshing" (25:25).

Do you recall standing at the mailbox waiting for the birthday card from Grandma which you were sure would contain treat money? Or being afraid to get out of earshot from the phone in case that special boy called for a date to the big dance? This verse reminds me of the father of the prodigal son who "saw him from afar off." This implies that the father must have been often turning his eyes to the horizon with the hope that his beloved son would be returning.

We know in our bones that this verse is true. Whether a letter, a call, a knock on the door, a telegram, or a skywriter, good news from afar is refreshing. Our hearts thrill at the receipt of the envelope with the law school admission office return address or the SAT or ACT testing office. Into the mundane workaday world comes news that in an instant can change the trajectory of our lives.

Perhaps good news from down the street or our neighbor is simply "more of the same" while news from afar has the exotic flavor attached to it. In Bible times, messengers were who brought news of battle victories, crowning of kings or birth of heirs. The best news of all time, the birth of the Messiah, was brought by angels, which literally means messengers. Some have testified to good news brought by angel messengers in our day—certainty that a loved one in hospital would recover, that a soldier in battle in Afghanistan was safe after a fierce firefight or that a long expected family member was returning to begin reconciliation.

This verse provides hope, past, current, and future that good news is still available.

# MARCH 1

## Proverbs on Relationships—Wise Children

"A wise son makes a father glad; a foolish son is the sorrow of a mother" (10:1).

Have you heard the saying, "A parent is about as happy as his/ her unhappiest child?" Since parents feel such responsibility for their children, it is difficult to untwine our states of mind from the experiences of our children. We feel such joy and pride when they "have it together," living happy productive lives of adult responsibility. On the contrary, it is difficult not to be miserable when our children are miserable, whether brought on by themselves or circumstances beyond their control.

"In the fear of the Lord there shall be hope for his children" (14:26). This seems to grant special blessings on the righteous—the hope of having favored children. While Proverbs does not consist of promises but rather general observations on how life operates, we love to draw hope from this optimistic verse.

"The father of the just rejoices" (12:24). What pride we take when our children are obedient to God's law and living a good life! This knowledge brings a deep seated pride and joy in our children. Stated another way, "If your child is wise, the parent will rejoice" (12:15). Parents of adult children recognize that while they try their utmost to shape and mold their children while they are within their sphere of influence, once a child is emancipated, a parent's influence is highly limited. Children necessarily pass through the time of separation from parental influence, often despising advice from parents in their twenties, but hopefully emerging on the other side of "separation" with renewed respect and gratitude for their parents' hard work over twenty years in caring for them and raising them to the best of their "lights" at the time. Parents are not perfect, but it is so gratifying when their children mature responsibly.

# March 2
## Proverbs on Relationships—Foolish Children

"A foolish son is the anger of the father and the sorrow of his mother" (17:25).

In contrast to the previous verses about wise children, there are several verses comparing the grief and heartache arising from observing our children growing astray. "A foolish son is the grief of his father" (19:13).

"By his inclinations a child is known if his works be clean and right" (20:11). Those who have taught Sunday school, Vacation Bible School, or even babysat for neighbors, the truth of this verse can be observed. It is easy for teachers or those in close contact with children to determine early on which children have a pure heart and those which have a rebellious foolish heart. Teachers do their best to guide and correct children, but studies show that most values have been formed by age four. This illustrates that parents will always be the primary influencers of their tots. While peer pressures and later life influences can derail someone on the right path, this verse indicates that one's basic ethics/conscience are mostly developed and evident by the time he/she is very young.

Contrasts between the personalities and good or bad inclinations of children can be spotted easily by those observing closely. While even good children can have meltdowns when tired or hungry, their basic inclinations of kindness or meanness seem to be "set" very early in life. While the "It takes a village to raise a child" saying has become a political hot potato, it cannot be disputed that extended family, teachers, coaches, neighbors, and all those who interact with and are in a position to influence a child have a responsibility to do their best to make the child a better person and thus our world a more positive place.

# MARCH 3

## Proverbs on Relationships—
## Correction of Children

"The rod and reproof give wisdom, but the child that is left to his own will brings his mother to shame" (12:15).

There are many Proverbs advising parents to correct their children out of love. "He that spares the rod hates his son" (13:24). This makes clear that to ignore our children or let them run wild is harmful to them; lax tolerant attitudes do not bode well for children. Even the most liberal child psychologist advocates careful monitoring of a child's conduct and correction when necessary. "Folly is bound up in the heart of a child; the rod of correction shall drive it away" (22:15).

Physical punishment may be "out of favor" in our modern culture and in our public schools, but many parents find that the biblical injunctions to correct in that manner are effective and positive in outcome.

"Chastise your son, despair not but don't kill him" (19:18). I believe this sets out the limitations of physical punishment: no permanent damage or injury should ever be undertaken. A spank on the backside with a wooden spoon seems to correct behavior. "Don't withhold correction from a child; if you beat him, he won't die or go to hell" (12:13).

The benefits of correction and instruction are clear. "Instruct your children and they shall give delight to your soul" (29:17). How pleasant it is to be in the presence of controlled families: families where it is evident they take notice of their children and closely monitor their behavior with a view to improving it in a kindly, consistent manner. To the contrary, when we observe in the supermarket or other public place an out of control child "running over" his parents, this brings grief to our hearts. Parents are in authority over their children and should not hesitate to correct or discipline for everyone's benefit.

# March 4

## Proverbs on Relationships—Grandchildren

"Grandchildren are the crown of old men" (17:6).

How we rejoice when our first grandchild is born! The feeling is indescribable to think about our legacy, the continuation of our family tree through our own beloved children. Grandchildren are a special blessing. Whether we are retired or not, we generally have more time than busy parents to dote on, influence, and rejoice in the lives of our grandchildren.

One special influence we can be is to pass along the family lore, the family stories to let children understand where they fit in the broader scheme of the extended family. The broader the perspective they have on their role and importance in their line, the more inspired they will be to "live up to" the family expectations and carry on with godly heritage to the next generation.

My grandmother and uncle were both fascinated with history, telling me stories early on about Indian Mounds discovered on our family farm in mid Missouri and Osage Indian tribes' activities in our area. Arrowheads, which washed out of our creek banks after heavy rains, increased the immediacy of the feelings that many other feet had trod the paths of our land. The more a child grasps the sense that they are merely one of many, I believe the more incentive the child has to listen to family traditions of religion and goodwill and follow in those footsteps. If a child has no sense of history and merely self focuses, this tends to lead toward selfishness and disregard of family legacies.

We should thank God for our grandchildren and do our utmost to show them love, make them feel special, and explain God's way of living and that it is designed by the creator of the universe for their benefit in maturing into a happy contented grown-up.

# March 5

## Proverbs on Relationships—Friendship

"A man amiable in society shall be more friendly than a brother" (18:24).

We should strive to be friendly to one and all. The person who exhibits a friendly attitude goes far in life, business, and social relationships. "Grace and friendship deliver a man" (25:9). Courtesy displayed to a law enforcement officer making a traffic stop goes a long way in "delivering" the driver from a ticket. A pleasant attitude in the business world is just as important as competence and work ethic to an employer.

"The good counsels of a friend are sweet to the soul" (27:9). Lunching with a friend can so lift our spirits. Whether married or single, we all need friends. This also reminds us that we should keep old and dear friends and not let relationships slide. "Don't forsake your or your father's friend" (27:20). This reminds us that old family friends are important as well. Not just our generation of friendships but those of our parents are important to loyally maintain.

Friends not only encourage us but also call us to task and keep us on the straight and narrow if we have the grace to heed their advice. The criticism of good friends, if sincere and good-hearted, can keep us out of bad experiences. "Like iron sharpening iron, so a man sharpens a friend" (27:17). Friends can tactfully "call us to task" about a planned life move that appears way off course or out of character. Friends who have our best interest at heart should be listened to and their advice thoroughly mulled over. If a friend is envious or critical out of jealousy, their advice is suspect, but if they love us and want to see us succeed, their advice may be invaluable, especially if our own perspective has become warped.

# March 6

## Proverbs on Relationships—Siblings

"A brother that is helped by his brother is like a strong city" (18:19).

The old saw about blood being thicker than water comes to mind. The older we get, the more we appreciate the uniqueness of our sibling relationships. Siblings are the only ones who had the same upbringing, the same family heritage, and understand why we are the way we are. While friends come and go, only siblings share years of playtime—years of family vacations and years of attending the same school, church, family weddings, funerals, and reunions.

When two siblings look out for each other, the strong effect is multiplied—"like a strong city." There are no more loyal bonds than the shared years and shared memories. In some respects, our siblings may understand us and have a clearer picture of what shaped our personality than we do.

Yes, sibling rivalry is a real influence, but when we compare our relationships of friends to siblings, siblings are in a special sphere. Love 'em or loath 'em, the lifelong influence of a sibling cannot be denied.

I believe this verse encourages us to strive to be loyal and helpful to our siblings. We should strive to overlook, forgive, and outgrow petty childhood differences and focus on the years we have in common, the memories that no one in the world but siblings know about. Even if just for the sake of old times, we should overlook the faults of siblings, the political differences, and do our utmost to reconcile and smooth relationships with our siblings.

And when that most difficult time arrives of settling together our parents' estates, dividing assets, we should likewise remember that people are always more important than material possessions. The relationships with our siblings should always take priority over our desire for "stuff."

# MARCH 7
## Proverbs on Relationships—Authorities

"A wise servant is acceptable to the king. He that is good for nothing shall feel the king's anger" (14:35).

In this day and time, the words *ruler, boss, leader,* or *employer* would be a good substitute for "king." This verse assures us that if we are a diligent, honest employee (servant), our work will be found acceptable by the boss, but if not, we can fully expect the displeasure of the boss. Employers look for and expect conscientious skilled workers and to keep a good relationship with our supervisor, we should work with a good work ethic.

Many verses detail the consequences of angering the "king" (CEO, boss, supervisor). "As the roaring of a lion so also is the anger of a king. His cheerfulness is as the dew upon the grass" (19:12). In other words, the fallout from an angry boss may be severe, but if we please the boss, we may bask in goodwill. "As the roaring of a lion so also is the dread of a king. He that provokes him, sins against his own soul" (20:2).

This verse shows the importance of staying within the good graces of our employer; it is our job to try to discern how best to work to satisfy the requirements of our employer. Otherwise, the consequences may be severe. Employees should strive to become competent in their areas of responsibility but also keep their ear to the ground to "read between the lines" to determine what will be deemed acceptable in completing our work.

The reverse situation is covered by "In the cheerfulness of the king's countenance is life" (16:15). Favor and rewards come to those who work diligently and competently to meet employer's expectations. Working hard and working smart are both expected both in biblical times and our own.

# March 8

## Proverbs on Relationships—
## Humility before Authorities

"Appear not glorious before the king and don't stand in the place of great men. It is better to be invited up than humbled before the prince" (25:6–7).

This verse makes clear that we should keep our nose to the grindstone faithfully completing our duties as our primary task rather than putting ourselves on display, "sucking up," bragging, and tooting our own horn. Bosses or CEOs can see through such cheap tactics and are not inclined to favor such a self-promoting employee. "It is unseemly for a servant (employee) to rule over princes" (19:10). This indicates that orderly relationships work best—that is, we should humbly perform our tasks assigned to us and not assert ourselves "above our station" or attempt to displace another. Backstabbing or treachery in work relationships do not pay off. What pays off in the long run is faithful completion of one's duties.

"The king's (boss's) clemency is like the latter rain" (16:15). "Latter rain" is an agricultural term referring to the rains that come after the fields are planted, thus bringing a fruitful harvest. If we perform our duties faithfully and are recognized for our faithfulness, without unduly calling attention to ourselves, in due time, the favor of the boss will be granted. "The hand of the valiant shall bear rule" (12:24). I believe this refers to not chafing under instructions from our duly constituted boss/supervisor. It is our job, as a faithful employee, to perform without complaint the reasonable requests of our boss that are within the scope of our duties. If we get too "high and mighty" and rebel against someone telling us what to do, this leads to failure and angers the boss. We are being paid for performance of our duties and should beware of getting too big for our britches.

# March 9

## Proverbs on Relationships—Righteous Rulers

"Wisdom and knowledge prolong a prince's life" (28:2).

Unjust rulers are subject to toppling; injustice more quickly dethrones a dictator. Common sense tells us that when a ruler or government rules with justice, considering the rights of their subjects, the people will be more satisfied and not be considering revolt. Stability in government is closely tied to the quality of the government, its overall justice.

"A wise king scatters the wicked and brings them to punishment" (20:26). The purpose of a righteous government is to pass laws to punish criminals and protect the rights of the innocent. So part of the job of a righteous ruler is to fairly discern righteous conduct from criminal conduct, legislate accordingly, and render punishment fairly in accordance with extant laws. Failure to do so allows the innocent to be overrun by wrongdoers, causing great dissatisfaction with the constituted government.

"Mercy and truth preserve the king (leader) and his rule is strengthened by clemency" (20:28). This echoes our verse of the day (above) and reinforces the principle that wise and fair leadership lends stability and longevity to a government or ruler. The reverse is "Take away wickedness from the face of the king and his throne shall be established with justice" (25:5). "Wisdom and knowledge prolong a prince's life" (28:2). In our day and time, when assassinations are not generally the way governments change, this verse would be equivalent to "prolong an administration" or tend toward reelection.

Anyone in a position of leadership, whether in government or business, should carefully familiarize themselves with these verses and act accordingly. All the verses reflect common sense, but it is certainly convicting to see these timeless principles laid out so clearly, in different words, but applicable to today's administrations.

# March 10

## Proverbs on Relationships—The Poor

"He that despises the poor reproaches his Maker" (17:5).

We are cautioned not to have contempt for the poor; negative consequences to us will ensue. "Do no violence to the poor because he is poor. Do not oppress the needy at the gate because the Lord will judge his cause and will afflict them that afflicted him" (22:22). The Lord's eye is upon everyone; he watches over all, and these verses seem to indicate he has special compassion for the poor. Jesus gave indication several places in the New Testament that special sympathy and kindness toward the poor were expected of his followers. These are not straight prohibitions; they are prohibitions with accompanying payback to those ignoring the prohibition.

The kingdom of God upon the earth envisions justice for the poor, so it is our job to help bring it about. "He that rejoices in another man's ruin shall not be unpunished" (17:5). We should not compare ourselves to the poor and gloat at their misfortune. Since there are three nearly identical Proverbs stressing not only the principle but also the negative risk to us if we disregard these Proverbs, we should take special heed.

"Better is the poor than the lying man" (19:22). This verse seems to carry an implication that the poor man may not be poor due to his own actions; poverty may at times come to anyone if medical conditions, disability, accident, or other disasters ensue without misconduct on the part of the afflicted. Lying, in contrast, is an intentional act which contravenes the Ten Commandments. In short, known disobedience to God's law is sure to bring negative payback while merely "being poor" can be a neutral condition. While often one's own neglect or misconduct can result in poverty, it can also result from force majeure. However poverty comes about, we are cautioned to treat the poor with kindness.

# March 11

## Proverbs on Relationships—Wise Wife

"He that has found a good wife has found a good thing, and he shall receive a pleasure from the Lord" (18:22).

Men, a prudent wife is from the Lord. Men should continually thank God and praise their good wives. The contrary admonition is, "He that drives away a good wife, drives away a good thing" (18:22). Although any person can cause irritation from time to time, spouses must take the long view and never lose sight of the blessing received from God.

We know that Proverbs chapter 31 lists the attributes of a prudent wife. The heart of her husband "trusts her"; she renders good to her husband and not ill. She is industrious, thrifty, a planner, and strong. She takes pains to look ahead and plan for her household in coming seasons. She is well dressed, a clever buyer/seller and manufacturer of handmade items. She has no fear of change of seasons or hard times due to her diligent insight and preparation. She is considered wise and her children rise up and bless her.

Above all, she reverences the Lord.

In contrast, the "everydayness" of married life magnifies the importance of avoidance of nagging. "A wrangling spouse is like a roof continually dropping through" (19:13). So then how is a roof continually leaking? It is irritating, unreliable, disgusting, a failure in its purpose. This comparison of attributes presents in a harsh light the effect of nagging upon one's spouse. Whether husband or wife, we know that continually nagging is quickly tuned out, making a relationship estranged. Stating a request once, clearly and fully, should be adequate. If our spouse chooses not to comply, we should think about other ways of accomplishing our need. Hire a repairman? Undertake the chore ourselves if it is within our capability? Accomplishment of a task in our time frame may not be worth a damaged relationship.

# MARCH 12

## Proverbs on Relationships—Fools

"A friend of fools shall become like them" (13:20).

Who we keep company with is most important to our conduct since our peers influence us more than we can imagine. Much thought should be given to who is within our circle of close friends; their impact is powerful.

Proverbs contains a variety of synonyms for a fool—rebel, scorner, wicked, the childish. One of the chief characteristics of a food is, "Fools despise wisdom and instruction" (1:7). Fools are arrogant, think they know it all, and do not need the advice or counsel of anyone. "The instruction of fools is foolishness" (16:22). That is, it is an utter and complete waste of time to try to convince a fool that he/she needs help or advice. The fool will only disregard this attempt and despise the person trying to convince him otherwise. "A fool receives not the words of prudence unless you say those things which are in his heart" (18:2). Again, the fool has no interest in hearing from others but seeks to reinforce his own worldview. Fools look for quotations, articles, or advice supporting their own perspective and disregard contrary comments.

"The fool despises his mother" (15:20). Thus, he or she refuses to take advice even from the person who loves them best and has their best interest at heart. Rebellion against authority often begins at home and soon follows into teachers at school, law enforcement officers making a traffic stop, judges in a courtroom, etc.

"He that walks in the right way and fears God is despised by him that goes by an infamous way" (14:2). This verse speaks to the natural enmity between a fool and a righteous person. The fool is guilty, and the proximity of a righteous person causes discomfort. Fools and righteous persons don't mix.

# MARCH 13

## Proverbs on Relationships—Neighbors

"Let your foot be seldom in your neighbor's house, lest he be weary of you and hate you" (25:17).

The name of the game is privacy! Don't we all know this from personal experience—we all need our personal space. A man's home is his castle! Emergencies are one thing, but social visiting should be kept to a minimum unless we see another outside in his yard perhaps. Dropping off misdirected mail is a helpful deed, but staying to visit is usually disruptive. We each have our personal agendas and chores to accomplish and interruptions are seldom welcome. We quickly wear out our welcome if we dream up excuses to stop and visit or, even worse, knock and visit.

We do have a special duty to our neighbor to watch out for unusual activity and notify authorities or neighbors if we can help. Did our neighbor inadvertently leave his garage door open after dark? A quick call is welcome. "Devise not evil against your neighbor, seeing he dwells securely by you" (3:29). This is a prohibition against doing harmful acts against our neighbor, but I believe this reasonably encompasses looking out for his or her best interests if something harmful endangers.

"The righteous is a guide to his neighbor, but the way of the wicked causes them to err" (12:26). If we learn of some development in the community that will affect our neighborhood, it would be neighborly to make sure our neighbor has heard the news if we can advise him/her in a pleasant, nondisruptive way.

"Don't go beyond ancient boundaries" (22:28). This admonition sets out the importance of respecting property lines. The setting of fences or shrubbery or landscaping should be carefully within boundary lines, and if we are unsure of them, a survey is warranted to avoid unnecessary disputes.

# MARCH 14

## Proverbs on Relationships—The Jones

"The ways of every covetous man destroys the soul" (1:19).

Are we caught up in the "keep up with the Jones" syndrome, continually comparing our "stuff" with our neighbors? Envy is toxic, says this verse, and self-destructive. Comparison does nothing but cause hard feelings in us and in others. Comparison kills contentment, the state for which the righteous should strive.

"A covetous man shall destroy the land" (29:4). Envying another leads to strife, which leads to arguments, which leads to disputes, which leads to legal claims, which leads to lawsuits, which leads to judgments, and which leads to long held resentments and bitterness. Proverbs makes clear that if a thought involving comparison and envy passes through our mind, we should immediately capture and dismiss it. Dwelling on it leads to entrenched hard feelings in a downward spiral of negativity and bad consequences.

"Fools covet things which are hurtful to them" (1:22). Coveting anything is worse than counterproductive; it is harmful. Remember that coveting makes the top ten—the Ten Commandments. "You shall not covet your neighbor's wife, nor his ass, nor his servant, nor anything of his." Focus on self-improvement and logs in our own eyes—not the new BMW sitting in the neighbor's driveway, nor the new pontoon boat sitting in his side yard.

While we might have thought our new landscaping was a thing of beauty, when our neighbor puts in a pool and spa and gazebo, our pride becomes tainted by envy, bringing a sense of bitterness to our mouth. These days, comparisons seem to center around our children's accomplishments. Witness the common bumper sticker, "My child is an honor student at Rockwall High." Fathers of Little Leaguers can work themselves into a frenzy when another's son is allowed to play more than ours. Turn your attention elsewhere!

# MARCH 15

## Proverbs on Relationships—Meddlers

"All fools are meddling with reproaches" (20:3).

Do you have a habit of involving yourself in another's problems? Sticking your nose in when it's not your fight? Proverbs warns against this. We know from personal experience that good seldom comes from this type of interference. We have enough problems of our own without commenting on a situation or criticizing another's actions when we are not involved.

"The just is first accuser of himself" (18:17). We should be focusing on our own conduct, improving those areas of our character that are lacking, rather than looking outward. Unless we are asked for our counsel, we should refrain from accusing others of deficiencies. "He that is pure, his work is right" (21:8). The work of the righteous is to continually align his/her character with biblical principles—not go looking for deficiencies elsewhere.

"Among the just grace shall abide" (14:9). This reminds us that even when we do see and are tempted to judge the deficiencies of others, the best course is to extend grace to others. No one made us judge, jury, and executioner. God is the ultimate judge of all.

"The root of the just shall not be moved" (12:3). Our firm foundation is living a life of integrity, compassion, and grace. When conduct of those around us is less than desirable, what does that have to do with us? We can stand secure knowing that we are responsible for our own conduct but not that of others around us. We should stick to our knitting—learning more and more from scriptures about how best to live and applying it to our own life. Have you been tempted, when you gained insight into a particular spiritual principle, to try to change everyone around you? Avoid meddling.

# March 16

## Proverbs on Relationships—Friends

"Thine own friend, and your father's friend, forsake not" (27:10).

This verse points to the importance of loyalty in our long-term relationships. "Our father's friend" refers to long held relationships, stemming over generations. Loyalty is a virtue we should strive for. "A friend loves at all times" (17:17).

How should we respond to a fault in a friend? "He that covers a transgression seeks love. But he that harps on a matter separates chief friends" (17:9). Everyone in life will get on our nerves at times, rub us the wrong way, or do something irritating to us. If we are to keep friends, we must extend grace and realize that no one is perfect. In order to maintain a long-term friendship, we must focus on the positive and minimize the negatives.

However, we should carefully choose our friends in the first instance. "Make no friendship with a man that is given to anger, and with a wrathful man you shall not go" (22:24). Perhaps anger is contagious, or perhaps we will be caught up in the negative consequences of a friend's expression of anger, if we are with them, causing danger to ourself. We cannot help but be influenced by someone's character if we often are with them. We are cautioned to seek out friends who will be good examples.

Sometimes, we will have occasion to hear unwelcome observations from a close friend. They will tell it like it is for our benefit. "Faithful are the wounds of a friend, but the kisses of an enemy are profuse" (27:6). Our egos may be wounded by constructive criticisms of a friend, but we can be sure a true friend will only speak in such manner for our betterment. Recognizing the objectivity and sincerity of such criticism, we would be well to heed it.

# March 17

## Proverbs on Relationships—Peers

"Have the sense to stay away from evil men who want you to be their partners in crime" (2:11).

At some point in our lives, we may be pressured by our peers to join them in shady activities. We must have the good sense to decline and to see clearly the potential consequences of that downward path. Cutting a legal corner here, ignoring a requirement there could lead to disaster and a ruined reputation.

More is said about these unwholesome peers. They are "Men who turn from God's ways to walk down dark and evil paths, and exult in doing wrong, for they thoroughly enjoy their sins. Everything they do is crooked and wrong" (2:12–15). We must use discernment especially in selecting business partners or those involving financial dealings. Check backgrounds through Better Business Bureau? Get ample references. Expedience in achieving a deal or a goal is no excuse for ignoring our gut feelings of danger in associating with someone who has no fixed principles of integrity.

"Follow the steps of the godly instead, and stay on the right path, for only good men enjoy life to the full; evil men lose the good things they might have had, and they themselves shall be destroyed" (2:20–22). Biblical consequences are clearly laid out. Selection of the right path, especially when we are young and inexperienced about human nature and personality indicators, is crucial to a good life.

"A life of doing right is the wisest life there is. If you live that kind of life, you'll not limp or stumble as you run. Carry out my instructions; don't forget them, for they will lead you to real living" (4:11–13).

Forks in the road of life are more clear cut than we might think, and if we lose sight of guiding principles, a review of Proverbs is in order.

# March 18

## Proverbs on Relationships—Harlots

"He who goes into a strange woman shall never return to the paths of life" (2:16).

There are many verses in Proverbs on the horrendous dangers of committing adultery and the many temptations encountered along the way of life. "He that keeps an adulteress is foolish and wicked" (18:22). "A harlot is a deep ditch which will kill." "He that maintains harlots shall squander away his substance" (29:3). In other words, giving in to sexual temptation will get us off track, ruin our health, reputation, and finances, and set us on an inextricable downward spiral.

The wicked are more susceptible to these temptations, but we are all enticed. "Adultery shall catch the wicked and bind him fast with the ropes of his own sin" (5:22). "The adulteress' house inclines to death and her paths to hell" (2:16). This is about as straightforward as it gets. These verses are hard-hitting and extreme, revealing that it is extremely difficult, if not impossible, to get one's life back on track if this sinful detour is chosen.

While we might realize that harm to reputation and marriage is inevitable, another dimension that is clearly addressed is financial ruin. "Those who consort with harlots, your labors shall go to another's house" (5:3). Whether through alimony to one's wife following divorce, bad business deals due to loss of integrity, or loss of opportunities due to reputational damage, our pocketbooks are affected.

The ultimate consequence is death! "Adulterers shall die because they have not received instruction" (5:23).

On the other hand, remaining loyal to one's spouse is life giving. "Let your health be blessed—rejoice with the wife of your youth" (5:18). Many modern medical studies prove that monogamy improves our health and loving relationships improve our mental states as well.

# MARCH 19

## Proverbs on Relationships—Counselors

"Hear counsel and receive instruction that you may be wise at your end" (19:20).

When we are young, we have teachers and parents and Sunday school teachers conscientiously advising us on the best way to live. When we are older, we sometimes think we don't need any advice. This thinking is a mistake, as there is always someone older, wiser, and more experienced in whatever course we are considering. Our egos should never get in the way of listening to, considering carefully and heeding good counsel meant for our benefit.

"Plans are strengthened by counsel" (20:18). If we are setting out on an important life change of direction or entering a course for which we have little experience, we should intentionally seek out experts in the field, those "ahead of us" on the journey to gain the benefit of their experience, without having to suffer failures and pitfalls on our own. We can save ourselves much grief and regret by searching for books, articles, interviews, blogs, and other sources to guide us. That is why TripAdvisor is so popular! "There shall be safety where there are many counsels" (24:6). The more people we talk to, especially those with known Christian character, the more secure we can feel about charting our intended course. "Keep the law and counsel and you shall walk confidently and your foot shall not stumble."

Receiving and attending to expert counsel boosts our confidence and allows us to proceed forward without undue second guessing and insomnia. Even if the advice we receive goes against our intended course, it is better to know now than later when it is too late. "A reproof avails more with a wise man than a hundred stripes with a fool" (17:12). Better to receive bad news while we can still avoid the pitfall.

# MARCH 20

## Proverbs on Relationships—The Fool

"The fool shall serve the wise" (10:23).

How are we to relate to those who disregard God's principles and wisdom? Although fools are prone to self-destruction, there are surprising observations made in Proverbs about their relationships with the wise.

The natural order of God's universe is that there is a natural enmity between the fool and the wise or righteous person. "Fools hate them that flee from evil things" (13:19).

While the righteous person may be tempted to try to "save" or set right the course of the foolish, it is clear that this is a waste of time. "The instruction of fools is foolishness" (16:22). "A fool receives not the words of prudence unless you say those things which are in his heart" (18:2). "Do not instruct a fool because he will despise you" (23:9). A fool has no use for good advice, takes no notice of righteous examples and even the usual management advice of praising *good* deeds when noticed is wasted on a fool. "It is futile to give honor to a fool" (26:8).

"The folly of fools is imprudence" (14:24). "Wisdom is too high for a fool" (24:7). God's wisdom for living is set out in black and white clearly for those who care to learn, study, and apply it. But fools don't bother to even search for wisdom, much less heed it when seen. "The thought of a fool is sin" (24:9). The fool's thoughts do not attempt to find the wise way but only the way they determine. A fool is blind to better paths in life, even though they are right in front of him or her. Why? Pride. "In the mouth of a fool is the rod of pride" (14:32). That is the root of the problem and the reason the righteous end up on top and the foolish end up serving the wise.

# March 21

## Proverbs on Relationships—Deceiver

"Practice not evil against your friend when he has confidence in you" (3:29).

Those who double-cross friends or commit treachery against a companion are evildoers. Friends expect loyalty from friends since they have made themselves vulnerable and revealed sensitive information. Persons who abuse such relationships and misuse confidential information are disfavored. Later, attempts to make right the damage are futile. "It is ruin to a man to destroy good men and thereafter to retract" (20:25). We all know that the headline accusing a person of wrongdoing is never truly counteracted by the later article on page 5 reporting that the accused was found innocent. The damage has been done since bad news sticks to minds like glue.

We only harm ourselves when we mistreat friends in this way. "A man that speaks to his friend with deceitful flattery spreads a net for his feet" (29:5). We embroil ourselves in dirt and soil our own reputation when we wrongfully seek to discredit another.

Our evil intentions will be found out when we slander or libel another. "He that covers hatred deceitfully, his malice shall be laid open publicly" (26:26). Lack of integrity is revealed in a variety of ways whether facial expression, tattletales, inconsistent writings, and—in this day—Facebook posts that seemingly can never be erased and live forever in cyberspace.

While we may think to gain advantage over our enemy by badmouthing him or her, the damage soon redounds to us and disgraces the speaker as evil motives appear. God's principles cannot be thwarted; his eternal laws of reaping and sowing will "out." Even New Agers who speak of karma recognize that bad deeds done to another will bring on the doer's head negative consequences.

We should strive to be faithful friends and avoid practicing any deceit.

# March 22

## Proverbs on Relationships—Faithfulness

"Many men are called merciful but who shall find a faithful man?" (20:6).

This verse indicates that truly faithful persons are hard to find, few and far between. We should strive for faithfulness since this pleases God. "They that deal faithfully please Him" (12:22). Rewards naturally follow. "He that is the keeper of his master shall be glorified" (27:18). In our day, we don't speak of masters but of employers, bosses, CEOs, or leaders. In other words, faithful employees who keep their nose to the grindstone and faithfully perform their assigned duties in a skillful and diligent manner will be recognized, promoted, and treated right which enhances both the reputation of the employee and their employer.

"A faithful messenger greatly refreshes the sender" (15:13). It is comforting knowing that when you know the person you select for an important task, to deliver an important message or represent you in an important forum, can be counted on. You will not lose sleep over the accomplishment of the assigned task. You will not have to worry about the outcome. Faithful agents are invaluable and, once discovered, are retained in close proximity for future assignments.

We know from common experience that faithfulness is so uncommon that those in positions of responsibility take notice of it. Christians should realize that this trait is a good indicator of their character and therefore should strive to present the best witness possible as a representative of Christ. Faithfulness in work, faithfulness in volunteer and church responsibilities, and faithfulness in family life are essential attributes of a dedicated Christian. In this way, we can signal to the world that we are different and better than the average employee; we can "let our light shine" and stand out in the crowd of common folks.

# March 23

## Proverbs on Relationships—Enemies

"When the ways of man shall please the Lord, He will convert even his enemies to peace" (16:7).

When we conform our character to reflect the attributes of Christ and strive to live peaceably with our enemies, we will receive divine aid in our endeavor to keep the peace. This verse reflects special divine intervention that will come about when we do our part. "He that fears the commandment dwells in peace" (13:13). Our relationships in all aspects of our lives should improve when we study wisdom and apply it to our lives, even relationships with our adversaries.

"Strive not against a man without cause when he has done you no evil" (3:30). Instead of letting minor irritations bloom into full fledged strife, the wise person smoothes over offenses, does not dwell on them, and positively tries to improve all relationships. Dwelling on a person's good points instead of focusing on the bad in grace allows the other person a do-over to improve their conduct.

"All the paths of wisdom are peaceable" (3:17). Peace should characterize our conduct and behavior in all our relationships. When others realize we aren't anxious to criticize, jump on their mistakes, and keep a sharp eye out for ways in which they've fallen short, their stress level will lower, allowing entrees of reconciliation. Perhaps our conduct will be an example to the other partner in the relationship. Teachers and social workers have learned the tactic of lowering the volume and sharpness of their voice in direct contrast to the loudness and anger of the listener. A soft answer turns away wrath and naturally de-escalates and tends to defuse a volatile conversation. We can do much, with our wisdom and godly conduct, to smooth relationships, exhibiting love with our voice and attitude.

# MARCH 24

## Proverbs on Relationships—The Proud

"One who boasts but does not fulfill his promises is like thunderstorms without rain" (25:14).

Proverbs has many verses which make clear that pride is a deadly negative factor which can kill relationships. No one likes a grandstander! Even worse is someone who boasts about his ability to accomplish something or fulfill a role but does not follow through. Since we have all been burned by such a promise, we should all be wary of boasting about events beyond our control or events we are unsure of fulfilling.

The worst of negative consequences come to the proud boaster. "The Lord will destroy the house of the proud" (15:25). We've all heard the saying, "Pride goes before a fall." Proverbs is the ultimate source of this maxim. "Pride goes before destruction and the spirit is lifted up before a fall" (16:18). This is the full restatement of that shorthand piece of wisdom. "Every proud man is an abomination to the Lord" (16:5).

Similarly, "He that makes his house high seeks a downfall" (17:16). "He that exalts his door seeks ruin" (17:19). "Humiliation follows the proud" (29:23). All these verses embody that single principle that nothing good results from broadcasting our pride and arrogance. "The proud and arrogant is ignorant who in anger works pride" (21:24).

Pridefulness puts people off, holds them at a distant, and puts them in their place. Pride is toxic to relationships of all types whether a spouse, child, coworker, or person we are trying to help. Condemning their conduct by negative comparison with ours tends to harden their position, making it more difficult to establish a working relationship. We warm up to folks when we feel we are peers, but we resent and avoid those who set themselves up as better than others.

# March 25

## Proverbs on Relationships—Pets/Animals

"The just regards the lives of his beasts" (12:10).

Did you realize that Proverbs not only addresses relationships with persons but also our pets or animals under our care? What a comprehensive book! The wise person considers carefully what is in the best interest of his/her pets and provides for their care. The wise person does not ignore them and leave them to their own devices. He "regards" their lives. I believe this means we are obligated to learn about how best to feed, exercise, and look after them and take steps to diligently and consistently care for them. The careless person ignores them; the mean person kicks the dog when he walks in the door after a bad day.

The wise person realizes that beasts are dependent on us so we must not fail in our obligations of compassion and care. Pets are also dependent on us to obtain the necessary affection. When we are to be gone, we must select carefully a responsible substitute provider: kennel, neighbor, caregiver. We should be scrupulous in taking them for their annual veterinarian checkup, and if we become no longer able to care for them due to illness or other responsibilities, we should carefully select a rescue organization to find a caring home for them.

Similarly, our field or farm animals—horses, cattle, chickens, ducks, pigs, and the like—deserve our attention and care in good weather and bad. If we assume responsibility for them, we must follow through. If we give pets or livestock to children, we have a duty to carefully train them in the animal's needs and how to meet those needs.

In the Old Testament story of Jonah, God was clear that he not only was concerned about the people of Nineveh facing destruction if they were unrepentant but also the many animals in the city. God cares for animals and expects wise persons to do the same.

# March 26

## Proverbs on Relationships—Parents

"The father of the just rejoices" (12:24).

Do you want to make your parents happy? The Ten Commandments stress the importance of honoring one's parents so that it will go well with us. "A wise son makes a father glad; a foolish son is the sorrow of a mother" (10:1). Our conduct in life does not only concern ourselves and our Creator but also our parents. We never get too old to be concerned about the conduct of our children. Conversely, we, as children, should always keep in mind that our behavior, our reputation, reflect upon and strongly affect the emotional life of our parents. Keeping in mind that everything we do influences our parents is a straightforward way of respecting our parents. Keeping in mind that kudos make them happy and blots on our life disappoint and even depress them is one spur to laudable behavior and a deterrent to misbehavior.

"If your child is wise, the parent will rejoice" (12:15). Many verses in Proverbs discuss the close relationship between the acts of children and the emotional state of their parents. "A foolish son is the anger of the father and the sorrow of his mother" (17:25). Notice how closely this verse parallels the verse quoted in the first paragraph, but notice the difference. Gladness and anger are results of children's behavior—both good and bad behaviors affect the emotional state of the parent.

"In the fear of the Lord there shall be hope for his children" (14:26). Consistent discipline of children and raising children to know and respect the commandments of God is a parent's best means of ensuring responsible adult behavior which leads to pride and satisfaction on the part of parents in their old age. Even with a rocky start, a parent not raising children by the "Book" can change his/her ways and begin to relate to his/her children in a righteous manner. Grace is always available for fresh starts.

# MARCH 27

## Proverbs on Relationships—The Righteous

"The righteous are merciful and show mercy" (13:13).

The righteous relates to everyone in their life according to the law of love: children, parents, peers, those in authority, the poor, one's spouse. The characteristics of the righteous reflect the character of God: compassionate, longsuffering, patient, loving, kind, loyal, and charitable. "He that is pure, his work is right" (21:8). The employer of the righteous should be able to place trust in the employee and not have to continually look over his/her shoulder to ensure assigned tasks are diligently and honestly performed.

Righteous friends do not backstab or double cross; instead, they go beyond the call of duty and act as a steward, putting the interests of the other above one's own. "Among the just, grace shall abide" (14:9). *Just* seems to be used as a synonym for *righteous* throughout Proverbs. A righteous person acts with justice and therefore can be termed "just." *Good man* is another common synonym for the *righteous.*

"The good man shall be above the fool" (14:14). Whether in terms of evaluations at work, reliance, and promotions into positions of trust, character "tells." All persons in authority seek persons on which they can completely rely. Just like Joseph in the Old Testament was quickly identified by Pharaoh as one who, while able to interpret dreams, also showed judgment, intelligence, and—above all—character. Thus, Pharaoh quickly promoted Joseph to be high right hand man to initiate and implement grain storage measures to prepare for seven years of drought since he could foresee that Joseph would not be "skimming" grain for his own enrichment but acting for the good of the Egyptian people as a whole.

"When it goes well with the just, the city shall rejoice" (11:10). Not only in relationships with individuals but also in public and government affairs, character is evident, rejoicing the people.

# MARCH 28

## Proverbs on Relationships—The Generous Person

"Riches make many friends" (19:4).

Wealthy individuals are sought after by many: to make charitable donations, to serve on corporate boards, to fill nonprofit positions, to fulfill church leadership roles, and to serve in government. Why? We instinctively assume that if one can competently manage money and have the discipline to save and accumulate, both native intelligence and good judgment must be present. Of course, we hope the generous person will also write big checks to the organization seeking out his/her time. For many reasons, a wealthy person is in demand.

"The rich rule over the poor; the borrower serves the lender" (22:7). In financial transactions, the person with the cash holds the leverage. The potential borrower with hat in hand at the local banker is well aware of this disparity. The banker on the back side of the desk holds all the cards. The poor man, in debt, must sometimes work for years to pay off the bank loan or the private note.

"The rich man seems to himself wise, but the prudent poor man shall search him out" (28:11). Wealth can lead to arrogance and a sense of superiority, but the wealthy person who can keep wealth in proper perspective, recognizing the true source of wealth, sets an example that others, rich or poor, study and emulate.

"He that has pity on the poor honors his Maker" (14:31). A righteous wealthy man must always recall that our Creator gives us power to accumulate wealth. "The soul that blesses shall be made fat" (11:25). This echos the reaping/sowing principle pervasive throughout scriptures, both Old Testament and New Testament. Generosity always rebounds and leads to return blessings.

"Some distribute their own goods and grow richer; others take away what is not their own and are always in want" (11:24). Wealth plus generosity is an upward spiral by divine decree.

# March 29

## Proverbs on Relationships—The Angry Person

"He that provokes wrath brings strife" (30:33).

Anger is a telltale sign of a person who has some major maturing to do before that person can be a decent role model for others and a sure sign of someone to avoid establishing a relationship with.

An angry person can wreck a work group, cause deep divisions on a corporate board, break up a family, and—along the way—create major disunity and heartache. Beware of befriending a habitually angry person. While everyone loses their temper from time to time, an irritable person fast on the trigger of anger has an uphill battle in life and wreaks difficulty in all their relationships.

"He that is easily stirred up to wrath shall be more prone to sin" (29:22). Once red hot anger takes ahold of one's brain, logical thinking and rational responses go out the window. Cursing, slander, lies, and cover-up frequently result, causing messes that can take lifetimes to set right. If we have an anger problem, we should pray for patience. Thomas Jefferson said that if angry, count to ten and if very angry, count to twenty before responding. "Anger has no mercy when it breaks forth. Who can bear the violence of one provoked?" (27:4). Anger is like toothpaste emerging from a tube; once out, it cannot be put back in; damage is done in an instant. Angry words, angry actions cannot be undone. While one may ask forgiveness, it may take months or years before the one bearing the brunt of another's anger can grant forgiveness. In any event, one can never forget damage wreaked by an uncontrolled tongue or fist.

"The anger of a fool is heavier than stones or sand" (27:3). I believe this refers to the way that anger weighs on the spirits of those confronted with it. It cannot lightly be ignored or forgotten.

# MARCH 31

## Proverbs on Relationships—The Proud

"Every proud person is an abomination to the Lord" (16:5). The verses in Proverbs concerning the proud are harsh and direct. "The Lord will destroy the house of the proud and will strengthen the borders of the widow" (15:25). Wow! Destruction is about as serious a penalty as it gets. Of course, we should examine ourselves to guard against self-destructive pride but also avoid associating and befriending those with excessive pride. "He that makes his house high seeks a downfall" (17:16). The reigns of Louis XIV in France and the Chinese emperor come to mind. The greater the disparity between excessively rich and prideful versus the poor peasants, the greater the likelihood of revolt and destruction of the governing class. Similarly in Russia, the Czars held massive amounts of jewels, dachas, and furs while the peasants starved. Class struggle and bloody revolutions followed.

"He that exalts his door seeks ruin" (17:19). When driving in the countryside or city and seeing high walls, locked gates, and security devices, these protections signal the thief or dishonest person that something "good" must be inside that is worth trying to steal. In comparison, the moderate estate invites no such speculation about the riches hidden inside. "The proud and arrogant is ignorant who in anger works pride" (21:24). Pride often leads to touchiness and anger. How dare that person question my position!

Proverbs strongly warns against boasting. "Boast not for tomorrow, for you don't know what tomorrow will bring" (27:1). Our job is to focus on today, living it as well as we can in light of God's rules for living. Excessive obsessing about tomorrow takes our eyes off today and undermines job number 1. "One who boasts but does not fulfill his promises is like thunderstorms without rain" (25:14).

# APRIL 1

## Proverbs on Attitudes—Rebellion

"Fools despise wisdom and instruction" (1:7).

The telltale sign of a fool is a rebellious spirit. The first rebel was Satan—prideful, believing he knew more than God and unable to humble himself to be under God's authority. If a student in class or an employee in a workplace or a child displays this attitude, those in authority should use strong measures to apply discipline and warn of the potential consequences of such conduct. Unteachability—the attitude that "no one can tell me anything" is self-destructive in the extreme. Rebelliousness displayed to a law enforcement officer during a traffic stop can land the driver in jail in a heartbeat! Then the arrest is on one's record, affecting future employment forever.

"A reproof avails more with a wise man than a 100 stripes with a fool" (17:12). Discipline is generally resisted by the rebel heart, but if we are in a position of leadership over the individual, our child, our employee, or our student, we must try to talk sense into the person. "Wisdom is too high for a fool" (24:7). This means the fool has no interest in learning from others and especially being criticized by others, for the fool already knows it all. "A scorner seeks wisdom and finds it not" (14:6). *Scorner* is a frequent synonym for *rebel* in scriptures. A scorner scorns anyone or anything purporting to instruct him and even if the rebel attempts to learn, the set of his heart cuts against the attempt.

"The foolish pulls down with his own hands that which is built" (14:1). This shows the height of self-destruction coming the way of a rebellious fool. Families, classrooms, and institutions all suffer from hosting a rebel in their midst. "A friend of fools shall become like them" (13:20). Thus, we are warned from adopting a rebel as a close friend.

# APRIL 2

## Proverbs on Attitudes—Complaining

"Remove from you a negative mouth and let detracting lips be far from you" (4:24).

No one cares to be in close proximity to a habitual complainer. Whether about the weather, one's health issues, one's family, or coworkers, people remove themselves from the company of a complainer. This is also directly contrary to the Psalms frequent admonition to be joyful, the telltale mark of a mature disciple of Christ. Complaining is also harmful to our health due to the close relationship between our attitudes and our body. "A sorrowful spirit dries up the bones" (17:22). We were designed for joy, and our bodily functions and systems are improved and lubricated by a positive spirit.

"All fools are meddling with reproaches" (20:3). If our goal in life is to become Christlike, we should be intentional about choosing to display a good attitude and conscientiously avoiding negativity. If we want to have friends, we must be friendly, not a continual griper. If a complainer doesn't currently have his own problems to gripe about, complainers frequently "reach" and stick their nose in others' issues, the definition of meddling.

One aspect of self-control is controlling what emerges from one's mouth in the form of complaints. Whether we are just letting off steam, speaking out of boredom or are in the mood for a fight, if our comments are not designed to positively impact and improve a situation, we should simply refrain from speaking.

Complaining can generate negative effects upon the speaker. "A curse without cause shall boomerang" (26:2). Criticism that is baseless shall not harm the accused but reflect dishonor and lack of integrity upon the criticizer.

In order to break a habit of complaining, we must take positive steps to replace potential criticism with positive remarks. Whether in the form of post-it notes on our bathroom mirror, car dashboard, or phone base, reminders to avoid negativity can get us started.

# April 3

## Proverbs on Attitudes—Pride

"Every proud man is an abomination to the Lord" (16:5).

This verse is a direct, hard-hitting condemnation of undue pride. Many verses echo this principle and warn of the consequences of prideful actions or attitudes. Boasting is a common speech pattern of the proud, but it is warned against.

"One who boasts but does not fulfill his promises is like thunderstorms without rain" (25:14). Thunderstorms cause commotion, anxiety, and concern but do not produce anything worthwhile or desirable. Thus, boasting does not lead to good fruit or beneficial results. It offends people; it causes resentment in hearers but does not produce any good thing. "Boast not for tomorrow, for you don't know what tomorrow will bring" (27:1). Often, we have a tendency to live in the future, boasting to our friends about our next planned vacation, our next special outing, tickets to a big upcoming concert. But many things could happen between now and then burying those plans. Wait until the event is in the past before posting on Facebook about it, bragging to neighbors or tooting our horn.

"The proud and arrogant is ignorant who in anger works pride" (21:24). A common emotion that kindles anger is quick offense, and a close analysis of a tendency to be easily offended is that one's pride has been pricked. Touchiness, easy irritability are symptoms of over-active pride.

Pride sets us up for a downfall. This phrase from Proverbs has entered our common vocabulary. "Pride goes before destruction and the spirit is lifted up before a fall" (16:18). This is often condensed to "Pride goes before a fall." "Humiliation follows the proud" (29:23). This verse describes the point in time after the fall when we are humiliated and brought low. "He that makes his house high seeks a downfall" (17:16).

# APRIL 4

## Proverbs on Attitudes—Quarrelsome

"Strive not against a man without cause when he has done you no evil" (3:30).

If we follow this principle, we will rarely be the originator of quarrels. Only if someone has intentionally "done evil" to us are we justified in challenging another. Otherwise, the righteous person is called to overlook an offense in love. This is the loving response to potential offenses—let it go. We ourselves are not always perfect, so why should we expect perfection from others? Feelings get hurt, intentionally at times, but more often unintentionally. Our world would be a better place if we train our responses to be patient, kind, and forgiving.

"He that fears the commandment dwells in peace" (13:12). Focusing not on our feelings this moment when we feel offended, but the long-term view incents us to recall that we usually must deal with the offender on a daily, weekly, or monthly basis. Why ruin a relationship over one small offense? If we get our back up and take offense at the slight "cut," we will end up a bitter old person without friends. No one likes to have to walk on pins and needles for fear of offending a thin skinned person. When we respond irritably to an offense, we stir up our emotions in a negative way, causing our innards to seethe and roil. Such upset has negative effects on our bodily systems as well as our emotions. "Joy follows those who take counsels of peace" (12:20). Life will go much smoother if we train our reactions to maintain peace.

What about those enemies that we simply cannot do anything right to please them? Is there hope? I think one of the most positive verses in Proverbs is, "When the ways of man shall please the Lord, he will convert even his enemies to peace" (16:7). Let's focus on our conduct, and let God change our enemy's heart.

# APRIL 5

## Proverbs on Attitudes—Simplicity

"The Lord's communication is with the simple" (3:32). What does *simple* mean when used in Proverbs? A connotation of childlike faith, trust in God and focus on God instead of world culture is the likely meaning. "The simplicity of the just shall guide them" (11:3). Instead of being tugged this way and that by the unstable values of our world, if we learn, follow, and trust in the principles for living set out in Proverbs, the possible detours off the correct path narrow, and our way becomes clear.

What are the benefits of simplicity? "The Lord will protect those who walk in simplicity and guard the ways of the saints" (2:7). This promise of protection offers great comfort to God's people. Other benefits relate to our progeny. "The just that walks in simplicity shall leave blessed children" (20:7). Even wealth does not counteract the benefits of simplicity. "Better is the poor man who walks in his simplicity than a rich man who is perverse in his lips and unwise" (19:1). Wealth is not a top level virtue; simplicity is. In weighing and balancing various pursuits in life, it is instructive to note how highly simplicity rates. Another similar verse is: "Better is the poor man walking in his simplicity than the rich in crooked ways" (28:6). In other words, wealth should not be our goal; simplicity should be. Understanding God's Ten Commandments and the more detailed nuances of godly living expressed in Proverbs "pays" more than single-minded pursuit of wealth.

Longevity is another benefit. "The simple shall continue in the earth" (2:21). Simplicity leads to the more general benefits of wisdom set out in Proverbs: health, abundance, joy, and peace. We are not easily led astray but can give God's principles for living priority in all our endeavors.

# APRIL 6

## Proverbs on Attitudes—Gratitude

"Count your blessings and be satisfied with what you produce" (27:27).

An attitude of gratitude is desired by God of his children. He created a beautiful world, marvelous bodies, nearly unlimited mind capacity and hearts that can be filled with his best blessing, love, if we will maintain correct focus.

Sometimes, we focus on our troubles, aches, pains, and relationship difficulties and lose sight of our blessings. It is easy to get sucked into a downward spiral of self-pity and regrets: "Nothing ever goes right." While clinical depression may have metabolic causes, many depressives are in their miry pit due to long habits of focusing on the negative instead of the positive. Even if we can, upon awakening, get in a good habit of devoting the first two minutes of our day, before rising, to thanking God for the priceless gift of another day, we vastly strengthen the possibility of a healthy attitude to carry us through the day. Sometimes, we don't know where to start in offering gratitude. We can begin where we are; thanks for the soft pillow upon which we lie, the cool darkened room in which to relax, the warm body of our companion (pet or human) lying beside us, a job or task to accomplish that day and food in the fridge to eat for breakfast.

Gratitude journals are all the rage, and many recent books have been published about the benefits of and the systematic ways to catalog our blessings. There is a clear mind/body connection between a grateful attitude and good health. Gratitude is the bedrock of worship; how can we worship a God when we feel our life is worthless or hopeless. Some wags have commented that humans had to invent a god in order to have someone to thank for the gift of creation. Think on the profundity of that.

# APRIL 7

## Proverbs on Attitudes—Humility

"Appear not glorious before the king and don't stand in the place of great men. It is better to be invited up than humbled before the prince" (25:6–7).

How embarrassing to present ourselves at the head table of a banquet, assuming we are a big shot, and be utterly mortified when escorted to a less prestigious seat in front of the whole room of attendees! We should avoid making assumptions about our own importance only to be knocked down to true size.

"Where humility is, there also is wisdom" (11:2). Understanding one's true importance or place in the universe, having a correct perspective on our lot, is the beginning of wisdom. All children of God are of equal divine worth in his sight, so it offends God's sense of justice for us to "lord it over" others created by him.

Great blessings are promised to the humble. "The fruit of humility is the fear of the Lord, riches, glory and life" (22:4). Paradoxically, the way to receive honor is not to strive for it but to humbly serve. "Humility goes before glory" (15:33). "Before a man be glorified, his heart is humbled" (18:12). "Glory shall uphold the humble of spirit" (29:33). These verses track with Jesus's several gospel sayings reflecting God's upside down economy: the greatest of these is the one lowly serving others.

"It is better to be humbled with the meek than to divide spoils with the proud" (16:19). Humility is truly a virtue worth striving for. Focusing on ourselves and our accomplishments is contrary to God's desire that we love others, loving our neighbors as ourselves. Loving others causes us to think first about whether there is anything we can do in a loving manner to make their life more pleasant.

# APRIL 8

## Proverbs on Attitudes—Joy

"A joyful mind makes age flourishing" (17:22).

Joy is one of the truest indicators of a mature Christian. Even when advanced in age, with accompanying aches and pains, our minds can remain on Christ and his coming kingdom, bringing a smile to our countenance and a joyful spirit to our dealings with others. Despite adverse circumstances, long years of habits of gratitude and focusing on the source of our life, God helps us to maintain our equilibrium through the stormy seas of life. Short-term problems do not undermine our true confidence in the hope of heaven when every tear shall be dried and every bodily pain cured. We look forward to eternity with our loved ones in the most beautiful of locations. We will not have to rush to accomplish our daily chores since eternity stretches ahead of us.

But joy arises not only from contemplation of the hereafter but also giving credit where credit is due. All our abundant blessings, including our very existence, flow from God and his wonderful love of his creation.

Counselors frequently urge two ways to renew our joy in living: nature healing of our spirits by spending time in creation, and refocusing our priorities on others, not ourselves. Teenage depressives are shocked out of navel gazing by weekly prescriptions: assignments to "spend five hours helping someone this week." The phenomenon of "helper's high" alters our perspective and lifts our mood since our emotions and bodies were designed to love others.

We are not designed to retire in our senior years and tend solely to our personal fulfillment. There is no retirement age for God's principles of loving our neighbors and making our life's goal not merely our own happiness but being a blessing to those living nearby or with whom we have contact.

# APRIL 9

## Proverbs on Attitudes—Greed

"He that is greedy of gain troubles his own house" (15:27).

Greed is an insidious sin that undercuts desired Christian values since it takes our focus off Christ and serving others to "more, more, more." Greed begins to concentrate one's mind on how to obtain more instead of how to remain content with what we have. "He that makes haste to be rich shall not be innocent" (28:20). This describes one of the main dangers of greed: we are tempted to bypass honesty, laws, and fair dealing, doing anything it takes to gain more, more, more.

"Better is a little with the fear of the Lord than great treasures without contentment" (15:16). While we should be a conscientious employee or business proprietor, we must maintain balance. Everyone knows innumerable families ruined through overwork, workaholism, and neglect of loved ones. "Labor not to be rich; set bounds to your prudence" (23:4). Families need attention just as do business ventures. Rabbi Harold Kushner in his book *When Everything You've Always Wanted Isn't Enough* describes his deathbed conversations with hundreds of parishioners. To a person, he recounts, none regretted not spending more time at work; nearly all, however, regretted not spending more time with their loved ones. We can avoid such deathbed regrets by striving for balance in our lives. Some of the wealthiest persons in the world have been the most unhappy; Howard Hughes, the reclusive billionaire, comes to mind. It is clear there is no direct correlation between happiness and great wealth.

"Substance got in haste shall be diminished but that which little by little is gathered with the hand shall increase" (13:11). This verse puts the kibosh on get rich quick schemes; instead, diligent consistent labor and saving is the biblical path to wealth and contentment.

# April 10

## Proverbs on Attitudes—Peace Loving

"All of the paths of wisdom are peaceable" (3:17).

This verse, if deeply contemplated, reveals that living by God's righteous principles leads to peace. How? Our Creator—who designed our minds, spirits, emotions, and bodies—created us to function best when reflecting the designer's values: loving-kindness, joy, contentment, and peace. When our lives are aligned with the Creator, we revel in the knowledge that we are living God's way, consciously or subconsciously. Life goes smoother, and we optimistically live not in fear but in hope of future blessings, rewards, and heaven.

It is this simple: God's rules for living exist whether we know and follow them or not. Either we smooth our way by living according to these principles or we break ourselves on the rules. We ignore them to our peril. We may think we can bypass or ignore life's rules, but they are inevitable and apply to all.

We can "kick against the goads" and struggle through life, rebelling and objecting to righteous virtues, but our path will be infinitely more pleasant and blessed if we peaceably abide in the vine: Christ.

"He that fears the commandments dwells in peace" (13:13). We have no guilty conscience keeping us awake at night, no fears of godly punishment, no anxiety wringing our stomachs painfully. Instead, we have peace and confidence in God's future blessings, and even if we struggle through hard times, we have hope that God will be with us through thick and thin, sickness and health, wealth or poverty.

God's mandate to offer forgiveness to all is one of the chief components bringing peace to our lives. Some folks remain tied up in knots over offenses dealt years ago, ruining their chance for peace in enjoying today. Similarly, worry destroys our enjoyment of a today lived in peace.

# April 11

## Proverbs on Attitudes—Compassion to Poor

"He that despises the poor reproaches his Maker" (17:5).

The Lord created the rich and poor. Christ said in the gospels that the poor will always be with us. Therefore, we will have continual opportunity to display this Christian virtue of compassion to the poor.

Poverty is not the worst thing that can happen to us. "Better is the poor than the lying man" (19:22). Diligence in employment or our financial circumstances is a virtue, but dishonesty and lack of integrity are deadly.

Gloating about our financially secure circumstances is discouraged. "He that rejoices in another man's ruin shall not be unpunished" (17:5). "Do no violence to the poor because he is poor. Do not oppress the needy at the gate because the Lord will judge his cause and will afflict them that afflicted him" (22:22). This verse condemns injustice often leading to poverty but does not excuse our Christlike duty to come to the aid of the poor.

What shall we do to aid the poor? "He that has pity on the poor honors his Maker" (14:31). "A merciful man does good to his soul" (11:17). "He that is inclined to mercy shall be blessed" (22:9). Thus, generosity is beneficial to us as well as the one helped. Similarly, the "Soul that blesses shall be made fat" (11:25). Generosity redounds to the benefit of the giver. When we help others, we gain peace for ourselves and the confidence that we are living in accordance with godly principles. Many can attest to the truth of this principle: gifts to others boomerang and we ourselves are blessed.

"Don't withhold from doing good if you're able. Do not procrastinate charitable acts" (3:27). Many folks wait until the last business day of the year to write charitable checks for tax deduction purposes; God prefers we regularly practice generosity all the year through.

# APRIL 12

## Proverbs on Attitudes—Hope

"The just has hope in his death" (14:32).

What is the worst thing that can happen to us? Have you ever contemplated this question?

Dying is certainly not the worst thing when we have hope in heaven. Dying without salvation is surely the worst thing. Dying bankrupt, dying friendless, dying alone, and dying painfully are of minor consequence when placed up against the eternal hope of life with Christ and our loved ones in heaven. So many of our traditional early American gospel songs originated with slaves in miserable circumstances who could assuage their tough days with the hope of heaven. "Beulah Land" and "When We All Get to Heaven" are examples, but there are many. Older hymnals contain many more hymns focusing on life hereafter, since life in the past was sadder with high infant mortality rates, serious illness before the development of antibiotics and vaccines and lack of social safety nets.

"The house of the just shall stand firm" (12:7). This indicates that the righteous man living correctly does not live in fear of the ups and downs of life but remains on an even keel placing hope in eternity. "The house of the just is very much strength" (15:6). Similarly, this confidence in the future lends stability to the household when parents are not terrified of circumstances but have rock solid hope. "The root of the just shall not be moved" (12:3). Stability, firmness, constancy, and hope are characteristics of a righteous household. Night terrors, fears, and worries can be minimized when eternity is our promise.

"The fear of the Lord is unto life and he shall abide in abundance without being visited by evil" (19:23). Hope is life giving; fear is seriously destructive. Hope is life giving to our bodies and prolongs life.

# April 13

## Proverbs on Attitudes—Teachable

"He that yields to reproof shall be glorified" (13:18).

We must exert care our whole life to remain teachable—to not get so big for our britches that we cannot be influenced by good counsel or constructive criticism. "A wise man shall hear and shall be wiser: he that understands shall possess governments" (1:5). Our ears must remain open, but more importantly, we must take teachings to heart. Whether a new Christian just learning the ropes or a pillar of the church who has completed years of Bible study, there is always something we can learn to self-improve from the Bible, from wise commentaries or even youth who have a fresh perspective.

"The mind of the just studies wisdom" (15:28). Our Christian life is a journey; we never arrive until the day we cross over the Jordan to eternal life. There are manifold rewards for those whose mind remains impressionable. "The learned in word shall find good things" (16:20). Self-satisfaction, confidence, and spirituality should naturally increase as we study, listen, and soften our hearts. "The learning of the wise is easy" (14:5). We will not have to struggle as do nonbelievers. The Holy Spirit illuminates biblical passages and commentaries for easy application to our daily problems in life. "Wise men lay up knowledge" (10:14).

"The ear that hears reproofs of life shall abide in the midst of the wise" (15:31). "He that yields to reproof possesses understanding" (15:32). Ironically, the wisest among us often seem to be the most hungry for additional wisdom, searching for it in both sacred and secular writings and lectures. "Good instruction shall give grace" (13:15). Who among us does not desire more grace to be exhibited in our lives? Hard-hearted individuals who reject any criticism, guidance, or teachings are hurting themselves.

# April 14

## Proverbs on Attitudes—Watchful

"The prudent man bypasses evil" (27:12).

The wise person watches the road ahead, conscientiously scouting for pitfalls to avoid in life. In contrast, the fool charges ahead without thought of consequences. "Turn your foot away from evil and He will make your courses straight and bring forward your ways in peace" (4:27). To be able to turn our foot from evil, we must be vigilant to detect evil in persons, circumstances, and locations. "Make straight the path of your feet and let your eyes look straight on and all your ways shall be established" (4:26).

"I will show you the way of wisdom and lead you by the paths of equity so that when you run, you shall not meet a stumbling block" (4:11). We can increase our powers of observation first by understanding the will of God as revealed in scripture but also by calling on God to direct our path and reveal to us dead ends. "Keep the law and counsel and the Lord will be at your side and will keep your foot that you won't be taken" (3:26). Prudence requires we think through our plans, laying them alongside scriptural truth to discern any deviances, allowing us to timely correct our course.

"The steps of men are guided by the Lord" (20:24). This verse is doubly true when we seek God's direction and help in increasing our powers of observation. Observation is easier when sufficient light is cast upon the forward path. "The path of the just as a shining light goes forward and increases to perfect day" (4:18). Light is a gift of God to the righteous illuminating our way. Life becomes an upward spiral of additional wisdom leading to increasingly holy conduct and desire for further instruction. Wisdom begets wisdom which brings a holy life.

# APRIL 15

## Proverbs on Attitudes—Confidence

"In the fear of the Lord is confidence of strength and there shall be hope for his children" (14:26).

Living in accordance with the biblical wisdom principles naturally gives one confidence in life. This verse says so, but we know this from experience as well. God, our Creator, who thoroughly understands us soul and body, knows what is best for us, so his rules for existence are for our benefit. We suffer no guilt; we hold no regrets; we do not waste energy second guessing ourselves when we are aligning our life with God's design and will for our lives. The absence of guilt, regrets, and doubt in and of themselves decrease our stressors. The Holy Spirit "confirms" with our spirits that his way is the best way.

"He that walks sincerely walks confidently" (10:9). Sincerity arises when we live authentic, God fearing lives, reflecting actions pleasing to God. We are not hiding our left-hand actions from our right hand but, more importantly, our brains and hearts. We are not fearing discovery in some misdeed, treachery, or double crossing of a family member or business associate. Our lives can be transparent within ourselves and to our closest acquaintances. Worries are decreased; optimism is increased and our lives are an open book to our heavenly Father, our superiors in the working world, and our children.

"Keep the law and counsel and you shall walk confidently and your foot shall not stumble" (3:23). This concept is illustrated by the example of a law enforcement officer stopping us in traffic. When we know we were driving within the speed limit and following known traffic regulations, our blood pressure does not skyrocket when we spy red lights behind us. We theorize that, at worst, we have a burned out taillight or turn signal. However, if we have illegal substances in the car and were speeding and running a red light, our heart nearly jumps out of our chest when we are stopped. Conduct makes all the difference.

# APRIL 16

## Proverbs on Attitudes—Covetous

"The ways of every covetous man destroy the soul" (1:19).

Jesus in the gospels reminded his disciples in several ways and times that we should focus on godly, not material things. Store up our treasures in heaven, not on earth. Several Proverbs baldly assert this principle that covetousness is a key trait of a fool, not of a righteous person. Righteous persons should, of course, make an intentional effort to refocus their priorities on things of God, serving others and increasing our wisdom. Fools, however, characteristically prioritize getting and getting and getting of material things—both to bolster their own pride and arrogance and to win the competition with the Jones. The irony is that even if they win the competition, the pursuit is destructive of their own soul!

"Fools covet things which are hurtful to them" (1:22). "Things" can be construed in the literal sense in this verse. Righteous persons covet wisdom, knowledge of God, and a closer relationship with the Holy One. Righteous persons covet justice for all, peace in the world, and unity, especially among believers.

"A covetous man shall destroy the land" (29:4). Adolph Hitler comes to mind with his never ending imperialistic desire to add to Germany's territory. First, he coveted the oil rich lands adjacent to the Fatherland, then the breadbaskets of the Ukraine, and finally all Europe. This verse was literally fulfilled with the carpet bombing of leading German industrial cities and the Rhineland. Many dictators covet absolute power, but this desire backfires and leads to their downfall. When a ruler's desires become excessive—such as the over-the-top extravagance of the Chinese emperor—class, envy, bitterness, and resentment of the common people who are living in the other extreme often lead to overthrow. Russian oligarchs today using the recent capitalistic regime change for their own benefit are similarly at risk.

# APRIL 17

## Proverbs on Attitudes—Critical

"Remove from you a negative mouth and let detracting lips be far from you" (4:24).

While it is sometimes difficult to zip our lip when negative thoughts come to mind, there is a six-inch gap between our brains and our lips, so there is a "saving distance" that enables wise persons to consider carefully before they open their mouths in criticism. Whether criticism of persons, actions, the weather, or someone's stated plans, criticism is rarely helpful. Criticism has inherent within it judgment, and we are not designated judges in chief but lovers in chief. When we undertake to criticize another, we may not be aware of all the surrounding circumstances or underlying motivations behind the action. Our criticism may damage in a severe way our relationship with the person; in any event, it generally serves to cast us in a negative light.

"All fools are meddling with reproaches" (20:3). This clarifies that reproaches usually, by definition, are meddling. Reproaches insert our opinions into the lives of others. Only in the case of our own children or those for whom we have natural responsibility are we in a position to consider putting voice to constructive criticism and then only in a loving way. As a witness for Christ, we must consider diligently whether proposed criticism will undermine our example as a loving Christian. WWJD?

If we find ourselves in a position where constructive criticism is warranted, evaluate seriously the tone of our words. "He that rebukes a man shall afterward find favor with him, more than he who deceitfully flatters" (28:23). Honesty is essential; positive motivation is essential. Are the proposed words for the true benefit of the hearer? Or only to "get it off our chest?" Sometimes, clearing the air is essential to a home or business environment. These instances, however, are few and far between.

# April 18

## Proverbs on Attitudes—Hard-Hearted

"He that is hardened in mind shall fall into evil" (28:14).

How does hardness of heart/mind manifest itself? Unforgiveness is a primary way—grudge holding, lack of desire to listen to others' opinions, rebellion, close-mindedness, refusal to listen to advice, or wisdom—the list goes on and on. The hard-hearted person gradually loses correct perspective and sees issues only from his/her perspective. This hardness damages the "ears" and leads to self-destruction.

"The desire of the wicked is the fortification of evil men" (12:12). Evil men focus on their own desires, grabbing power and stuff. If another evil person wants to accrue some of the reflected glory of another powerful person, they support the evil leader out of self-interest. The "bag man" of gangsters hopes to follow in the boss's footsteps one day when the boss is knocked off. Therefore, they do whatever is expedient to solidify the leader's authority. Cabinet members of corrupt leaders, lieutenants of wicked generals, and subordinates of evil dictators have lost sight of fairness, justice as applied to the populace, and are instead envisioning the perks and revenue flowing their way from proceeds of one-sided transactions.

"When the wicked rule, the people shall mourn" (29:2). If government contracts are thrown to friends or offshore accounts are established with missing public funds, these evil deeds at some point become apparent. The attitudes, especially hard-hearted attitudes, of those in positions of command cause auditors and investigators to become suspicious of government operations leading to discovery.

"The wicked loathe them that are in the right way" (29:27). Since the goals, desires, and aspirations of wicked men are 180° to the goals, desires, and aspirations of righteous men, they are naturally at odds. "There is no love lost on a man of violence to others" (28:17).

# APRIL 19

## Proverbs on Attitudes—Contented

"Count your blessings and be satisfied with what you produce" (27:27).

Have you known coworkers who were so busy raising complaints about their failure to receive a raise or promotion that they failed to accomplish their assigned work? Always worrying and agitating about the next year's increase can detract from single minded focus on the work at hand. I believe this verse advises that our priority should be uncomplainingly applying ourselves to our "to-do" list and that faithful consistent effort, not agitation, is the better way to be recognized for our service.

Being grateful for our regular salary is a better path than perpetually dreaming about more, more, and more. If our boss senses our ingratitude, perversely, that incents him/her to bypass us for that next salary bump. Just like a grandmother giving holiday gifts to a grandchild, if the child fails to sincerely let the grandparent know how happy they are with the gift, they put themselves in the position of being less likely to receive a gift in the future. It is human nature to want to be generous to those whom we genuinely believe to be grateful for past kindnesses.

One common saying is that gratitude is the bedrock emotion of happiness. There are those who never seem content or satisfied with anything good that comes their way. Brushing off blessings as "nothing much" is a poor habit to get into. It is better to take conscious steps to intentionally be grateful and show gratitude both to God and to those who shower us with unexpected blessings. If God judged us on our righteousness, we would always fall short of his perfect standards. Therefore, it behooves us to exhibit gratefulness for our very life and our salvation—total undeserved gifts of God.

# April 20

## Proverbs on Attitudes—Touchy

"He that is easily stirred up to wrath shall be more prone to sin" (29:22).

This verse reminds us of 1 Corinthians 13's love chapter: "Love is not irritable, touchy or rude."

News accounts of flash fights between law enforcement officers and those stopped for traffic violations leap to mind. If drivers would take ten deep breaths, push down their hair-trigger temper, and speak respectfully to the officer, far fewer resisting arrest charges or even shootings would occur. It is our job, as mature Christians, to intentionally work on increasing our self-control with the help of the Holy Spirit.

Our life and arrest record can quickly spiral out of control if we let our emotions exceed our rational thinking. Righteous wise persons think about the impact of their actions on the future, not on the immediate satisfaction of speaking all our mind or poking someone in the eye. "He that provokes wrath brings strife" (30:33). Strife is completely opposed to our Christian duty to respond with love—loving our neighbors as ourselves. Strife raises our blood pressure and causes us severe regrets and sleepless nights.

"A spirit that is easily angered; who can bear?" (18:14). We must avoid gaining a reputation as a "fly off the handle" personality. It is far better to be honored as a person of patience, understanding, and mercy both for our own benefit but more so as an example to all those observing us, especially children. Kids who fight or shout back at the drop of a hat come to the attention of the principal for the wrong reasons. Our goal is to come to the attention of the principal for reasons of scholarship, citizenship, and sports excellence. Getting our name in the paper on the police blotter because of neighborhood rows will stick in others' minds even if later retractions or mitigating circumstances come to light.

# April 21

## Proverbs on Attitudes—Faithful

"Blessed is the man who hears me and who watches daily at my gates" (8:34).

Daily attention to devotions, daily prayers of intercession and petition, and daily gratitude to God upon arising and retiring are the surest ways to strengthen our closeness to God and bring maturity into our Christian walk. We have numerous other daily habits—exercise, bathing, housecleaning—so it behooves us to schedule, calendar, and develop habits of spiritual discipline in our lives. If we are a habitual type of person, we can develop holy habits to increase the chances we will accomplish our regular devotions to God.

Systematic reading of Proverbs and Psalms lends itself to completion in a calendar month. Proverbs has thirty-one chapters, so we can develop a habit of reading the numbered chapter corresponding to the day of the month to increase our wisdom and understanding of God's principles for living. Similarly, Psalms has 150 chapters, so reading five chapters a day will lead to completion in a month. Proverbs focuses on wisdom from our Creator; Psalms covers the gamut from praises to putting words to frustrations about life or ill treatment by enemies. Nearly always, one of the five daily Psalms corresponds to our mood or spiritual need that day.

Scriptures divided up into daily texts to complete the Bible in one year are another useful faithful way to become, year by year, better acquainted with the whole scope of the Holy Book. Many disciples consistently subscribe to short daily devotions, listen to Christian radio scriptures of the day, or sign up for verse of the day e-mails. In every way that we incorporate regularity into our life, not leaving scripture reading/study to "a spare moment" that never seem to arrive, we further our faithfulness, which we know is pleasing to God. Blessed is such a person.

# APRIL 22

## Proverbs on Attitudes—Foolish

"A fool will laugh at sin" (14:9).

Proverbs has many synonyms for foolishness: rebellious, scorner, wicked, unrighteous, abominable, imprudent.

Chief characteristics of a fool are refusal to hear or pay attention to advice of counselors, a know-it-all attitude, and a disgrace to his/her parents. "The soul of the wicked desires evil; he will not have pity on his neighbor" (21:10). (See hard-hearted attitude earlier this month.) "A parable is unseemly in the mouth of fools" (26:7). It is unseemly since a parable is not taken seriously by a wicked person. "A fool laughs at the instruction of his father" (15:5). Families are God's design to teach authority and obedience to children. If a child does not heed and respect the advice of parents in the first instance at home, that child is bound for trouble in kindergarten, grade school, high school, college, the military, on the job, and in marriage. It all begins in early training. "Wisdom is too high for a fool" (24:7).

To benefit from good advice, a person must first recognize that they can benefit from learning. If the fool believes they are fine as is, no improvement is necessary, they will never grow and mature. "A fool receives not the words of prudence unless you say those things which are in his heart" (18:2). A fool tests advice by comparing it with his/her own thoughts. If they challenge those thoughts, the first impulse is to completely discount that advice. When you observe a person who staunchly refuses to listen to points of view different than his/her own, beware. "A friend of fools shall become like them" (13:20). Associating closely with those who disrespect legitimate authority and who decline to acknowledge the need for any expert opinion is risky business.

# April 23

## Proverbs on Attitudes—Friendly

"Grace and friendship deliver a man" (25:9).

Our way in the world is smoothed in every respect by a friendly, open attitude. Why carry a chip on our shoulder when we have ultimate cause to rejoice? If we catch ourselves frowning or spiraling downward into negativity, it helps to find a friend to encourage us. "Like iron sharpening iron, so a man sharpens a friend" (27:17). Friends encourage one another, but they also "call one another" on issues when that is prudent. If we notice a friend getting offtrack, we can act as a friend in lovingly calling attention to that fact out of sincere goodwill. "The good counsels of a friend are sweet to the soul" (27:9). A true friend acts in our benefit, whether bestowing good news or constructive criticism.

Many a driver has avoided receiving a moving violation ticket by a friendly, respectful attitude when stopped in traffic. It is so important to model this behavior to our children and stress to them the riskiness of ill-advised behavior in critical moments of life.

Many a potential long, messy lawsuit has been avoided by timely, courteous invitations to private negotiation. If we get our "back up," this severely lessens the chance of a mutually beneficial settlement. Heartache, expense, and months of drawn-out misery can result unless we soften our heart and think on the long-term aspects of the relationship.

Friendly people recognize that people are precious—more precious than wealth. It is not worth sabotaging family relationships to fight over inheritances, over valuables left in a relative's home. Instead of a Mexican standoff, it is better to draw lots to take turns choosing antiques, family heirlooms, or unique sentimental items. Why jeopardize offending forever our loved ones by jumping the gun and secreting valuables before the whole family has arrived? Love is forever; wealth is not.

# April 24

## Proverbs on Attitudes—Envious

"Envy is the rottenness of the bones" (14:30). We might read this verse and take it as a metaphor, but based on recent medical science, it surely has literal application as well. Discontent, frequently caused by envy of others, bodes ill for our physical well-being. Who knows but in the future cancer, high blood pressure, shingles, and other stress-related illnesses will be shown to have a direct relationship to our non-peaceful state of mind caused by envy.

"Don't envy sinners" (23:17). Perhaps the implication here is that it is laudable to envy Christians further along in their Christian walk. We could emulate them and model our behavior on them to be inspired to improve our own behavior.

Envy of others' material possessions is particularly warned against. Envy leads to worry, a wholly unproductive state of mind, which can run amuck to ruin today, even when the worry relates to events of tomorrow. Envy of others' physical attributes is likely unproductive since our looks are inherited and only alterable/enhanceable to slight degree.

A helpful question to ask is: is this issue within our control? If so, we can apply ourselves more diligently to our job to increase our income, look for a new job, or take concrete steps to improve our position in life. But if the issue is not within our control, envy is particularly futile. This analysis brings to mind the serenity prayer that distinguishes between those things we can change and those we must remain content to let lie.

"Eat not with an envious man because he has false imaginings and his mind is not with you" (23:6–7). This warning bears on who we choose to associate with. Since eating, breaking bread, is one of the intimate human acts denoting a friendly relationship, we should decline to socialize with those who resent us, judge us, or envy us for good or bad reasons.

# APRIL 25

## Proverbs on Attitudes—Cheerful

"A happy face means a glad heart; a sad face means a breaking heart." (15:13)

"When a man is gloomy, everything seems to go wrong; when he is cheerful, everything seems right!" (15:15)

Christians have profound reason to be ultimately cheerful, but it is the day by day living that gets us down at times. When we are sliding down to the "dumps", it is our job to try to redirect our focus to something optimistic, so we don't undermine our Christian witness. Listing mentally or on paper our reasons for hope and a future (Jeremiah) can help. Aches, pains, financial reverses, and bad news can put us on the downward slide, but we are masters of our minds and with practice, we can begin to search for an upside: God delights in us (Psalms)! Our names are recorded in the Book of the Lamb (Revelation)! We are children of God, designed uniquely by Him and loved eternally by him! More practically, our God has unlimited resources: the cattle on a thousand hills are mine! (Psalms) God is reachable via the prayer "hotline" 24 x 7! He never takes a day off nor slumbers, nor sleeps!

We should not hesitate to call on our loved ones for practical help, but if we are at a loss, feeling like we're at a deadend, prayer for relief and help is available without cost or delay. Many Psalms are prayers of lament by King David or others bewailing a current hopeless looking situation, so we can take comfort that we are not the only person feeling sad and frustrated. Reading Psalms of lament helps put our situation in perspective. We are one of many humans who have experienced bad times but the all powerful, all knowing, merciful God has his ear tuned to our cry.

# APRIL 26

## Proverbs on Attitudes—Industriousness

"The thoughts of the industrious bring forth abundance" (21:5).

Do you want to be more creative? Get more accomplished? Then begin the work. Step 1 of a project is often the most difficult. Creativity builds on itself when we get the ball rolling. God has a way of multiplying our efforts if we will put forth diligent effort.

"Have you seen a man swift in his work? He will stand before kings and not be obscure" (22:29). This signifies honor that shall be bestowed on those who become expert in a craft or field through application of consistent diligent effort. "According to the works of his hands, it shall be repaid him" (12:14).

Rather than sitting around bemoaning our lack of standing or position, expend energy improving our skills, studying, practicing, and planning. It has been proven that virtuoso musicians generally work ten times harder than ordinary musicians. They practice long hours due to passion for their gift but also due to resolve to achieve great things with their God-given gifts. "In much work there shall be abundance" (14:23). The law of reaping and sowing is particularly applicable in this area. God's universe is designed so that our sincere faithful efforts are rewarded. "The soul of them that work shall be made fat" (13:4). This word represents abundance also—the theme of this devotion. Just as light follows dark, so abundance follows industry, diligence, practice, and dedication. "Well does he rise early who seeks good things" (11:27). When we sleep in, the day is half gone, and our opportunity to improve our skills, impress our bosses, and set good examples for our children is halved.

Industry and abundance have a direct relationship, as shown by these several similar verses. If we have a propensity to laziness, perhaps taping a verse on our bathroom mirror will help.

# APRIL 27

## Proverbs on Attitudes—Perverse

"A perverse man scatters abroad strife; and a whisperer separates chief friends" (16:28).

*Perverse* means "cantankerous, contrary, disputatious." Have you ever known a contrarian who seems to delight in disagreeing with others? Picking fights? Debating issues? Some folks enjoy taking the opposite view just to begin or continue an argument. Perhaps they think this makes life more interesting, or perhaps they just want to be the center of attention. This attitude is not favored by God.

"For the perverse is an abomination to Jehovah; but His friendship is with the upright" (3:32). Perversity puts us at odds with others and is directly contrary (pun intended) to God's way of love. A perverse attitude seems 180° opposite of Jesus's teaching of overlooking faults of others, smoothing quarrels in the interest of peace and loving our neighbor. This stance undermines our Christian witness.

If you catch yourself starting to open your mouth to dispute an issue, think carefully about whether it is a bedrock issue of faith or merely a matter of personal taste. There is no harm in good naturedly debating our favorite brand of coffee, our favorite restaurant or movie, but if we are challenging another's family values or personally held cultural beliefs, we must consider carefully whether we will offend or anger our listener. It is likely not worth it to cause offense. Our mothers likely reminded us not to debate politics or religion at the dinner table. There is true wisdom behind this admonition. Dinner is a special time of communion with others—the breaking of bread signifies special intimacy and fellowship. The feeling of unity can be easily disrupted by dredging up divisive issues.

Often, we have a good friend, but we have learned through prior experience not to discuss politics or other sensitive areas with them. We can focus on all the tastes we have in common and leave the rest alone in the interest of brotherhood.

# April 28

## Proverbs on Attitudes—Helpful

"The righteous is a guide to his neighbor; but the way of the wicked causes them to err" (12:26).

There are sunny souls among us who are constantly attentive to the needs of their friends and neighbors and are always on the lookout for how they may help another. They are an inspiration to others. Helping others makes us respect ourselves; we are designed by our Creator so that endorphins are released when we accomplish good deeds. Thankfully, such organizations as Scouts intentionally instill the value of helpfulness and performance of kind deeds into the character of their young members. We, as parents, must be especially conscious of the example we are setting when we encounter others, especially the elderly or weak.

Helpfulness is the first step on the way to justice. Helpfulness springs from a sense of underlying goodwill toward others, leading to right treatment of others. "He that follows justice is beloved by the Lord" (15:9). "He that is pure, his work is right" (21:8). When we treat others with respect, as children of God, as God's beloved, we draw his blessings. He delights in our fair and kind consideration of others. "The good man shall be above the fool" (14:14). This viewpoint of goodwill toward others is a major distinction between the righteous person and the fool, who focuses solely upon him/her own sphere and desires.

Kindness and justice toward others is contagious and spreads to our sphere of influence. "When it goes well with the just, the city shall rejoice" (11:10). Even when we're in a large city, stuck on an elevator or subway with our eyes turned downward, if one person lightens the mood with a compliment or positive remark, others are immediately affected and become more lighthearted. Let's let our light shine in helpful ways!

# April 29

## Proverbs on Attitudes—Seeking

"He that seeks after evil things shall be oppressed by them" (11:27).

This verse brings to mind discontented people who act in ways that lead to addiction. If one seeks after drugs or alcohol or porn, they may eventually consume us and displace other good things in life. Addictions ruin our balanced perspective, causing us to disregard healthy pursuits and become tunnel visioned in our single-minded addictive desires to get more, more, more of the self-destructive thing.

What do we think of first upon awaking in the morning? What runs through our mind upon lying down at night? What is simmering in our consciousness when we're idling at a traffic light? If we are striving to seek after better things, we can follow practices established by monks in ancient monasteries. They sought to train their minds to focus on God or breath prayers using external cues. At the beginning of every hour when the clock chimed, they would intentionally turn their mind upon gratitude toward God for their blessings or petitions to God interceding for others. If we have a grandfather or chiming clock, perhaps we can do the same.

Some disciples use location cues to remind them to seek after God. One friend who commutes to work each day uses a certain highway exit to remind him to pray for his employees, coworkers, and business. When he passes that exit, it's time to discipline oneself to seek God's guidance and protection and blessing on the planned day's activities. Are you a walker or jogger? We can establish certain landmarks to act as prayer cues: a certain park, building, or intersection.

In any endeavor when we have routine and repetition in our life, we can take advantage of that routine to turn it to our benefit in establishing daily reminders to seek more fully after God.

# APRIL 30

## Proverbs on Attitudes—Reverence

"There is no wisdom, prudence or counsel against the Lord" (21:30).

When we take this verse deeply to heart, we get our perspective in proper order and realize how all powerful, awesome, and sovereign is our God. Therefore, our proper attitude naturally becomes reverence. Discouragement and frustration result when we begin to think that we are in control and that our desires are supreme. Instead, this and other verses from Proverbs and especially from Psalms remind us of the supremacy of God, the comparative insignificance of ourselves, and therefore create an attitude of respect and worship for our Creator.

"The Lord is maker of both rich and poor" (22:2). "The hearing ear and seeing eye, the Lord made them both" (20:12). "All the ways of a man are open to his eyes; the Lord is the weigher of spirits" (16:2). In short, he made all, he knows all, and he sees all. The hundred-dollar theological terms are omnipotence (all powerful), omniscient (all knowing, all seeing), and omnipresent (present everywhere). Whether we use sophisticated terminology or words that children can grasp, it is important to daily get our proper view of our God correct.

This perspective also takes some of the load off. We are not ultimately in control; He is. "As the divisions of waters, so the heart of the king is in the hand of the Lord. However He wills, He turns it" (21:1). The righteous person can rest securely in the knowledge that God has things under control. Even in times when we fret about the ineffectiveness of our leaders or the conflict in our world, we can sleep better knowing that God is in charge. Yes, we are put on earth to accomplish the furthering of his kingdom on earth, spreading his love, bringing improvements in earthly situations of his children, but we must recognize that ultimate outcomes are in his hands.

# MAY 1

## Proverbs on Living Well—Carpe Diem

"The fear of the Lord shall prolong days; the years of the wicked shall be shortened." (10:27)

This Proverb does not stand uniquely. Several other verses in Proverbs and Psalms make this point that living well, obedient to God's principles for living, extends our lives as a general rule. "Forget not God's law and keep his commandments for they shall add to you length of days" (3:2). Our popular culture emphasizes so much proper diet, maintaining our body, following doctor's orders for prescriptions and periodic tests, but—more important—is following God's prescription if we truly aspire to advanced age.

"Hear my child and receive my instruction that years of life may be multiplied to thee" (4:10).

But what shall we do with these increased years? *Carpe diem* is a Latin phrase meaning "seize the day," made famous by a Robin Williams movie where he played the role of a literature professor instilling this notion into his students. Many philosophers through the ages have expounded upon this thought. Our own Ben Franklin wrote in Poor Richard's Almanac: "Do not squander time, for of such is life made." The bottom line is that every single day is a gift of God and if we do not use it well, we are making light of that gift. All this philosophizing boils down to: what is our purpose on earth? How can we please God in living each of our days?

Furthering God's kingdom on earth is one primary purpose. How can we bring to pass the expansion and knowledge of God's kingdom? All Christ's teachings in the New Testament focus on this basic goal: to express love and kindness to those we meet, to help and serve others, and to be his hands and feet in this world.

# MAY 2

## Proverbs on Living Well—Diligence

"The soul of them that work shall be made fat" (13:4).

When we are productive and accomplish much, it does so much to boost our self-esteem and confidence. Diligence seems to be an upward spiral. The more we accomplish, the more motivation and self-confidence we have to do more and on and on. Diligence brings honor in addition to improved sense of self-worth. "Have you seen a man swift in his work? He will stand before kings and not be obscure" (22:29). Since the Bible teaches that humility is a virtue and pride is a sin, we should not work for the primary purpose of receiving honor and recognition, but those things naturally follow according to Proverbs.

"In much work there shall be abundance" (14:23). God blesses our efforts and is pleased that we are making the most of the days granted to us. "He that tills his ground shall be filled with bread" (28:19). "The hand of the industrious gets riches" (10:4). There are enough verses of this ilk to feel assurance that working hard is the best way to provide for our future and the future of our loved ones. "According to the works of his hands, it shall be repaid him" (12:14). This is simply the age old law of reaping and sowing. Whether one calls it karma, the natural laws of the universe, or we give credit to God for establishing this divine principle, it simply works. Try it and see!

Satisfaction also flows from a job well done. "He that tills his land shall be satisfied with harvest" (12:11). When we work hard, it feels wonderful at the end of a productive day to think back on our accomplishments and avoid any regrets about a misspent day. Work pays in so many ways.

# May 3

## Proverbs on Living Well—Health

"The fear of the Lord is a fountain of life to decline from the ruin of death" (14:27).

There is a clear relationship between living obediently to God's principles and good health. A fountain of life denotes freshness, renewal, cleanliness, and abundance. Our Creator designed our souls along with our bodies to work in conjunction. They both work optimally when we live according to the Laws also created by our God. Joy, peace, grace, forgiveness, loving acts contribute to internal well-being, thus allowing our immune system and other systems that we may not yet even fully understand, to tick along per the "design manual." Grudge holding, hate, wicked deeds, regrets, guilt, and meanness weigh heavily on our minds that carries through to our physical health.

"Your body shall rejoice when your lips speak aright" (23:16). Thus, right speaking: encouragement, praise, optimism, hopeful speech blesses our bodies and causes them to flourish. "Soundness of heart is the life of flesh" (14:30). Soundness carries with it the essence of obedient righteous living. It is not as though our "flesh" was created by a different designer than our minds and souls. They are all a piece, intertwined, and related in ways that science is only beginning to verify. The longer we live, the more we experience and understand this close relationship. Let's let this understanding work for us, not against us.

The bottom line is God's laws are God's laws. We, his creatures, can either live smoothly and effectively in accordance with those laws, or we will stub our toes and lives on those laws if we disregard them. They are what they are, so we, the created ones, must adjust to them. They preexisted us; our job is to discover those laws and apply them to our lives so that we may flourish both soul and body.

# MAY 4

## Proverbs on Living Well—Living Humbly

"The fruit of humility is the fear of the Lord, riches, glory and life" (22:4).

Wow—just look at the abundance arising from humility. Mother Teresa comes to mind. She surely was one of the most humble persons of our age: having no assets, no popularly recognized "power" or authority. However, in our time, she, a humble nun working in the poorest of missions caring for the dying, is arguably the most revered person in our generation. She consistently topped polls as the most admired person in the world! She exemplifies this Proverb, in God's upside-down economy.

"Before a man be glorified, his heart is humbled" (18:12). Striving for humility is counterproductive; instead strive to serve others and do God's will. Striving for humility essentially undermines humility. Strive instead to daily do with diligence the tasks which bring about the kingdom of God on earth. "To the meek the Lord will give grace" (3:34). God blesses the undertakings of the humble, the servant, and the consistent doer. "Humility goes before glory." Our job is to perform our tasks, not seeking the limelight. Recognition and blessings of God naturally follow.

"Where humility is, there also is wisdom" (11:2). In short, humility is the premier mark of the wisest person. While our society values the wisdom of PhDs, philosophers, and well-known writers, often these people are supremely arrogant. The public can easily detect this arrogance, which tends to backfire. Those who refrain from seeking the limelight generally prevail ultimately. We naturally revere those reticent saints who do not make it a point to let everyone know what wisdom they possess.

We recall Christ's example of taking the towel and washing his disciples' dusty feet, just after they had been discussing among themselves who would be greatest in heaven. What conviction! One knows they never forgot his teaching by example in the Upper Room.

# May 5

## Proverbs on Living Well—Honesty

"The lip of truth shall be steadfast forever" (12:19).

Governments stay in power, leaders get reelected, pastors are retained, teachers' contracts are renewed, employees are promoted, professors receive tenure—all when they live honestly. Steadfastness in life, work, marriage, and extended families is worth striving for.

The opposite consequence is stark. "The deceitful man shall not find gain" (12:27). The thief may think he is taking a shortcut to wealth, but it always backfires. "No good shall come to the deceitful son" (14:15). "He that deceives the just in a wicked way shall fall in his own destruction" (28:10). Things fall apart, guilt weighs on the mind, sleepless nights naturally follow, and jail cells become our home if we live by deceit. "Crooked weights and measures are abominable before God" (20:10). Injustice and cheating are not minor offenses in God's eyes but "abominable." That term pulls no punches.

Whether in the sphere of business transactions, grading student papers fairly, disciplining our children or employees correctly and consistently, or taking shortcuts to try to get ahead, dishonesty never pays in the long run. Cheating the IRS? Concealing a wrecked car with new paint? Mislabeling manufactured goods? All these petty dishonesties are not petty in God's eyes or, for that matter, the eyes of the law. If we are in business for the long haul, in marriage for the long haul or in friendships for the long haul, honesty is the better path. "Steadfastness" gets us along in this world and gets us to heaven.

"The robberies of the wicked shall be their downfall because they would not do justice" (21:7). Once reputation or respect is lost, it is nearly impossible to regain a sense of personal integrity or trustworthiness in the eyes of others. And don't forget: our sovereign God sees all!

# May 6

## Proverbs on Living Well—Abundance

"The substance of a just man shall be precious gold" (12:27).

Gold is viewed as the most valuable material in the world due to its characteristic of never decaying or tarnishing. Wedding rings are formed of gold. Our currency was initially backed up by gold. Cathedrals were gilded. Capitol domes shone. Gold standard implies the ultimate in luxury. One current fad is to include gold flakes in high-class martinis as a symbol of top drawer elegance. Thousands of pioneers headed west and to Alaska to find gold, considering it the quickest way to wealth. Yet we cannot eat it. In a true depression or end times, we cannot even trade it since no one else can live on it. It is just pretty to look at.

Yet this is a mere analogy in Proverbs. It was chosen as reflective of the substance of a just man since our culture lusts after gold so strongly. In God's eyes, the substance of a just man is ultimately precious.

We, if we are righteous, are ultimately precious in God's reckoning.

If gold is not the type of abundance to strive for, what is? Scriptures make clear that peace, joy, right living, grace to others, generosity, and love are signs of God's abundance in our lives—signs that God's Holy Spirit indwells us making our lives overflow with his virtues, his character, and his blessings.

"One is as it were rich when he has nothing and another as it were poor, when he has great riches" (13:7). This Proverb shows us that the wealthiest of persons can be utterly miserable if they lack the fruit of the Holy Spirit: patience, self-control, peace, and love (Galatians). Conversely, the poorest person with few possessions can be blissfully, abundantly happy when these gifts flood their lives.

# MAY 7

## Proverbs on Living Well—Joy

"Joy follows those who take counsels of peace" (12:20).

Joy—some think of joy as the absence of negative issues: lack of worries over money, health, relationship woes, concerns about our purpose of life. But even if we have none of those worries, does their absence leave us joyful? True joy is the mark of a mature Christian and springs from hope in life eternal, sure knowledge that we are living in obedience to God's design for our lives and assurance that our names are written in the Book of the Lamb.

Joy springs from asking the ultimate question: what is the worst thing that can befall us? Death of loved ones is one of the worst, but even that blow is somewhat mitigated by the knowledge that there is life hereafter. Even those Christians suffering the ills of cancer and chemo often say their lives are blessed with peace and patience like never before. Suffering produces righteousness, which produces character, which produces peace and joy.

How can we increase our joy? Concentrating on taking in daily doses of God's promises to those he loves is a good start. Psalms is chock-full of such promises, but they abound in Proverbs and elsewhere in scriptures. Reveling in these promises produces hope and faith, which leads to joy. Joy is the natural expression of a heart filled with the Holy Spirit and devoid of heavy worries about the future. God's promises of abundant provision cancel worries and dread of the future. God's promises to always be with us alleviate fears of abandonment and loneliness. God's promises of protection in this world and the next blunt our midnight tossing and turning about life's circumstances.

"He that fears the commandment dwells in peace" (13:13). Peaceful existence naturally produces joy and gratitude.

# May 8

## Proverbs on Living Well—Strength

"The house of the just is very much strength" (15:6).

This assurance gives the righteous person confidence in the future. Similarly, "The root of the just shall not be moved" (12:3). Steadfastness, strength, and stability are all advantages gained by the mature Christian. "The just is delivered out of distress" (11:8). Trials come to all in this earthly life, but like the man who builds his house upon the rock, instead of the sand, a firm foundation provides security. "The just is as an everlasting foundation" (10:25). "The house of the just shall stand firm" (12:7).

Where do we go in time of troubles? "The just run to the name of the Lord and shall be exalted" (18:10).

Our prayers are heard and heeded. "He will hear the prayers of the just" (15:29). This gives added confidence that when troubles come we have a place to go and someone who cares and has the power to alleviate our situation.

Knowing that we are approaching life from a position of strength with an all-powerful God at our back is such an "upper." We are to live not as people without hope but exhibiting confidence reflecting our sovereign God.

"The good man leaves heirs, sons and grandsons" (13:22). This is further evidence of the stability of the "house" or line of the righteous person. In order to have heirs, we must have intact families who are capable of maintaining stable relationships and nurturing healthy children. Our physical and mental health and strength are improved, leading to viable heirs. Thus, not only our generation but also future generations are affected by our choices to live righteously, justly, and obediently, thus deriving strength.

Strength is an individual benefit, but its effects carry on through generations and "houses" of righteous persons.

# May 9

## Proverbs on Living Well—Pursuit of Wisdom

"The pursuit of wisdom is better than of silver and wisdom's fruit is pure gold" (3:14).

Again, Proverbs compares something with precious metals, the ancient world's most valuable commodity. While some may think that silver and gold are preferable and would solve all their problems, how empty would be a life with silver/gold but lacking wisdom. "Get wisdom because it is better than gold; purchase prudence for it is more precious than silver" (16:16). How do we purchase wisdom and prudence? Literally, we can buy books, go to courses of study, listen to lectures by eminent theologians, and spend our time watching Christian DVDs and listening to Christian radio. All these things will increase our wisdom, in addition to our daily meditation on scriptures.

What does the wise person learn? "A wise man fears and declines from evil" (14:16). A wise person learns the pitfalls in life and how to avoid them, how to be observant in learning from the failures of others without experiencing them ourselves. "The heart of the wise seeks instruction" (15:14). "The mind of the just studies wisdom" (15:28).

What are the benefits of wisdom? "The learned in word shall find good things" (16:20). "The wise of heart receives precepts" (10:8). "Wise men lay up knowledge." Wisdom saves us from wasted effort. Wisdom enables us to pray correctly in accordance with God's will, which means God is more likely to answer our prayers. Sin blocks our prayers (see 1 Peter); obedience makes our prayers a delight to God.

We have the blessings of God. "Blessed is the man that finds wisdom and is rich in prudence" (3:13).

An upward spiral of wisdom, right action, and reward results based on the eternal concept of reaping and sowing. Our efforts at searching for wisdom will be rewarded. "If you shall seek wisdom and incline your heart to know prudence, you shall understand the fear of the Lord and find the knowledge of God" (2:5).

# May 10

## Proverbs on Living Well—Transparency

"The hearts of men are laid open to the wise like a reflection in water" (27:19).

Those filled with the Holy Spirit have the gift of discernment, which often allows them a peek into the motives of others. Most people do wear their heart on their sleeve or their motivations in their eyes. Our faces naturally reflect what is in our minds and it is easy, not just for those trained in body language but ordinary Christians to discern whether a person is righteous or evil. If we are aware and observant, the wisdom of God allows us this view of the hearts of others.

But transparency works in other ways. God, of course, is all seeing and all knowing, so he is always able to determine our motivations. If we are honest and speak truthfully, we don't have to remember what we said earlier; the truth remains the truth. Abraham Lincoln made a famous comment about the ease of not having to trouble ourselves trying to recall the earlier "version" revealed yesterday. Life flows along more smoothly if we are able to discern motives of others and our sincerity can shine through without the effort of cover-up.

If a child refuses to meet our eyes when questioned or a teenager hurries to his/her room upon arrival to avoid conversation, it is pretty easy to tell that something unpleasant has occurred. It does not take a psychologist to reach that conclusion. However, an added layer of discernment can, with experience and wisdom, be discovered and utilized in everyday living. One theologian commented that in meeting others, "The Christ in me recognizes and responds to the Christ in you." Sometimes, the beaming faces of well-grounded Christians announce the state of their hearts before a word is spoken or an introduction made.

# May 11

## Proverbs on Living Well—Self-Control

"He that rules his spirit is better than he that conquers cities" (16:32).

An ounce of prevention is worth a pound of cure. Watching our tongue or our fists and avoiding a confrontation is ten times better than wading into a fight and having to untangle the terrible negative consequences that ensue: apologies, retribution, regrets, broken noses, knocked out teeth!

Road rage is epidemic on the highways of our urban areas. As in Psychology 101, demonstrations that too many rats jammed in a cage get hostile but room to spread out avoids rat fights transfers to too many humans on too few roads. Wise persons recognize that giving way to our frustrations is not the high road (pun intended). Flipping the bird, tailgating, honking, and flashing of lights are best avoided since the response of the other driver is totally unpredictable. We or our passengers could get shot, have a wreck, and get arrested. At a minimum, our blood pressure will shoot up, and we will have trouble focusing on our true job for the day, mulling over and over in our minds the arrogance and wickedness of "the other guy."

Patience and thinking through the consequences of an evil act we are considering will convince us that overlooking a slight, intended or unintended, pays dividends.

If we are a student in a hurry and impatient of anyone in our way, we must consider that an accident, an arrest, and an incident could prevent us from getting into that professional course we anticipate, will likely raise our insurance rates, and cause grounding or punishment at home. Immediately, we will be late for our class or job and may suffer injury that affects us forever and causes untold regrets.

"A man who can't mind his speech is like a city without walls" (25:28). Impatience on the highways is one thing, but uncontrolled speech can damage relationships meant to be permanent.

# May 12

## Proverbs on Living Well—Soul Keeping

"He that possesses a mind loves his own soul" (19:8).

*Soul Keeping* is the title of a marvelous spiritual book by a great professor and philosopher Dallas Willard of California. But several Proverbs focus on this concept. "It is the part of man to prepare the soul" (16:1). In other words, there are deliberate steps we can take to improve our soul, preparing it for eternal life and more abundant life on earth. "He that keeps his soul keeps his way" (16:17). This refers to the maintaining of our walk of life on the narrow pathway that leads upward to eternity.

"The spirit of a man is the lamp of the Lord which searches hidden things in your soul" (20:27). The Holy Spirit operates to reveal to us areas of unholiness that need to be confronted and dealt with, repented, and corrected. As we study Scripture, as we pray and ask God to reveal to us defects in our character, areas we have not yet turned over to God, he will answer and prompt us in the way of righteousness.

"He that keeps his own soul departs far from arms and swords" (22:5). Peace should be our goal; the way of peace has nothing to do with arms and swords. Violence is abhorrent to the Christian, and personal physical confrontation is rarely the way to solve any of life's problems.

Care and nurturing of our soul is done in the expected ways: regular worship attendance, daily devotions, and scripture meditation, challenging the mind by listening to the words of great preachers, breathing in inspiring Christian music and books and intentional avoidance of compromising situations and evil influences. A pursuit of holiness is intentional. We should ask for direction, help, and strength in our Christian walk to improve the state of our soul.

# May 13

## Proverbs on Living Well—Peaceful Rest

"Keep the law and counsel and you shall sleep without fear and rest in sweet sleep." (23:24)

When we are young, we may be kept awake by colicky youngsters. When we are in midlife, the stresses and strains of family and work life may bring insomnia. And one of the banes of old-aged folks is the failure to sleep through the night, perhaps due to aches and pains or the side effects of medicines.

Life on earth has its nighttime disturbances. But Proverbs assures us that if we live obediently, we will be saved from the disturbances arising from guilt, regrets, grudge holding, fear of discovery of our evil deeds, and a host of other mental ills.

If we are prone to insomnia, we appreciate doubly the blessings of a restful night of sleep. We should give thanks for every such night. Learning to lay our cares at Jesus's feet each evening before sleep is an intentional way to lessen our load. After all, he's awake 24/7. Have you ever considered how dreadful it would be to not be designed in such a way as to have eight hours of dark in which to refresh and renew? If we had to slog through our daily grinds continually without arising and finding a beautiful sunrise and knowledge that "His mercies are new every morning," life would seem endless and discouraging. I am thankful we are designed such that our brains and bodies get a rest. "Give it a rest" is an expression that we should take to heart when our eyes are drooping in the evening. How exhausting it would be to be expected to just keep on plodding. Our brains are like computers that must "defrag" and compile in orderly form all our new knowledge, memories, and experiences gained that day. Sleep is precious. Let's thank God for it and how our bodies are designed to need sleep.

# MAY 14

## Proverbs on Living Well—Confidence

"Keep the law and counsel and you shall walk confidently and your foot shall not stumble" (3:23).

When we are living true to the precepts God has designed for our best life, we can avoid many of the worries and fears of the future and dread of the unknown. God's laws are not designed to stop us from having fun but for preserving our lives, our reputations, our health, and our personal relationships. Self-destruction is the natural consequence of failing to learn and apply God's design for living. Note also that in addition to keeping the law, mention is made of keeping counsel. This likely refers to the advice of good pastors and advisors who are spiritually mature and far along in their Christian walk. Not everything is addressed in the Bible; some current issues need interpretation by religious leaders.

"He that walks sincerely walks confidently" (10:9). "Sincerely" equates with authentically, without need for masks and cover-up. Transparency is another description of this concept. We avoid straining to recall which version of the "truth" we told to our neighbor when we stick to the truth from the beginning. Guilt and fear of being caught are nonissues.

"In the fear of the Lord is confidence of strength and there shall be hope for his children" (14:26). This verse brings in an additional notion of strength. Our confidence is strong and can withstand criticism, put-downs, and challenges. We do not have to spend our time worrying whether we have chosen the right path when we are closely abiding in God's Word and applying it to our lives. We will never please everyone in life, but we can certainly worry less about the need to please everyone when we are secure in our knowledge and application of God's laws.

# May 15

## Proverbs on Living Well—Resilience

"The just shall spring up as a green leaf" (11:28).

This is an inspiring verse and an encouraging thought. Even when bad things happen to us in life (think Job to whom the worst things happened), we are able to regain our equilibrium and hope in the future when God has our back. The natural consequences of doing the right thing are that we regain our position, our health, our self-confidence, and our zeal for vital living in the future. Life is a series of ups and downs for all of us; we encounter surprising twists and turns in life. This verse assures us that our downs won't last as long if we are just, righteous, and living according to his rules.

Resilience is an important skill to implant in our children. Assuring them that, as Adam Hamilton frequently recites, "The worst thing will not be the last thing," goes a long way to reestablishing them on the upward path of life. A good-night's sleep, an afternoon nap, a heartfelt hug, and some wholesome food all are good ways to set us again on the way of hope.

The righteous realize after study and exercising their faith that the end of the Book reveals victory of his blessed ones—us! The good guy wins! Christ our Redeemer rides in on the white horse just like the fairy tales. The end of days is not a cause for alarm and sleepless nights but anticipation of our ultimate honor and glory and uniting with Christ.

While depressives may require medication and counseling, much recovery of natural balance in life can be regained by focusing on the eternal promises of God. Yes, we will be judged, but Jesus will be our advocate, and he has already marked us for the "save" column. Our names are in the Book of Life.

# MAY 16

## Proverbs on Living Well—Beloved

"He that follows justice is beloved by the Lord" (15:9).

Karl Menninger, compassionate psychologist of the world-famous Menninger Clinic in Topeka, Kanas, was convinced that love is the cure for most ills—love given and love received. How much more then would we be cured of our daily ills to absorb deeply in our psyche that we individually are the beloved of the Creator of the universe, the all-holy, all-powerful, all-knowing God. Being a child of God in addition to our own well-cherished child is an all-important concept to impress upon the minds and hearts of our children and grandchildren or students or charges under our responsibility. Suicide would be reduced if persons reminded themselves daily, hourly of this eternal fact.

It is almost too much for our feeble minds to fathom that we are even known to, much less observed and understood, by our Lord. Mother Teresa stressed that the worst ill that could befall the dying on the streets of Calcutta was not having inadequate medical care and attention but apathy of those passing by. Being ignored and uncared for, dying alone, and unseen is utterly demoralizing. Hindus were impressed with the precious word that the eye of God was upon them and that they were loved by Christ and his servants in the form of caring nuns of her order. Even when the person was so far ill that medical intervention was useless, the order brought the dying to a place cool, clean, refreshing with attentive nuns to attend to what comfort could be given in the form of cool cloths, healthful food and drink, and watch care.

All humans were created with a craving to be loved. Even if the whole human race ignores us and passes us by, we are assured that we are loved by God.

# MAY 17

## Proverbs on Living Well—Vitality

"The fear of the Lord is unto life and he shall abide in abundance without being visited by evil." 19:23

It's easy to spot someone who exudes vitality—love of life, love of others, excitement for the future and joy in daily living. Don't we all strive to reflect this attribute? Psychologists and counsellors speak of acts and words that are "lifegiving". We can all identify with moments in our lives when parents, grandparents or other loved ones have spoken words of heartfelt encouragement that wonderfully boosted our self esteem and gave us that "oomph" to give it one more try. Barnabus, Paul's advocate and helper, exuded this trait of being an encourager. We know how wonderful it is to be on the receiving end of such words or acts: encouraging notes received unexpectedly, a delivery of flowers when we are ill, a well chosen gift that thrills our soul. Based on the Golden Rule, we should therefore be constantly thinking how we can bless another going though a bad time with a lifegiving gesture.

Conversely, we have all suffered from death dealing words or acts from bullies, toxic persons who can never seem to have a good word, or naysayers. Despite the sticks and stones maxim, we all know the powerful impact of words: good or bad.

Picture in your mind the most singularly vital person you know: smiling, caring, full of abundant life! Study closely their actions and words. That person can become a role model to improve our vital behavior. "Among the just grace shall abide." (14:9) Grace is another aspect of vitality: tact, diplomacy, the ability to smooth feelings and bring unification. Those who bring vitality and grace to any gathering are always welcome, for we know how scarce they are. Let us strive to become one!

# May 18

## Proverbs on Living Well—Stability

"The just is as an everlasting foundation" (10:25).

It is difficult to overemphasize the essential nature of a firm foundation. "The house of the just shall stand firm" (12:7). "The root of the just shall not be moved" (12:3). All these verses describe one important difference between the unprincipled fool and the righteous, just, law-abiding person who tread the godly path of life. Building contractors and architects understand well the importance of a firm foundation. Bridge builders and Gustave Eiffel spent as much time on getting the foundation right as on the overlying structure. The larger the structure, the more essential it is that a foundation be level, deeply rooted and of good tensile strength.

The weighted bottom roly-poly toy comes to mind. When the bottom is so much heavier than the top, a child simply is unable to knock it down. It springs right back up when hit.

Of course, we are all familiar with the house on the sand, house on the rock analogy used in scripture to point out the essential difference between the God-principled and the unprincipled.

"The habitations of the just shall be blessed" (3:33). Since our home is the seat of our family life, this reference to habitations speaks not only of a structure of a residence but also of the structure of a family filled with God-fearing parents and obedient children. God designed us to be nurtured in families, and it is the rare high-achieving person who does not spring from a firm, supportive family background.

"The tabernacles of the just shall flourish" (14:11). Now we broaden our view from home to church or other holy places. A tabernacle was the place where God was present to meet with man. A flourishing sense of self, home, and holy place goes a long way to supporting a fine blessed life.

# May 19

## Proverbs on Living Well—Safety

"The horse is prepared for the day of battle but the Lord gives safety" (21:31).

This verse speaks of safety in upcoming battle, but safety in upcoming life is what we likely crave. God's sovereignty and watch care over all aspects of our life is addressed in scripture. What is safety to you? Enough food, money to pay our bills, ongoing good health, and security in our "castles?" Freedom from want, from assault, from enemy attack? We hope that in all areas of our daily lives we will experience safety.

I believe this verse recognizes that we are expected to do all within our power to prepare for whatever is upcoming in our lives: retirement, old age, and other challenges. "The horse is prepared" implies that someone must do their part to prepare the horse. The cavalry soldier must feed, shoe, water, and groom his horse to prepare. Likewise, we must learn about finances, save, develop self-discipline, and prepare in all reasonable ways for events we anticipate in our lives. But the big "but" is that all men's plans are subject to override by our sovereign God. "As the divisions of waters, so the heart of the king is in the hand of the Lord. However he wills, he turns it" (21:1). The king may fancy himself as ruler of all, but the joke is on him! God is the true ultimate ruler of all. All endeavors of humans are puny compared to the plans of God, which take into account a breadth of worldview, an infinite view forward in time ("a thousand years is as a day," says Psalms) and factors that never enter our one-dimensional minds.

God has resources that we are not even aware of to keep us safe, provide protection, and get us out of difficulties. Let us thank God for our safety brought about by his sovereignty.

# May 20

## Proverbs on Living Well—Tactful

"To speak a word in due time is like apples of gold on beds of silver" (25:11).

The emphasis in this verse seems to be on the "just right" timing of a word. Job's friends did the right thing for a solid week: they sat with him in silence, mourning with him the loss of his children, herds, health, and prosperity. This is important to note when we go to comfort our loved ones in time of loss. Many words are not necessary; just one or two loving expressions of loss are fine. Our presence and a warm hug are needed more than torrents of wordy attempted explanations.

When your husband returns from a hard day at the office or your child suffers a hurtful snub from a friend, often, some quiet time to process and recover are needed before words of sympathy can even be heard. Knowing when to say something and when not to say something is the work of wisdom. Ecclesiastes recognizes that there is a time to speak and a time to be silent. Our job as friend to the grieving is not to express what is on our mind but to quietly perceive what may be needed by our friend. We are so used to just opening our mouth and letting words pour out; it takes mature tact to know when to put a sock in it. Tact is the quality of focusing on the other—not ourselves, in order to assess the situation and give the other a chance to explain, vent, or grieve.

Tact is very akin to grace—a graceful way of living that is appreciated, not resented, by the hearer. If we have had a severe quarrel with our spouse, it is the very soul of tact to permit a cool down period before the gut issues are addressed in a rational manner. Generally, one spouse will be a pouter and one a shouter. The requirement of the pouter, to go away and brood for a while in order to regain equilibrium, must be honored above the tendency of the shouter to vent. Further damage to the relationship is inevitable if the shouter proceeds. Think carefully about the timing of our words so they will be valuable as gold.

# May 21

## Proverbs on Living Well—Marriage

"He that has found a good wife has found a good thing, and he shall receive a pleasure from the Lord" (18:22).

Do we stop to consider the many blessings we have due to a spouse in our life? Generally, spouses complement one another. One is talky; one is the strong silent type. One is technical; one is emotional. Even in more practical areas, one loves outside pursuits; one loves inside pursuits. One is patient; one is a hard charger.

Even when our differences frustrate one another, clear thinking reveals that our spouse was sovereignly matched with us to complete our deficiencies and vice versa. There are so many areas in which I feel completely incompetent. I give thanks often for a spouse who can diagnose the car trouble, have the patience to research the IRS code on deductibility issues, choose the correct fertilizer for the yard, etc. Although our spouse might wish we were different at times, we are the way we are, and that fact ultimately is for a good reason—to complete and complement us.

Almost all married couples I know are very different from each other. Perhaps that is God's plan so that their children will "turn out in the middle." Maybe this pattern keeps the human race from getting too "type A" or too laid-back. Especially in raising young children, often when one spouse is at their wit's end, the other is unbothered and can step in and take over to allow the other to regain calm.

When our spousal frustrations are on the rise, we must remind ourselves that spouses are a blessing from God meant for our good. Perhaps the spouse's characteristics are just the thing we need to smooth our rough corners, recognize our weaknesses, and become more godly.

# May 22

## Proverbs on Living Well—Softness

"A soft tongue breaks hardness" (25:15).

A sharp retort or an unthought-out response generally escalates a potential dispute. Often, a simple pause brings about de-escalation. A considered modulated tactful response can go a long way into preserving relationships at home and work.

Of course, a soft tongue generally accompanies a soft heart. How do we keep our hearts and tongues soft? Humility is key. Shouts and verbal attacks spring mostly from hurt pride. Therefore, if our pride is kept under control, our tendency to produce quick hurtful responses is greatly lessened. Humility results from a proper perspective of our role in the cosmos versus God's sovereignty. When we consider that we are unable to create any new thing without the basic resources created and provided by him, our pride diminishes.

"He that is hardened in mind shall fall into evil" (28:14). The converse is easy to recognize. If we keep our hearts and tongues and spirits soft, our chance of falling into evil falls. Regrets result from a hard answer, a damaged relationship, the failure to accept an apology, the building of a wall. Blessings result from a sincere heartfelt apology, the offer of restitution if one has done wrong, soothing words and soft actions that create love, not hate.

Anger is such a dangerous thing. It can quickly spiral out of control resulting in thrown punches, black eyes, arrests, and road rage. Softness literally puts a damper on; let's think of it as a big squishy pillow on the fire of anger. Grudge holding by many prevents angry hard words from being assuaged. Softness in the first instance alleviates the hard task of finding a way around or through a damaging quarrel.

Praying for God to keep our hearts soft is a laudable act. Devouring scriptures will work to transform our hard hearts into downy pillows of softness.

# MAY 23
## Proverbs on Living Well—Wealth

"By instruction the storerooms shall be filled with wealth" (23:4).

What instruction does this refer to? I believe this verse refers to the wisdom of God as revealed in Proverbs and the scriptures. Living in obedience to God's Word results in abundance and blessings, both material and nonmaterial. Some believers seem to doubt that this verse is literal, arguing that it refers only to nonmaterial wealth. I take it at face value since many other verses in Proverbs echo this thought.

Wisdom results in right living, more stable families, non-estrangement from one's extended families, promotions at work, honor, and recognition due to integrity and honorable character. All these factors tend to produce wealth. We are more likely to receive an inheritance from our forebears if we treat them kindly and with love and respect. Diligence is repeatedly stressed in scripture. Diligence and character work together exponentially to produce wealth.

Instruction also relates to the law of tithing. The last chapter of Malachi is very clear about the effect of consistent tithing on wealth. God invites us to test him on the principle of cause and effect: tithing producing abundance. See if I do not open the windows of heaven and pour out so many blessings as there won't be room to store them.

Avoiding addictions increases wealth. Avoiding angry fights avoids lawsuits and law-enforcement consequences, preserving wealth. Raising loving responsible children increases wealth. In nearly all the ways we can think of being obedient to God's laws, wealth ensues. Instruction in self-control, moderation, and avoiding excess preserves wealth. Preserved wealth multiplies to increased wealth.

While the "name it and claim it" mentality has been ridiculed as unlikely to increase wealth, this verse is very clear that learning God's wisdom and applying it consistently will increase wealth and blessings.

# May 24

## Proverbs on Living Well—Faithful

"They that deal faithfully please Him" (12:22).

Faithful people are scarce as hen's teeth. "Many men are called merciful but who shall find a faithful man?" (20:6). We know from personal experience that faithfulness is hard to find. Those who are faithful please the Lord and, of course, please those who depend on them. Volunteerism is a tough field due to how lightly many hold their responsibilities. If we volunteer for a position or a responsibility, we should treat it as seriously as paid employment. We should arrange our doctor appointments, family visits, and other personal business to put our volunteer position first, just as we would if we were a paid employee.

"A faithful man shall be much praised" (28:20). Those in positions of authority should give due honor and recognition to faithful volunteers, realizing that their time is valuable as currency. Now that our average life span is lengthening, some of us have thirty years after retirement in which to volunteer. America is renowned for the high percentage of retirees who do significant volunteering in their golden years. "He that is the keeper of his master shall be glorified" (27:18). When we loyally work to achieve the goals set by our boss, we can expect to receive due recognition. A loyal employee or volunteer works not to achieve his/her personal goals but those set by the person in authority.

"A faithful messenger greatly refreshes the sender" (25:13). It is a wonderful feeling to know we can count on the person entrusted with an important message. It is a great comfort. Battles may turn on safe delivery of an important message. Vital business transactions similarly may depend on timely delivery of a message. And back to our theme verse: another's eternal destiny may depend on our delivery of the gospel to another.

# May 25

## Proverbs on Living Well—Peace

"Turn your foot away from evil and He will make your courses straight and bring forward your ways in peace" (4:27).

True inner peace is so rare in our culture. Everyone seems to be rushing hither and yon that few take time to contemplate the state of their soul. We are promised peace if we are obedient and listen to God's direction for our lives. The verse and song comes to mind: "Be still and know that I am God." Achieving a state of peace entails turning off outside stimuli—radios, TV, iPods, DVD players—and letting the beauty of scriptures and the beauty of nature heal our souls. Sometimes, we don't realize how unpeaceful we are until an illness or injury forces us to slow down and depend on others to provide for us.

Striving after material possessions and more of everything kills our peace. Studying God's repeated promise of provision can multiply our peace. Christ's preaching in Matthew about the lilies of the field and the birds of the air should cause us to slow down and examine the reason we are striving so. He assures us that he is aware of our need for food, clothing, and shelter and that we are infinitely more valuable in his eyes than is a sparrow. If we are in need of something (versus in want of something), we should pray for our daily provision, and God has promised to answer for we know that is in accord with his will.

"All the paths of wisdom are peaceable" (3:17). "He that fears the commandment dwells in peace" (13:13).

"When the ways of man shall please the Lord, He will convert even his enemies to peace." We have many scriptural promises of peace, so if our level of peace is low, we would do well to review them and take them to heart.

# May 26

## Proverbs on Living Well—Optimism

"The path of the just as a shining light goes forward and increases to perfect day" (4:18).

This verse sets out perfection as our end! What joy and hope that observation brings. "The wise servant shall prosper in his dealings and his way shall be made straight" (14:15). We are perfectly justified in being a Pollyanna, optimistic about the future, when our hope is grounded in Christ and his biblical promises. Prosperity, provision, peace, and a future are in store for the wise.

"I will show you the way of wisdom and lead you by the paths of equity so that when you run, you shall not meet a stumbling block" (4:11). Not only are we promised positive things but also avoidance of many negative obstacles in our life. If we remain in God's will, we can expect our future, both on this earth and in heaven, to be better than if we were outside his will. As a general observation on life, the way of the righteous is better in every respect than the way of the fool. Rewards are promised in this earth as well as heaven for our good deeds, and our fellow sojourners on earth will likely honor and respect us.

"According to the works of his hands, it shall be repaid him" (12:14). The law of reaping and sowing operating in the realm of earth applies so that if we are working for good and acting with love, we can rightly expect blessings to be repaid. Therefore, we can confidently look forward with optimism to a rosy future. Diligence is a factor contributing toward optimism. "He that tills his ground shall be filled with bread" (28:19). Again, whether in agricultural or other forms of work, diligence leads to abundance, causing us to have optimism about our future.

# MAY 27
## Proverbs on Living Well—Guidance

"In all your ways think on God and he will direct your steps" (3:6).

The closer we are to God, the more likely we are to receive and recognize his guidance and direction in our daily lives. "Lay open your works to the Lord and your thoughts shall be directed" (16:3).

When we pray, read Scripture, and listen for God's leading, we can expect guidance for our lives. When we are in the will of God, he directs our steps. Perhaps we awake in the morning with a new idea, perhaps we read in a book a line that sets us on a new way of thinking, or perhaps we talk with someone on a bus, plane, or elevator that is just the missing piece we needed to initiate a new phase of our lives. There are a series of books called *Godwinks*, which contain vignettes of divine coincidences, holy convergences, or seemingly miraculous meeting of needs. Divine coincidences or "God-incidences" are termed *Godwinks* where we receive a subtle nudge from God in a direction in his plans for us.

"His will is in them who walks sincerely" (11:20). If we sincerely seek his will and are open to his answers, his will will be revealed at just the right time and manner. "I will show you the way of wisdom and lead you by the paths of equity" (4:11). "Make straight the path of your feet and let your eyes look straight on and all your ways shall be established" (4:26). If we are striving to walk the Christian path and immerse ourselves in his Word, it is as though a beam of light illuminates the path forward. His Word is a lamp to our feet and a light for our path forward (Psalms).

# May 28

## Proverbs on Living Well—Well-Spoken

"Incline your ear and hear the words of the wise and apply your ear to my doctrine which shall be beautiful for you, if you keep it in your heart, it will flow in your lips that you may trust in the Lord" (22:17–19).

Proverbs has so many verses covering both good and bad speech: gossip, criticism, rash promises, angry words, comforting words, etc. So much of our lives is "lived through our mouths." "I give you thoughts, knowledge and words of truth" (22:21). If we wish to have a mouth full of blessing, not cursing, we should diligently apply ourselves to gaining knowledge from Proverbs about what is desirable and what is painful. "The man of understanding is of a precious spirit" (17:27). Therefore, precious and appropriate words will proceed out of his/her mouth, for we know that out of the abundance of the heart, the mouth speaks. By their fruit, you shall know them. Much of the fruit we bear is evident in the words that we speak. Are our words primarily helpful, necessary, edifying, uplifting, encouraging? If so, our hearts have likely been transformed by the Holy Spirit.

"The prudent man bypasses evil" (27:12). Much evil is revealed by the words we speak. If we find ourselves cursing, criticizing, judging, and demeaning others, we must reexamine our hearts and redouble our time of prayer and meditation. There is a direct cause and relationship between the condition of our hearts and the speech proceeding from our lips. Our goal in this life should be to witness to others using pleasant, apt, and convincing words reflecting the pure condition of our hearts. "A wise man thinks humbly of himself" (30:1). Therefore, our words should be spoken with all humility and wisdom.

# May 29

## Proverbs on Living Well—Blessedness

"Blessed is the man who finds wisdom and is rich in prudence." 3:13

A synonym often used for blessed is happy. Blessedness is when quiet joy bubbles up from our soul, even when in the midst of mundane daily activities. When we are driving, walking, shopping or lying in bed in the early morning, we have a sense of "rightness" and joy—we feel we are where we're supposed to be and on the right path for the future.

Of course, obstacles and troubles enter our path and take our focus off of our blessedness. Distractions in our daily living threaten our sense of peace. But the more mature a Christian we are, the quicker we are able to refocus on the upside and minimize the downside. The more habitual our thoughts and prayers of gratitude to God, the more blessings naturally flow into our lives. Gratitude begets more blessings. We feel in step with the universe and the "music of the spheres". That music resounds in our soul whether our attention is fully listening to it or not. Awareness of God smooths the way for acknowledgement of our blessings and their source. We can virtually float on air as we go about our daily responsibilities. A smile blossoms on our face readily when addressing the local store clerk, the mailman or that grumpy neighbor.

Instead of habitually rehearsing our gripes in our mind, we gradually learn to refocus on future expected blessings. Letting go of the past and its pains and hurts may be difficult at first but with practice and the benefits of healthfulness, sense of freedom and optimism, it becomes the path of choice. Blessedness is closely linked to hope—our ultimate hope of salvation hovers above all petty life trials.

# May 30

## Proverbs on Living Well—Fearlessness

"He that hears my word shall rest without terror and enjoy abundance without fear of evils" (1:33).

Are you prone to sleepless nights of tossing and turning, worrying about the "what-ifs?" Pure hypotheticals? Long shot possibilities which might affect us or our loved ones? The cure for such fears is immersion in God's Word and especially his promises of protection and safety. The verse above shows the clear relationship between knowledge of scriptures and, as teens says, "no fear." Do you know others who are inveterate worrywarts who could benefit from a list of God's promises of his watch care? If you have a topical index of Proverbs, perhaps you could copy these verses to lend assurance and lessen their negativity.

Our worries may be exacerbated by listening to too much news, reading too many crime novels, perusing the Internet news headlines, etc. Garbage in, garbage out is the programming maxim, but it also applies to what we fill our minds with. While I listen to a few minutes of national news headlines on National Public Radio while in the car, I find it unnecessary to read the newspaper accounts of all the local murders, rapes, and muggings in the nearest big city. We can exaggerate fears in our children by leaving local news on TV which they overhear. While we should all take reasonable precautions to lock our houses, cars, and property, it is counterproductive to dwell on the worst things which could happen.

When you awake at night and have difficulty getting back to sleep, turn every worry into a prayer. Worry is harmful to our bodily systems; negativity increases our likelihood of illness due to the strong mind/body connection. The prayer of a righteous person, however, is powerful and effective (James).

# MAY 31

## Proverbs on Living Well—Priorities

"The pursuit of wisdom is better than of silver and wisdom's fruit is pure gold" (3:14).

"Wisdom is more precious than all riches and to be desired above all things" (3:15). These verses are crystal clear that wisdom is valuable. The metaphor of silver, gold, and all riches are used since these three are deemed by our popular culture as the *most* desirable things to pursue. Proverbs shows the contrary: that wisdom is of more value than any of those. If that is true, should we spend more time reading Scripture, listening to good sermons, devouring books of commentary and devotion than accumulating riches or precious metals?

If we truly took these verses to heart, wouldn't sports, entertainment, shopping move down our list of daily to-dos, and studying Scripture and watching DVDs on biblical wisdom slide up our list of priorities? It has been said that if you want to see where one's true priorities lie, look at one's calendar and checkbook register. Are there more social events than Sunday school, Bible studies, and lectures? Are we purchasing more clothes, shoes, cars, and entertainment than spending money at the Christian bookstore? These two indicators cut right to the heart of what is important in our lives.

Do you always have a book of biblical wisdom or devotions next to your bedside or recliner? If not, reconsider whether to check out the latest Max Lucado, Chuck Swindoll, or Rick Warren book on Amazon or at the big box religious literature rack and pick up something to inspire you. We should always have something handy to challenge our thinking and nudge us down the Christian path.

What magazines do we subscribe to? Consider subscribing to *Daily Bread, Guideposts, Angels on Earth*, or another inspirational magazine to keep in the car when we're waiting in line at the drive-through. Let's pursue wisdom in all the ways we can as a top priority.

# June 1

## Proverbs on Direction—Eyes

"The path of the just as a shining light goes forward and increases to perfect day" (4:18).

There are many ways we receive God's guidance and direction in our lives. We have five senses so we may receive direction through several senses. The most obvious which comes to mind is our eyes: reading, especially God's wisdom in his Word. But this verse calls to mind a spotlight, which illuminates one step at a time on our path forward. "For [our parents'] advice is a beam of light directed into the dark corners of your mind to warn you of danger and to give you a good life." (6:23).

Our eyes respond to highlights in our Bibles or religious books. I urge you to adopt a system of colors or symbols to catch your eye and increase your awareness of patterns and repeated themes in scripture. Are you a rainbow user: yellow, pink, blue, and green highlights indicating different subjects? I use several capital letters in the margin to indicate verses on common themes: W for wisdom, P for promise, L for life, V for victory, O for obedience, etc. Once marked, it is easy to see how frequently a theme is addressed and to relate different books of the Bible in addressing a common theme. Proverbs especially overlaps with Psalms, Ecclesiastes, and James (the New Testament practical wisdom advice akin to Proverbs). Then if you're preparing a Sunday school lesson, a Bible study talk or a devotion article about a certain subject, it is easy to collect verses on a theme.

Do you underline key words? Use abbreviations or symbols? I use a clock face set on four o'clock to indicate the theme of carpe diem—that life is short and could end soon. A starburst indicates light. Two small circles indicate water or fountains. A small half sun denotes sunrise or sunset. It is fascinating to see how frequently these themes repeat and these symbols catch our eyes more easily.

# June 2

## Proverbs on Direction—Ears

"Whether you turn to the right or to the left, your ears will hear a voice behind you saying, 'This is the way, walk in it'" (Isa. 30:21).

This verse from Isaiah is so apt I chose to use it instead of a Proverbs citation. The next most obvious of our senses other than eyes is our sense of hearing. Perhaps we think it is our conscience speaking to us, the Holy Spirit, or the childhood admonitions of our parents. If we seek guidance and pray for direction, we should take time to still our hearts to listen for a response. Have you experienced an audible leading? Many mature Christians testify to warnings in the nick of time before a danger arose, attributing them to a guardian angel or divine spirit.

The more we input wisdom literature into our spirits, the more readily it comes to mind when we are weighing a particular decision. Perhaps we hear our pastor's recent sermon coming to mind or a teaching tape or Sunday school lecturer. Even the words to a Christian song play through our heads at time, providing inspiration and guidance.

Again referencing *Godwinks* books' tales, sometimes, the phone rings with advice from a friend or a Facebook posted meme or inspirational e-mail is exactly the thought to address our current need. *Guideposts* articles or devotions from *Daily Bread, Upper Room*, or other inspirational publications can be used supernaturally by God to bring God's will for our lives to the forefront of our minds.

Of course, as parents, we are ordained as instruments of discipline or counsel to guide the path of our children. But those in authority over us—counselors, therapists, pastors, or teachers—can give appropriate words of advice to many, but the word is perfectly applicable to our pending dilemma.

# JUNE 3

## Proverbs on Direction—Feet

"The steps of men are guided by the Lord" (20:24).

There are a great number of Proverbs which reference our feet, our pathway, our steps, or our walk. "In all your ways, think on God and he will direct your steps" (3:6). "Keep the law and counsel and the Lord will be at your side and will keep your foot that you won't be taken" (3:26). "Turn your foot away from evil and He will make your courses straight and bring forward your ways in peace" (4:27).

"His will is in them who walks sincerely" (11:20). Our life is lived one day at a time, one step at a time. Narrow is the way that leads to life eternal, but wide is the path to destruction. Often, we get frustrated when God does not reveal the "big plan" to us but merely the next small step. Just as in the wilderness over forty years, God never revealed the exact destination to Moses, or the new home to Abraham, God delights not in playing "hide the ball," but in increasing our dependence on him. Like Saul being led on the Damascus Road after being struck blind or like a child holding tightly to a parent's hand, when we only see the next step clearly, we necessarily must stay close to God, the revealer of our path forward. His ultimate desire is that we keep close to him, so this is one good way to bring dependence about.

"Make straight the path of your feet and let your eyes look straight on and all your ways shall be established" (4:26). How do we make straight the path of our feet? This brings to mind early chapters of Proverbs strongly cautioning against being enticed to a life of crime by our evil peers. Heed God's Word and familiarize ourselves with it to guide our feet aright.

# JUNE 4

## Proverbs on Direction—Thoughts

"Lay open your works to the Lord and your thoughts shall be directed" (16:3).

How comforting and intimate is this promise that God drops thoughts inside our minds when needed. But notice the condition: we must share with God our plans and needs if we expect thought guidance. "In all your ways think on God and He will direct your steps" (3:6). Again, we take the intentional step of approaching God and requesting his direction if we expect his direction to follow.

I have noticed that if we pray and seek guidance just before we sleep at night, we will have a fresh insight upon awakening. Whether it is the way our God-created minds work, allowing creative abilities to work with the "pending issue," or whether it is sovereign watchful God (who never sleeps!) on overtime providing needed answers, this phenomenon has been mentioned by several Christians.

"The Lord hears the prayers of the righteous" (15:29). This gives us confidence that our requests for guidance will be heard and addressed by our all-seeing, all-hearing God. Even though he is of sufficient power and scope to run the mechanics of the universe, he is of such an intimate caring nature that he attunes his ear to the concerns of each of his beloved children.

In my experience, receiving brand new, sometimes, surprising new thoughts is the second most common way to receive direction from God after Scripture. I have been thrilled at the unique interesting thoughts that have come to mind which seemed beyond anything I could have dreamed up on my own. God, you see, has the larger picture, looking down from 30,000 feet (so to speak) while we have the 180° level view. We might think of the surprising power of Google Earth as a parallel.

# JUNE 5

## Proverbs on Direction—Parental Advice

"Keep your father and mother's commands in your heart and they shall lead you" (6:22).

Why is parental advice reliable? At the very least, we know they love us more than anyone else in the world so they have our best interests at heart. God ordains parents to be the prime authority in children's lives, so no matter how old we are, we still replay "tapes" in our heads of what our parents' advice would have been. Parents have by definition lived longer than their children, so that fact alone ensures they will have more experience in interpersonal relationships and the ways of the world. In addition, they know us better than others around us, especially our peers, since they have watched us grow and develop from day one. Love of us and intimate knowledge of our characteristics go a long way to validate their advice.

Children often reflect many of their parents' attributes and abilities, so our "likeness" to our parents is a third reason that parental advice may be more apt than that of teachers, counselors, or peers. Our parents have lived where we lived for early years of our lives, shared in many life experiences, and understand our motivations and uniqueness. This overlap fits them to understand our pending dilemmas and puts them in a special relationship lending itself to good advice.

Children, once grown and self-sufficient, are not obligated to abide by parental advice but should consider and listen respectfully to opinions of parents for all the above reasons. "The wise in heart will receive commandments" (10:8). The wise in heart remain teachable and recognize that God's will for our lives may well come to us through words of our parents.

Children, listen to your parents, is advice that never grows stale since God often works through parents.

# June 6

## Proverbs on Direction—Blockages

"He is a shield to those who walk in integrity, guiding the paths of justice" (2:7).

Sometimes, our path forward is not revealed in a positive way, but we are guided by closed doors, ended opportunities shunting us in another direction. Much like the apostle Paul was prevented by the Holy Spirit from going to Asia, so he could be available to heed the call from Macedonia, God puts obstacles in our way. Like rats in a maze who continually have to adjust their route when they run around a corner, finding a wall, they must backtrack and find the single way forward.

Have you ever been frustrated about accomplishment of a plan, knowing in your soul that your way had to be right and then later acknowledging that if you had gotten your way, disaster would have ensued? Again, we are at ground level trying to understand circumstances involving timing, relationships, and future events while God is omnipotent and omniscient therefore seeing from all levels including future events. God's knowledge must be beyond that of the most sophisticated computer, factoring in effects on others, effects even on our future legacy, and considerations which would not even occur to us.

He is sovereign, almighty and all powerful; we are merely frail humans which limited minds. I have experienced frustrations in choosing a home in a new city, but being directed to another one, which looking back, was just the right fit for so many reasons. School districts, churches, neighbors all were part of God's plan in hindsight. When I stopped pounding on a closed door and accepted the revealed way forward, I sensed peace and "rightness," which surely were of divine origin. This sense of peace in following God's will is a common way his leading is evident. Accepting blockages in our best interest is a sign of Christian maturity.

# June 7
## Proverbs on Direction—Acknowledgment

"Trust in the Lord with all your heart and lean not to your own understanding; in all your ways acknowledge Him and He shall direct your paths" (3:5).

Notice the express condition in this verse. We must acknowledge him which leads to receipt of divine direction. Surely, we must, as a bare minimum, acknowledge him in our thoughts, realizing our need for holy inspiration. Better yet, perhaps this verse encompasses the need to acknowledge him outwardly: by word or action, in order to smooth the way for a heavenly finger-pointing of the correct path. If we were to take the next step and "put it all out there"—publicly let our "clan," our Sunday school class, our breakfast club, our family, or other small group know that we are seeking God's direction, expecting in faith to receive inspirational "Godwink" or other guidance, this exercise of our faith would surely be pleasing to God and inspire him to respond clearly. While it is doubtful God responds to intentional manipulation, I believe that so long as our request for guidance is sincere and well intentioned, God would desire to reward our faith with a clear nod in the direction he wants us to go.

While some testimonies about receipt of godly instruction are well nigh comical, who are we to limit the manner in which God responds? One college graduate was agonizing over which of two geographically diverse job offers to take: Wyoming or Michigan, and earnestly praying for direction while driving. At a stoplight just then, he looked up and saw a bumper sticker immediately in front of him saying, "Go, Michigan!" While most likely this was a team sports fan sticker, who is to say God does not or cannot work in such a manner? Especially if confirmed by wise godly counselors, such directives may well originate with God.

# June 8

## Proverbs on Direction—Illumination

"The path of the righteous is like a shining light that shines brighter and brighter until the perfect day" (4:18).

While some view this verse as one reflecting general optimism in the mature Christian's walk, much like an upward spiral of increasing holiness, most literally, this verse speaks of increasing light to clarify our way. If the hoped for light is metaphorical, then it can be understood as clarity in our next step forward—clarity received from scriptures on the page "standing out" in our study, from wise counsel from Christian advisors, or running across a perfectly apt paragraph in a devotional book we are then reading. Or "light" can be understood as the absence of doubt, gray issues, or uncertainty when facing a decision. Many Christians speak of a feeling of palpable peace descending when a hard choice is resolved; confirmation in the form of such peace is subjective, but those who let the Holy Spirit reign in their lives come to recognize its nudge.

As we gain more experience in life, especially if we are applying ourselves to study and apply God's wisdom for living, much light arises from the plumb line of simply knowing God's will for our lives because scripture lays out many correct choices. Illumination is such an ethereal word, but black and white principles are rampant in Proverbs particularly. We are reminded that many decisions in life do not require agonizing over—answers are in line with the Ten Commandments, the sermon on the mount, or the two overarching commandments to love God supremely, and our neighbor as ourselves. What further comes to mind are the once popular WWJD bracelets, a current reminder to think as though we were in Jesus' life—how would he respond?

Illumination is an inspirational term, denoting mental clarity, lack of confusion, and godly leading.

# JUNE 9

## Proverbs on Direction—Openness

"The wise in heart will receive commandments" (10:8).

The book of James promises that if we ask for wisdom, we shall receive it. Asking for wisdom is the first step in becoming wise. Systematically studying and digesting Proverbs, especially those portions applying to the issues in our lives, will answer many dilemmas in life. However, this verse seems to promise that if the issue isn't directly addressed by scripture, the wise will be guided in their decisions. No particular method is specified: listening to sermons, listening to radio teaching in the car, reading "all good books" as John Wesley encouraged, or searching the scriptures might show the way. Sometimes, we happen to run into an old friend or a person we respect when we're in the midst of a nerve wracking crisis, and something they say gives us peace of mind that the way we are contemplating is the correct one.

Sometimes, studying Proverbs or other scripture books in a different translation opens our eyes to a new dimension of understanding. Modern translations often lend a more understandable twist that directly addresses our uncertainty.

It is our job to be diligent in becoming wise using the inspired Word of God already existing, continuing in Bible study year by year and the wisdom in our heart will be pleasing to God, spurring him to meet our needs. This verse leaves open the door in the method we will receive guidance; likewise, our minds should stay open and alert to observe "input" arriving in our lives through different channels. Praying for Holy Spirit knowledge to discern God's desired path should not be overlooked. This reminds me of the story of the flood victim atop a building praying for deliverance. When the frustrated prayers of the victim reached his ears, God replied, "I sent a helicopter, a boat and an inner tube!" What were you waiting for, a floating gold Cadillac?

# JUNE 10

## Proverbs on Direction—Made Plain

"The way of the righteous is made plain" (15:19).

This is another bald observation that righteousness helps in our decision-making. Of course, righteousness results from consistent obedience to God's laws. A precursor to such obedience is being well acquainted and grounded in God's laws and precepts. Gaining such knowledge is not through osmosis—being in the presence of a saintly grandparent will help but is not enough. It helps to attend church to hear sermons preached explaining the scriptures, attend Sunday school or small group Bible studies to get input from other God-fearing Christians, feed on a steady diet of inspirational scripture-based commentaries or books. But there is no substitute for personal study and meditation on God's Word. Having a bedrock foundation of such precepts paves the way for exploration of new issues that we have not found addressed in scripture. Obvious extrapolation from clear dictates of God often leads to resolution of cutting edge issues.

Expressly praying for guidance and allowing time/space for an answer is key. We are reminded that praying is our job, but we must also turn off radio, TV, music, and conversation long enough to allow the still small voice of God to respond to our urgent pleas. Listening is essential to receiving plain advice in answer to prayer. Let's give God the courtesy of an opportunity to reply to our pointed prayers.

Sometimes, the path forward becomes plain when alternatives drop out of the running, are blocked, or become obscured. If we take a single step forward (in a way that does not foreclose other doorways), that movement in faith reveals shortcomings of other paths, leaving one straight ahead and plain.

Much like Joshua and the Israelite leaders stepping one foot into the Jordan, suddenly opening up the dry riverbed, movement forward can likewise make our ways plain.

# JUNE 11

## Proverbs on Direction—Integrity

"The integrity of the upright shall guide them" (11:3).

In thinking about this verse, we can be sure that if one path forward involves lying, cheating, stealing, or committing a crime, it should be immediately scratched from the list of alternatives. In some ways, life is not so hard. The person of integrity, the righteous person who has trained themselves to abide by God's precepts, can easily eliminate some options which might be considered by others in the world.

Living wisely does operate to simplify our lives and our decision-making in many respects. Committing to paper the alternatives we are considering in making an important life decision is helpful since our brains have difficulty holding a number of alternatives clearly in mind. Making a rudimentary pros/cons chart for each alternative clarifies our thinking and allows us to ponder each option in turn. Seeing something in black and white may jog our minds to recall a piece of scripture or a sermon point we've learned, allowing us to delete one or more alternatives as contrary to God's will.

The corporate world often uses the headline test in employee training: if I do X in the course of my employment and my supervisor, stockholders, regulators, or department of justice were to read about X on the front page of the newspaper, envision how would that affect my reputation, that of my company and even that of my industry? That stark reality of future consequences often helps to clarify the path forward. An essential aspect of integrity is not feeling guilt, not having to worry and stew over inevitable negative consequences if the action came to light. Persons of integrity sleep better and surely have lower blood pressure stemming from the absence of tension and stress of being "found out."

# June 12

## Proverbs on Direction—Straightness

"Turn not to the right hand nor left; keep on the straight path" (4:27).

This proverb seems to address the situation where options have been considered and a path chosen, but perhaps peer pressure, distractions, or snares threaten to knock us off the chosen path. What obstacles have you faced that have nearly knocked us off the path? Perhaps we take a public position, but immediate feedback is negative: will we have the courage to stay the course? Politicians are infamous for posing a "straw man" position and then waiting for media or constituent reaction before finalizing a policy. Is this an effective way to run a state, or even a country? There are times when despite anticipated negative pushback, we must resolve to maintain a well-considered position. Despite temptations to abandon the "right thing" because of complaints, if we did our homework in praying for wisdom, making sure our chosen path was in accord with scripture and the advice of godly counselors, we may just have to endure the slings and arrows of public opinion and stick with it.

In visualizing this verse, do you see a dirt path through the woods? A path along the beach between boulders and caves? A well-trod snowy track in the mountains? The practice of bringing to mind a physical location for operation of the verse may be helpful in strengthening our resolve.

Visualizing the future as clearly as possible is another incentive to accomplishing our chosen path. If our goal is graduation, marriage, a well-honored retirement, taking a shortcut detour through the swamps of sin can suddenly and irreversibly mar that end goal. Much like Olympians with closed eyes rehearsing their routines or psyching themselves up for the upcoming competition, reinforcement of the end goal can be very helpful. Heaven is our end goal: visualize that when considering a detour.

# June 13
## Proverbs on Direction—Commandments

"The Lord's commands are a lamp and the law is a light and instruction of the way of life" (6:23).

The Proverb is very straightforward about the basis for our decision making—the Lord's commands and law. Again, those commands and laws do not leap into our heads unless they are first read, studied, absorbed, and tucked away in our brains and spirits in a way that encourages them to jump to the forefront when needed. The use of two different sources of illumination—a lamp and a light—is interesting. At first blush, we may not think there is a true difference. However, I have heard sermons preached about potential differences. A lamp is generally in a fixed location, not generally portable like a torch (or today a flashlight). A lamp's function is to allow us to more easily read a text when we are sitting in our easy chair, when we are contemplating scripture, even when we are relaxed. On the other hand, a light is more atmospheric, more widespread, broader, higher, and more pervasive. It not only illuminates the very place we are now, but the next few steps down the path when we are moving forward.

"Instruction" is also mentioned in addition to lamp and light. "Thou shall not covet" is a very clear instruction. It clearly applies to us sitting on our front porch drooling over the fancy new car in our neighbor's driveway. But applied more broadly, is the instruction wide enough to apply to our sitting in our easy chair paging through the leaves of the new Neiman Marcus Christmas catalog filled with luxuries beyond our reach? Why waste our time getting ideas when we have no need and a dearth of means to acquire such things? Recreational shopping falls into this category as well. Let us heed commands and laws as guides for our direction in life.

# June 14

## Proverbs on Direction—Righteousness

"The righteousness of the perfect shall direct his way" (11:5).

At first blush, this proverb seems intimidating since few of us would characterize ourselves as "perfect." Can ordinary old still-maturing Christians benefit from this verse? Surely, we must discount this verse as beyond our reach.

Since we know that none of us in our human condition is perfect, maybe the only reasonable interpretation of this verse is that all who strive to consistently obey God's laws and who believe in Christ as the way of salvation are made perfect by his sacrifice. Other words for *righteous* are *wise*, *godly*, *saintly*, *obedient*. Good intentions are key since our hearts are open to God's eyes as in water. Even if our actions should fall short of perfection, if our hearts are dutiful and willing to obey God's will, our reward will be great. One of those rewards in this lifetime is confidence that we can know and understand God's will for our lives if our hearts are open to his leading. One aspect of abundant living is living mostly in certainty, not miserable darkness, about how to lead our lives. While there may be times of indecision in any life, a great many choices in life are guided by scripture which has been digested and internalized by the righteous person.

The Jan Karon line of Mitford religious novels has popularized the universal applicability of the "prayer that never fails": "may thy will be done" (from the Lord's Prayer). When our high schooler is utterly heartbroken about a romantic breakup, we have no clue whether to pray for reconciliation or that a "better fish" will spring from the sea. Therefore, the prayer that God's will be done is a righteous way to counsel both the child and to take to heart ourselves when we are praying for the child's comfort.

# JUNE 15

## Proverbs on Direction—Pondering

"Ponder the path of your life and let all your ways be established" (4:20).

"Ponder" has a flavor of deep meaningful thought on a subject. We often are too busy to stop and ponder, but we must schedule time once in a while, whether on vacation, sabbatical, during January 1 resolution making or otherwise, to not just get up in the morning and head out the door, without thinking why we are doing what we're doing but visualize the future. Are we choosing deliberately the path God wants us to? Is our path leading to a destination that we will be satisfied when we're on our deathbed that we have used our best talents and gifts in a way pleasing to God?

"Ponder" is opposed to just "going" down the path of life. Deliberate consideration of our goals, our intended destination and the reasons we are doing what we're doing is encouraged by this Proverb.

The arrangement of the verse implies that if we heed the call to ponder periodically, our life will be more "established"—perhaps more grounded, established on a solid Christlike foundation and intentional. We won't end up "there" and wonder how in the world our winding path led us there. We don't want to wake up at age eighty or when our health fails and have serious regrets about the bucket list we intended to accomplish but never completed. Of course, finances and family circumstances sometimes impede our progress toward our bucket list items, but if we have no goals or bucket list to start toward, we certainly will not accomplish our heart's desires.

Psychological studies have shown that if we commit our goals to writing, we have a 75% better chance of accomplishing them. Ponder the path of your life and write down your aspirations; then post them on your bathroom mirror, your dashboard, and your day planner, and "let all your ways be established."

# JUNE 16

## Proverbs on Direction—Acceptability of Prayers

"The Lord hears the prayers of the righteous" (15:29).

If we pray for guidance in our life, how can we increase the chances of getting a clear reply? We can diligently strive to improve our righteousness to increase the odds. There are many passages in Psalms and elsewhere illustrating the principle that God is more attentive to the prayers of the righteous, his dearly beloved. 1 Peter 3:7 speaks of our prayers being blocked by sin, as does Psalms. It would be logical for God to reason: why answer Sue's prayer if she is unlikely to accept and follow my answer since she doesn't yet follow my clearly prescribed laws.

The closer our walk with God, the more highly attuned to our slightest prayer he is. This correlation is weighty, and we should think carefully about the effect of our righteousness on the desires of our heart and our prayers in general. Perhaps a fun parallel is: God may put the prayers of the righteous person on his "favorites list" with a special "tone" for incoming prayers. Revelation speaks of golden bowls holding the prayers of the saints. Perhaps this is metaphorical description, but if not, maybe when the prayers of the righteous "hit the golden bowl," a special chime sounds! How imaginative to envision our prayers ascending to heaven and being addressed by hovering angels, anxious to bring our petitions to the attention of Christ or his minions. I read a vision of a person returning from a "near-death" experience who described radiant beams of golden light slicing through the floor of heaven; each time a beam appeared, a sonorous chime sounded and an angel hurried to the beam to see what was needed. When the person inquired (in the mental telepathy wordless communication that most NDEs describe) what the beams represented, they were the incoming prayers of the righteous.

# JUNE 17

## Proverbs on Direction—Guardrails

"Keep the law and counsel and the Lord will be at your side and will keep your foot that you won't be taken" (3:26).

This comforting promise brings to mind the guardrails on a bridge, the bumpers at the bowling alley, or the rumble strips on highway margins. Examine closely what it is that keeps us from going astray: keeping the law and counsel. Keeping the law entails making an effort to learn God's precepts, observe them, memorize them so they reside deep in our consciousness, and call them to mind when we are in a time of need. The second condition is keeping counsel: listening to sermons, our parents, our teachers, our elders, our pastors, our youth leaders. Necessarily, we must tamp down our "know-it-all" ego to heed the words of those senior to us, allow those words to percolate in our minds, and respect those giving such counsel.

What dangers does this verse guard against? Taken by whom? Any number of dangers surround us in our daily walk: potholes in the path of life, temptations that would lead us astray, momentary forgetfulness of the right path, peer pressure, and tunnel vision fixed on getting ahead monetarily.

What threatens to knock you off the straight and narrow path? Examining our own weaknesses helps us prepare to avoid being waylaid by them. If we have a problem with a certain person we are preparing to meet, resolving ahead of time to stand firm in our convictions might help. Bringing to mind those biblical passages or principles of wisdom applicable to the anticipated meeting will help cement them front and center in our minds so that we are not swept off our feet during the meeting. Preparation for life in general involves learning and reviewing God's law to serve as guardrails on our daily path.

# June 18

## Proverbs on Direction—Steps

"The steps of men are guided by the Lord" (20:24).

This verse emphasizes the overall sovereignty of God in our lives, leading and guiding us in accordance with his divine plan. If we feel uncertain about which direction to head, one criteria I have heard is "do the next good thing ahead of us." We may never catch a glimpse of our ultimate destination, but making sure the very next step is kind, helpful, and loving boosts our assurance that it is in accordance with God's will and will get us further down the path to his intended destination for us.

What is our purpose in life? Many describe that as merely being the hands and feet of Christ upon earth. Mother Teresa speaks of not worrying about what grand tasks we accomplish but undertaking small tasks with great love and care. Where do we put our feet for the next step? Being open to God's leading means reading our morning devotions with an eye for wisdom applying to our task at hand that day, listening to Christian radio perhaps to glean a word just right for a pending decision, and paying heed to those we meet whose words God may be using to guide our steps.

A firm foundation for our steps is laid by habitual attendance at church, Bible studies, small groups, and daily scripture readings. The way ahead will not appear so murky when we have embedded in our spirits the basics of God's will for our lives as lived by biblical examples: prophets, righteous kings, disciples, and apostles. Scriptural stories are so diverse, there is likely something applicable to our current situation if we will regularly study and listen to those stories.

We should daily ask God to guide our steps and then keep our ears attuned for his direction.

# June 19

## Proverbs on Direction—Priorities

"In everything you do, put God first, and he will direct you and crown your efforts with success" (3:6).

What a wonderful, comforting promise this is! Success is a loaded word: our culture quickly equates it with financial security, material possessions, fame, and youthful appearance. But Christians' definition of success is derived from obedience to God's way of living. Our priorities should reflect those of God—loving relationships, best use of our time and talents to serve others, humility and diligence in our assigned tasks.

We know from the lives of billionaires like Howard Hughes that material wealth does not necessarily lead to happiness or self-satisfaction. He ended up a germophobic recluse who was unable to complete the most basic tasks or relate to anyone around him. Habitual self-focus becomes toxic and is a downward spiral, for narcissists tend to pout and never believe the world is paying them their due. On the other hand, other focus brings satisfaction and assurance that we are doing God's will. We were designed for good works by our Creator. Our bodies, souls, and minds benefit when we are generous, caring, and helpful.

Our priority each day should be: how can I best exemplify the life of Christ? How can I boost God's will to first place in my life? If we find that we are spending the bulk of our time tending to our possessions—searching for things buried in our closet, maintaining our various vehicles, boats, and golf carts—perhaps we need to simplify our possessions so we can get back to the main thing.

The calendar/checkbook diagnosis comes to mind: what do these items reveal about the priorities in our lives? What does our daily to do list reveal about our priorities? Is the first thing that hits our hand in the morning our iPhone or our Bible?

# JUNE 20

## Proverbs on Direction—Good Hearts

"The heart of man disposes his way but the Lord must direct his steps" (16:9).

How do we prepare our hearts to follow God's way? Prayer is the main way we prepare our hearts. The primary effect of prayer is not to bring about the petitions we make but to soften our heart and align it in accordance with God's will. The more time we spend in prayer, seeking God's will, the more thoroughly the Holy Spirit can accomplish its renewing, transforming work. Our part is to do everything within our power to make our hearts godlike, which paves the way for God to more easily guide and direct us. We become more willing to be led and more observant of the ways in which God is leading us.

In addition to prayer, our hearts can be prepared by silence, meditation, and attention to God. Directing our minds to God, throughout our day, in the midst of whatever task we are undertaking, turns our periodic breath prayers into more disciplined constant attention. Brother Lawrence, the simple monk who labored in his monastery's kitchen and garden, developed this habit and famously wrote about this process of increasing our mind's communion with God. Some confraternities of monks are reminded to turn their mind to God each quarter hour with the clock's chiming in addition to our customary mealtime and bedtime prayers.

The Lord delights in those whose minds are stayed on him. He hovers over and attends to the lives of those communing with him. As a practical matter, if we seek the Lord's guidance, the Lord's eyes and attention will be on us to a greater degree if we are "meeting" with him in our spiritual disciplines, training our souls to commune with him.

# JUNE 21

## Proverbs on Direction—The Way

"I lead in the way of righteousness" (8:20).

The book of Acts recounts that one early name for the followers of Christ was "The Way." In contrast to the surrounding pagan culture of the Greeks and Romans who had hundreds of gods in their pantheon governing every aspect of life, this new strange Christian faith advocated focusing on a single invisible God who led them in the way of righteousness. How strange this way must have sounded at first to new converts. In one sense, perhaps simplification from a temple or shrine on every crossroad, every wayside on the Appian Way in Rome to a single universal invisible Creator who could be worshipped any place one found himself would be easier. Making offerings and vows to placate two hundred plus gods seems overwhelming. Reducing this obligation to a single way of righteousness almost sounds like a relief.

Where does righteousness lead? Righteousness causes one to pursue justice in our world, deal with others in a compassionate understanding way, look for opportunities to be of service, and improve our workplaces, homes, and neighborhoods. Most pilgrimage travelers hostels were established by Christians; most orphanages and hospitals were founded by religious orders. History reveals this clear pattern. While there are horrible historical interludes of Crusades, the Inquisition and not-so benevolent enterprises where true Christianity was replaced with "eye for an eye" vengeance, the vast majority of righteous Christian society brought hope and healing to their worlds.

Today, the phrase "bloom where you're planted" is a shorthand way to remind us that wherever we are, our calling in life is to bring comfort, hope, and healing, just as Christ did when he walked life's daily path. "I lead" indicates that we must be followers, so keep on the lookout for Christ's leading.

# June 22

## Proverbs on Direction—Away from Evil

"The path of the godly leads away from evil; he who follows that path is safe" (16:17).

Safety! Isn't that what most of us long for? Dream of? Hope for? How can we sleep peacefully at night without some assurance of safety? As parents, we want this for our precious children. Instinctively, most of us are predisposed to travel in the direction leading to greater safety. So how do we proceed?

How do we become more "godly?" Godly folks are full of godly wisdom, gained from yielding to the shaping of the Holy Spirit, praying, attending church, reading devotions and godly literature, and asking for an increase in wisdom in life. Every day, a good way to start the day is to remain open for opportunities to serve, asking God to direct us on the good path which leads to safety.

Even when we walk through the valley of the shadow of death, we should fear no evil (Ps. 23) since our path leads to safety. If our nature is of a fearful type, we can bring comfort to ourselves by concentrating on these uplifting promises of God's nature. He is a good God, desirous of a hope and a future for us (Jeremiah), blessing us with promises of abundance both materially and spiritually. We should have no fear of evil since our God is more powerful than forces of evil in the world. While evil is widespread in our world, God is in ultimate control and according to the book of Revelation, the guy in the white hat is victorious! While despair may envelope us from time to time, joy comes in the morning if we attune our spirits to God's wavelength which is the joy channel. Our path is upward, heavenward, away from evil.

# JUNE 23

## Proverbs on Direction—Established

"Make straight the path of your feet and let your eyes look straight on and all your ways shall be established" (4:26).

What does *established* mean to you? It brings thoughts of firm foundations versus wishy-washy principles. If we are established in the faith, we are past the point of decision; we are on the downward slope on the far side of a turning point. We do not agonize each morning about our basic purpose in life and our path forward. We firmly march toward our well-thought-out goals and are not distracted by petty happenings. We are not, like "tweens" are so subject to, rocked to and fro by peer pressure and the whims of popularity.

How then do our ways become established? By straightness. Straightness of footpath and straightness of vision. Straightness can be read literally, but it also carries a firm connotation of principled, well disciplined, and righteous. When we are young, we are inexperienced in decision making and can be easily led astray. We hope that by the time we are mature adults, we have seen others experience enough negative consequences that such negativity deters us from suffering the bad fallout for ourselves. A person who is straight has clearheadedly considered the consequences of diverse paths and, for the right reasons, chosen one over another. We have not willy-nilly wandered down one path but chosen it for rational reasons. Robert Frost's poem about choosing the road less traveled, making all the difference, is written from a hindsight point of view at an end stage of life. We, however, have the choice of "roads" to take from a forwarding looking perspective, a more difficult task.

Looking straight on carries with it the duty to carefully think ahead about a choice we're in the midst of to consider positive and negative consequences, asking God's guidance as we go.

# June 24
## Proverbs on Direction—Leading

"I will show you the way of wisdom and lead you by the paths of equity so that when you run, you shall not meet a stumbling block" (4:11).

This verse offers two action word promises: "show" and "lead." How does God show us the way of wisdom? Some Bible readers speak of God "illuminating" or highlighting to their eyes a certain text when studying. I have noticed repetition as a method. Perhaps a verse is in one's morning devotions, then it is read on the radio, and then it appears as the sermon text, all in the same day! When we receive a coincidental confirmation through repetition originating from diverse sources, maybe we'd better take a closer look. Likely these coincidences are "God-incidences." Or maybe we have read a verse fifty times, but on the fifty-first reading, we understand the application of the verse in a new way. Often, we have read something in a commentary, an article, or a *Guideposts* magazine that illumines the meaning of a verse in a way that had never before come to mind.

I inherited a ceramic container holding printed Bible verses that "lives" on the breakfast table, allowing me to peruse a verse each morning. I also have a religious calendar on my dressing table with a fresh devotion every morning. If these two coincide in subject matter, something may be afoot!

We must be alert to the nudge of the Holy Spirit as we proceed through our day, noticing accented precepts in sources as diverse as an article in the *AARP The Magazine*, an account of an alumni's life in our alma mater's materials or a National Public Radio "StoryCorps." Stars align rarely, but godly inspirations spring up in the most interesting ways, urging us to stop and consider closely where God is leading.

# JUNE 25

## Proverbs on Direction—Prosperity

"The wise servant shall prosper in his dealings and his way shall be made straight." 14:15

A servant necessarily serves someone. I don't believe this verse is limited in applications to employees or paid servants. We are all servants of the Lord in establishing his Kingdom on earth. Notice the adjective, however, "wise". Wise servants are those who listen intently to the plans and desires of the one they serve so they will more closely carry out the master's goals. They are agents, not principals, so they are not to work for their own best interests, but for those of their master. Their desires are subordinated to accomplishment of the master's plans.

If a servant is wise, two consequences result: prosperity and a straight path. Servants are logically rewarded if they diligently and sincerely carry out the work required by their master. I believe we are not only rewarded in heaven for what we've sown in this life, but also in this life. There are verses in many Bible books which note this correlation.

It is horribly discouraging to observe the lives of young people who have strayed off the path into immoral behavior, gotten seduced by the siren call of the culture, and reaped serious destruction and waste. The earlier in life we discover God's precepts and appropriate them for our lives, the more risky detours we can bypass and the straighter our way will be to Godly obedience and its reward, prosperity. John Wesley, the founder of Methodism, admonished Christians to make all the money they can, save all they can and give all they can. Prosperity liberates us to having an opportunity to be generous to those in need and to our church and charitable institutions. God loves a cheerful, prosperous giver.

# JUNE 26

## Proverbs on Direction—Answer to Prayer

"The Lord hears the prayers of the righteous" (15:29).

If we pray for guidance in our lives, how can we up the odds that we will receive guidance? By improving our righteousness. While we are responsible for learning and following the rules for living set out by our Creator, our righteousness naturally increases without specific effort by virtue of the Holy Spirit transforming our hearts. We should systematically study, meditate, read, borrow Christian DVDs, purchase devotional materials, and immerse our minds in inspirational movies and resources since inputs affect output. A steady diet of uplifting testimonies in *Daily Bread*, *Upper Room*, or other religious magazines will be a blessing to our spirits and incent us to firmly follow the path of blessing.

Are we spending all our time addicted to secular TV series? Romance novels? Sports channels? We must allocate room in our lives to bless our souls with godly "input" if we hope to increase our righteousness. Life is a journey to be planned, not just to stroll along in a directionless manner.

If we had even a small grasp of the limitless power available to us through fervent prayer, we would reorder our lives to prioritize a planned increase in the pursuit of righteousness. The effective fervent prayer of a righteous person avails much, according to James. If we dwell upon the omnipotent God we serve, we will be encouraged to make resolutions to improve the state of our souls, our righteousness based on the correlation between our godly state and God's inclination to attend our prayers.

We make resolutions to diet, exercise more, get a new car this year, and complete our wardrobe—how much more important it is to take positive steps to ensure we are progressing upward in our Christian walk.

# JUNE 27

## Proverbs on Direction—God's Will

"His will is in them who walks sincerely" (11:20).

Conforming our nature to God's is an ongoing work of the Holy Spirit. When Christ lives in us, our will is subsumed into his, and godly choices are easy. We don't have to agonize over every twist and turn in life; rather, we move forward confidently. Life's bumps {are lowered to} smooth our way, and we have assurance inwardly that we are marching upward to Zion. Not only have we learned from life experiences, but also Christian maturity saves us from learning the hard way. When God's will in our souls is not a tiny spark but a constant warm blaze, dilemmas lessen. We glide along instead of hitting all the potholes. A feeling of blessedness comes to those walking in the center of God's will.

Notice the condition in this verse: walking sincerely. *Sincerely* means without cover-up—to God or our loved ones. Transparency is another descriptor for this condition. Not kidding ourselves or ignoring our true feelings is characteristic of walking sincerely. Insincerity builds barriers to hide feelings, cover over bad thoughts, and defensively deny the truth. Sincerity has no need to bother with barriers/covers or defensiveness. It is open and free. A sincere heart greases the skids for God to indwell and direct our lives. There is no pollution to muddy the works nor unpleasantness to roil the waters of our peace.

Paul matured to the point of saying that it is not him but Christ who dwells in him. This is our aspirational goal: more of him, less of us. In the long run, our will becomes indistinguishable from Christ's. Life is less messy when Christ calls the shots because God has a higher and longer life view than we do—in fact an eternal view.

# June 28

## Proverbs on Direction—Head Butting

"There is no wisdom, prudence or counsel against the Lord" (21:30).

We may construct elaborate plans and schemes using our free will, but if the plans are not of the Lord, our way will be rocky. Effort will be required, and we may feel like we're pushing a four-hundred-pound boulder up a mountainside. If we feel a pervasive sense of unease when confronting a particular task and slight feelings of guilt, we'd better recheck our plans against biblical principles. If we are receiving advice from several peers but we simply cannot feel comfortable with it, we should directly ask God for illumination. If we feel like we're proceeding out on a long unsteady limb, perhaps we should retreat to the solid foundation of scripture for further consideration. If our souls are attuned to God's precepts, our spirits must be heeded when discomfort surrounds us.

How do we know if we're proceeding in the right direction? Is the plan in line with biblical principles? Have we consulted one or more godly counselors, especially those older and wiser than us? Have we researched similar experiences for past history? Our number 1 job in life is to understand God's will and try to follow it. If we're merely drifting along doing our "own thing," we will receive repeated signals when we're going astray. We may choose to block those signals with social distractions, partying, and alcohol or other substances to dull our awareness of godly guidance, but we do so at our peril.

When something is wrong, there will be signals if we choose to look and listen for them. Rarely are we caught off guard. Rather, if we are totally honest with ourselves, we buried our head in the sand to avoid receiving godly wisdom contrary to our desires. Trying to go forward contrary to God's will is like butting our heads painfully against a wall.

# June 29

## Proverbs on Direction—Lots

"Lots are cast into the lap but they are disposed of by the Lord" (16:3).

In ancient times, groups including priests at times made decisions by the throwing of lots, having full confidence that God's sovereignty extended even to their outcome. This little known verse may be "out of fashion," but its wisdom continues to this day. God's sovereignty remains supreme. We would be well advised to think creatively how this verse may be productively used in our lives today.

Drawing numbers out of a hat for priority in choices of various kinds is an effective way of fairly disposing of the goods in an estate without rancor or bitterness. If there are a limited number of slots for a performance, seats in a car, etc., drawing numbers (lots) seems just to all participants. "Luck" is not a concept Christians put much stock in; instead, this verse affirms that it is God who involves himself even in the outcome of so-called random methods for determination.

What hard choices face you? When a group of people are involved and there is not enough X to go around, drawing numbers blindly is a sensible method of resolution. Whether in the workplace or at home in extended family disputes, years of potential animosity and grudge holding can be avoided by use of lots. I have heard stories of years of estrangement resulting from one parent or heir unfairly jumping the gun to secret inherited furniture, assets, or valuables. Even though we know in our hearts that relationships with our loved ones are infinitely more valuable than so-called "valuables," it is difficult to expunge resentments which smolder after unfair splits of collections. Accusations of "Mom wanted me to have that" can be countered with simple drawing of numbers for orderly blind disposition. Try it, you'll like it! Be confident that God is intimately involved in these decisions.

# June 30

## Proverbs on Direction—Soul Maintenance

"He that keeps his soul keeps his way" (16:17).

Just like regular oil changes and maintenance smoothens the life of a vehicle, regular devotions, and prayer smoothens our way in life. In other words, it will be exponentially easier to choose the right path for our daily life if we are regularly communing with God and absorbing his will for our lives as expressed in scripture. Sitting at the feet of pastors, teachers, and scriptural commentators illuminates the Holy Word and embeds it deep in our souls. Then when crunch time comes, decisions are not gut wrenching but matter of fact and obvious. We keep easily to the straight and narrow path when we tend regularly to our soul.

If we are only praying in emergencies, it is difficult to separate the junk from the valuable. When we regularly establish relationship with Christ, it is natural and easier to discern a path forward that is righteous and ordained by God. Keeping our soul also involves not covering holy intentions with trash, not exposing our souls to unwholesome porn, hate-filled media, or bitterness. We do not have to read the local newspaper section on crime to expose ourselves to the salacious details of every murder, rape, and burglary. Feeding our souls instead with praise music, uplifting devotions, and spiritual nourishment will prepare it for the hard days that will surely come at some point in our lives.

Do we inundate our souls with talk radio or TV where conflict, compromised families, and violent arguments are the daily norm? Instead, choose peaceful soothing music that returns our attention to God and his blessings in our lives. When our eyes first open in the morning, habituate yourself to firstfruits of gratitude toward God as our beginning thoughts for the day. Our decisions will surely be easier.

# July 1

## Proverbs on Authority—Good Government

"Mercy and truth preserve the king and his rule is strengthened by clemency" (20:28).

In this month honoring the birth of our nation, it is interesting to note all the Proverbs dealing with wise government and its opposite. Although few nations are governed these days by kings, the precepts carry over generally to any form of government. If we love our country and want it to endure, those in positions of authority or even those of us voting for those in positions of authority should note well the experience gathered by King Solomon, the wisest of men with God-given wisdom. A government is much more likely to endure for generations if it is good to its subjects and has their best interests at heart. Abraham Lincoln, in his Gettysburg address, succinctly and elegantly described this concept as "government by the people, for the people."

Logically, this makes sense that if people's natural rights are being honored and they feel secure, are prospering and able to pursue their interests without government interference, they are wholly unlikely to foment rebellion or seek a different government. If the government is "straight talking," speaking truth, the people are unlikely to become disillusioned. A contrary example is the Vietnam War about which the Johnson administration, to ward off public disillusionment, engaged in a pattern of under reporting casualties for years on end. While the people were already unhappy with the war for policy reasons, it was so far away and so far removed from Communism's direct impact on our nation's interests, but this anger and disgust with a distant war exploded when this lying was revealed.

People are "big enough" to hear truth from their government, good or bad. Patronizingly, twisted government misconduct totally undermines the faith of the people in such government.

# July 2

## Proverbs on Authority—Humility

"Appear not glorious before the king and don't stand in the place of great men" (25:6).

This verse offers straightforward advice about how to interact with persons in high places. Do not act puffed up, posing as someone above your station in life. This tactic will backfire, causing you embarrassment, humiliation, and long-lasting shame. Do not try to outdress, outtalk, or outdo the VIPs in any manner. Be yourself; don't be a poseur. A humble attitude is best. This is reminiscent of the parable Christ spoke in the gospels about it being better to be invited up to the head table, than presumptuously seating yourself in an important spot, then being unceremoniously escorted away.

Despite the world culture becoming "flatter"—i.e. hierarchies of class and rank becoming less important—they still exist. We must as a practical matter acknowledge this and are wise to act in accordance with this verse. Solomon had retinues of retainers and caravans of spices, gifts, and tributes arriving regularly from all parts of the world. He observed the conduct of courtiers, slaves, and servants of every rank. He was well aware of the impact it had on him when a lowly person sought to ignore rank and hopscotch over an assigned position. That person's credibility would be shot for the near term and likely the long term.

In our daily lives, when invited into the corner office at work to discuss business, we should not get "above ourselves," which will boomerang and damage our reputations. This is timeless practical advice whether in the era of kings or Republics. Not only in the arena of government but also in our dealings at work, church, volunteer office, or hospitals, human nature has not changed so this piece of Solomonic wisdom is equally applicable.

# July 3

## Proverbs on Authority—Punishment

"A wise king scatters the wicked and brings them to punishment" (20:26).

Do you aspire to maintain an organization of integrity? Whether a government, corporation, nonprofit, or church, rooting out evildoers and banishing or punishing them sets the right example to govern an organization of respect and integrity. If a ruler or boss is not diligent in staying atop circumstances or is too lazy to devote attention to wrongdoing going on in the organization, the message sent to the ranks of workers is that integrity does not matter. It is essential that immoral conduct not be permitted to become widespread and supervision lax. The health of the organization, the morale of the employees is at stake.

If a CEO is so self-absorbed with his/her new limousine, golf tournaments, business lunches, and perks of position that he/she ignores wrongdoing in the trenches, the business will suffer at some point. Wrongdoing cannot be permitted to flourish lest the entire business become corrupted and ineffective.

Even in our own little fiefdoms in our homes, if parental discipline is lax such that one child bullies another or flagrantly disregards the family rules, the other children will quickly become resentful and disobedient to test boundaries. Children feel more secure when boundaries are clearly explained and followed.

The definition of a good supervisor is one who keeps close tabs on the organization, taking steps to discipline or fire persons not following company rules or being dishonest. The reverse will lead to chaos, legal problems, and distraction from the chief goal of productivity. Interpersonal relations work best when all are following the rules and distractions are avoided in resentment of others' disregard of those rules. Prompt and fair punishment is the most effective way to keep any organization in tiptop shape from families to Fortune 500's.

# July 4
## Proverbs on Authority—Truthfulness

"The king that judges the poor in truth, his throne shall be established forever" (29:14).

Why did the American colonists rise up to oppose King George of England? History tells us that most were unhappy about the principle of taxation without representation. Taxes on tea, on legal documents, and on luxury goods became oppressive since the colonists had no one representing them in Parliament. The people felt "put upon"—that they were merely a sponge to be further squeezed for the benefit of Great Britain. King George lost sight of the goal of good government to benefit the people it governs.

If a government desires to endure, this bedrock principle observed by Solomon three thousand years ago is still applicable. The era of Hitler in Germany, the era of Stalin in Russia, and the era of many modern African dictatorships whose governments are characterized by lies and deception could not endure because they lost the respect and trust of their rulers. Even Communism in all areas of the world has never remained true to its ideals. Although proposing the principle that all work and all share, the hypocrisies of Communist leaders always revealed that their late model Mercedes sedans, offshore bank accounts, and seaside villas were not enjoyed by the people. When the true state of affairs becomes known, the people lose any incentive to support such a government.

Governments who imprison and torture their subjects never publicly admit to it—they dissemble and cover up. Richard Nixon and Bill Clinton may have maintained their offices if they had truthfully confessed to their misdeeds instead of promulgating elaborate denials and cover-ups. People can accept flawed leaders but rarely lying ones. How a ruler relates to the "poorest" in the realm is a true indicator of his/her fitness for office.

# July 5

## Proverbs on Authority—Wisdom

"Wisdom and knowledge prolong a prince's life" (28:2).

If you are an officer holder and wish to be reelected or promoted, how do you best accomplish this? Whether the PTA, the homeowners association, or Congress, applying oneself diligently to learn as much as possible about the needs of your constituents, the departments of the organization, and the laws is a good start. Even more important is understanding human relationships—becoming a student of human nature. Studying Proverbs is an excellent way to gain wisdom not just in spiritual matters but in practical daily matters of how to get along and maintain relationships. If you become expert in a field, people look to you with respect and are anxious to retain the benefit of such experience.

If you fail to study and gain wisdom and knowledge, you are much more likely to be turned out of political office and to have a shorter life. In ancient times, a deposed prince was frequently assassinated. Therefore, political life and years of life went hand in hand. Today, in at least the western world, political leaders could be ousted and disgraced but remain alive. In third world nations, ouster still may equate with death. Thus, "prolong a prince's life" can be read literally or as political life and either interpretation contains truth.

Of course, harking back to January readings about the benefits of wisdom, wisdom and knowledge are generally associated with longer life, whether you are a prince or a peon. Thus, this principle applicable to those in authority can be extrapolated to the life of anyone.

Many benefits flow from gaining wisdom and knowledge, but the more power and authority one has at stake, the more responsible one should be in learning Proverbs and taking it to heart.

# July 6

## Proverbs on Authority—Topsy-Turvy

"It is unseemly for a servant to rule over princes" (19:10).

When someone usurps the position or authority of another, respect is lost and circumstances get confused. In ancient times, most princes gained power through kinship accession, so this verse addresses contrary situations. Primogeniture generally established who inherited, who became family patriarch, and who ruled a country. But even in today's corporations, seniority and putting in one's time is the usual stepping stone to a promotion. Those skipping these steps but still promoted are generally bitterly resented by those bypassed. While there may be good executive reasons for selecting a less senior person for a spot, it is nearly inevitable that his/her peers will resent the selection and will have difficulty putting aside such feelings in the course of future dealings.

The Old Testament is replete with sagas of third wives usurping the position of primary wives; mistresses being better loved than formal wives. All these "out of order" scenarios lead to heartache, dissension, undermining of authority, and disappointments. When Jacob honored his younger son Joseph above his siblings by having made the coat of many colors, extreme retribution ensued. When a prophet anointed David, Jesse's youngest son—in lieu of the older, taller, handsome older sons—bitterness was rampant. Negative consequences developed which affected that and later generations.

When Jacob, the grabby one, double-crossed his brother to receive the patriarchal blessing, the family was nearly split apart. When Abraham's mistress became the bearer of his firstborn, even though suggested by his wife Sarah, hateful conflict erupted.

When we are considering a promotion, bestowal of an honor or recognition in a manner that is out of order, we would be wise to think carefully about the natural fallout of such an action.

# July 7

## Proverbs on Authority—Intimidation

"As the roaring of a lion so also is the dread of a king. He that provokes him, sins against his own soul" (20:2).

We must recognize that kings, the FBI, teachers, law enforcement officers, and anyone in a position of authority wields power. Those under their authority are subject to that power. We ignore or flaunt that power to our detriment. We cannot expect to poke a roaring lion in the eye without suffering an attack or great hostility. Similarly, we cannot expect to flagrantly disregard the order of our superior without risk of arrest, discipline, imprisonment, or a damaged reputation. Even if we are in the right and their order is arbitrary, we must speak in a reasonable voice, act in an ordered measured manner, and "take up our complaint" through proper channels. We cannot simply run away, resist arrest, talk back disrespectfully, or worse.

Parents must strongly impress upon their children the importance of responding wisely to the teacher, principal, coach, bus driver, or policemen. Injustice can be pursued later, but immediate obedience is the watchword of the day. Those in authority are intimidating simply by virtue of their position, and the rest of us must acknowledge that fact. Even an unelected dictator must be heeded; otherwise, we may be at peril of our life.

It is simply unwise to let a confrontation escalate when it is not between equals. When one wields power and the other is subordinate, practical realities dictate prompt compliance. Whether we like it or not, that is how power structures operate. The person of wisdom accommodates this power structure and understands its functioning. We must keep our mouths and fists under control; good sense dictates a measured deliberate response. Biting one's lip and clasping one's hands is by far the better course.

# July 8

## Proverbs on Authority—Wise Servants

"A wise servant is acceptable to the king. He that is good for nothing shall feel the king's anger" (14:35).

If you want to come to the attention of the boss in the business world or otherwise, diligently perform your work in an intelligent manner. This is the path to honor and recognition and promotion. If you're slacking off and thinking you'll be able to hide your screwups or lack of productivity, think again. Poor performance is difficult to mask for very long; the truth will out.

Our relationship to our supervisors is based, to an extent, on our personal dealings and personality, but far more important over the long haul is the quality of our work, for good or ill. We are not being paid to be a fun loving person; we are being paid to accomplish a defined task. In the world of business or government, productivity is what ultimately counts. Bosses who like you can only protect low-performing employees so far; other employees, quality control managers, or customer complaints will bring home to roost our deficiencies.

If we want to be well liked and honored, we first must apply ourselves to learning all we can about how to do our job well and then methodically and consistently do the work. We are to work "as for the Lord," whether anyone is watching or not. Our all-knowing God is always watching. We are not put on earth to dilly dally or waste time but to use each moment in a way benefitting mankind and the furtherance of God's kingdom.

Diligence and being expert in a field is the path to honor. We especially should be thinking about setting a good example for our children as a worker that they can be proud of—at age three or eighty-three.

# July 9
## Proverbs on Authority—Justice

"Take away wickedness from the face of the king and his throne shall be established with justice" (25:5).

A wise king should be alert to creeping immorality in his kingdom; a wise government should keep tabs on criminality, both to deter would be criminals and to maintain a firm foundation for its people. A government cannot proclaim justice yet allow underhanded double dealing, bid rigging, bribery, or corruption to flourish. The credibility of an administration rests entirely upon dealing promptly and sternly with known misconduct.

Any Congress who wishes to be reelected must tend to housecleaning; any executive department which values its role must remain watchful of activities within its purview. The ego of rulers incents them to desire a favorable legacy; this desire helps powerful persons to stay clean. If bad actors are in charge and corruption runs rampant, the administration is unlikely to last.

This type of Proverb is not an admonition: do this, do that. It is a simple observation type of proverb. If this happens, that is likely to result based on Solomon's acquaintance with rulers and kingdoms. Solomon was wise enough to be interested in political regimes and to notice patterns: cause and effects in the ancient world around him. This proverb is not a promise; it is a simple correlation noticed based on experience.

The prophet Jeremiah admonished the Babylonian exiles to bloom where they were planted; likewise, we should work to improve local and state governments where we live to make the world a better place. We can help do that by being a whistleblower when needed, reporting misconduct, and insisting on justice from our governmental authorities at all levels. The kingdom of God is built on justice, so we should be a key part of its furtherance.

# July 10

## Proverbs on Authority—Multitude

"In the multitude of people is the dignity of the king and in the small number of people the dishonor of the prince" (14:28).

Again, this Proverb is an observation of the way things work; not advice. The rulers of the largest countries in the world are a priori considered most important. Generally, the senator from the most populous state, having the most constituents, holds the most power. The pastors of mega churches are sought by the media for comments more often than the neighborhood local pastor. The college professor whose lectures are audited by the most students holds sway at staff meetings. Numbers indicate respect and power. Unless the audiences are mandated (like Chairman Mao rallies in Red China), this principle holds true. Voluntary attendance at any event indicates that the attendee desires to receive tutelage from the speaker; the lecturer who has a handful of attendees is disrespected.

If you throw a party and no one shows up, that certainly detracts from one's dignity. However, if the line to attend your book signing extends around the block, honor is bestowed on the author by simple virtue of quantities of intended readers. Appearing on book best-seller lists are automatic claims to fame for the author. Word of mouth referrals resulting in large numbers of consumers, concert goers, or congregations automatically bestow dignity upon the public figure.

Jesus had thousands appearing on hillsides and following him around in the Galilee. He must certainly have possessed a clear charisma or special loving nature that drew people to him. Of course, some came to see a miracle performed, but once there, they obviously stayed to hear the substance of his teaching. We can judge our own effectiveness by how many appear to hear us speak, buy our book, or refer clients to us. This principle is as true now as three thousand years ago.

# July 11

## Proverbs on Authority—Criticism of Employees

"Don't accuse a servant to his master." Prov. 30:10

This verse is narrow in application but is fascinating. It seems to me that the reason this prohibition is included has to do with boundary issues. We are not the superior of the employee. if we have an issue with a person's performance, it is more professional and smacks less of "tattle taling" to take up the issue face to face, directly with the person. We may be misreading the situation entirely, so talking it out first would be more efficient. Once a criticism is unleashed to a person's superior, we may poison his/her reputation and we will look foolish if our evaluation is incorrect. Perhaps there is another factor we are not aware of that caused the person to act as they did. We are inserting our nose into a relationship of which we are not a part.

The employer or superior may resent our sticking our nose in a situation not our prime business. If we give the person a chance to explain or self examine and correct their conduct, a job may be saved. Especially if we couch our remarks in the form of constructive criticism, letting them know we have their best interest at heart, we may gain a friend instead of alienating two persons: the employee and the supervisor. We are not in the chain of authority in this instance: we are an onlooker who, admittedly, may be affected by the poor performance of the employee, but it is not our responsibility to blow the whistle on poor performance except in the case of those reporting to us.

As parents we know how painful it is for others to criticize our children, or even point out their defects. By picturing this feeling, we can more easily understand the purpose and meaning of this verse.

# July 12

## Proverbs on Authority—Parents

"A man who mocks his father and despises his mother shall have his eye plucked out by ravens and eaten by vultures" (30:17).

We first learn respect for authority at home. It is parents' primary task to inculcate respect for authority in toddlers who grow up to be citizens of the world. Parents are warned not to provoke their children to anger but to nurture them in the respect of God and men. This verse warns of a terrible end for those who do not learn basic respect when growing up. If a child goes off to school without having learned respect for adults, those above him in the natural order of things, he or she will surely face difficulties in getting along in the classroom or with the gym teacher, the coach, the band director, and the cafeteria monitor. All along our life's journey, we must interact with those in authority over us. Disrespect, insubordination, and rebellion are serious character flaws.

In the working world, few jobs are solo. Most employees are part of work teams, headed by team leads. While we can respectfully disagree with a proposed path forward and make our opinion known, if our viewpoint is overruled or disregarded, it is our job to perform our work diligently or resign. Backstabbing, stirring up resentment among coworkers by backdoor undermining of the boss will quickly lead to our being escorted out the door. Unity is essential in the workplace to further productivity and morale.

The same issues are found even in the local church. We may serve on committees and disagree with the view taken by the majority, but once we have reasonably and logically explained our position, if that position is not adopted, we must toe the line or resign. Challenging law enforcement officers can lead to arrest, jail time, or even death! Respect must be learned early at home or else!

# July 13

## Proverbs on Authority—Wicked Ruler

"A wicked ruler will have wicked aids on his staff" (29:12).

Leaders always set examples, and likes attract. If there is corruption at the top—of any organization, or government, large or small—people of character will not wish to be associated with such conduct and will naturally migrate off to other positions. Those inclined to wickedness, however, will not be bothered by such corruption and may be attracted to the ultimate power displayed by a wicked ruler. Greed, gain, and desire for personal promotion or privileges are frequent reasons a person will stick by a wicked leader. Longstanding loyalty, past dealings, and the "I'll scratch your back," you scratch mine mentality are common reasons a person not bothered by corruption will remain in the entourage of a wicked leader.

Thus, when we join any organization, company, church, or governing body, we should watch carefully for signs of integrity. If we spot wrongdoing, we should first confront the wrongdoer privately and try to change it; if that is not effective, we should report it through proper channels. If those steps do not bring about change and we foresee continued problems, we should promptly remove ourselves from the environment so our morals and reputation will not be tainted. The longer we stay, the more sleepless nights are bound to come worrying about moral dilemmas and saving our own skin. A good name lost is nearly impossible to recover. A poor job reference or lack of a reference will follow us and make it an uphill battle to secure a new position.

We must enter any new organization with our ears and eyes open; our future life, health, and career depend on it. Misdeeds tend to multiply, and the slide from minor to major can happen faster than we can imagine. Beware!

# July 14

## Proverbs on Authority—Great Leaders

"With good men in authority, the people rejoice; but with the wicked in power, they groan" (29:2).

The morale of a corporation, a family, a church, or a government—large or small—is dependent on the character of its leaders. Optimism springs up when an organization believes its leaders are trustworthy and have their best interest at heart. Hope for the future is evident. Plans are laid with expectation that they will come to fruition. Visionaries lay dreams for the next phase of the plan. Stakeholders get excited about new chapters coming to pass. Even when current problems face us, there is confidence that solutions will be found when good leaders are in charge. The calendar seems to spiral upward; the sky is the limit.

On the other hand, when the wicked are in power, we are hesitant to even look to the future. There is little confidence that things will improve; dread for the future weighs on our hearts. It is all we can do to think ahead or make definite plans because we fear the worst: the house will come tumbling down. Folks hunker down, envisioning ways to protect their own and maintain the status quo. Why waste time making plans for the future when we have no confidence that things will improve? Private property is in jeopardy. No one wants to take a risk and promulgate a plan, fearing their head will be lopped off by those in authority. Businesses decline to invest in a country where an unstable dictator rules; investors decline to buy more stock when instability seems to be the word of the day. Children stay in their rooms making as little noise as possible when an alcoholic raging parent is expected.

We all recognize the truth in this observation from our own life experiences.

# July 15

## Proverbs on Authority—Close to the Vest

"It is God's privilege to conceal things, and the king's privilege to discover and invent. You cannot understand the height of heaven, the size of the earth, or all that goes on the king's mind!" (25:2–3).

This Proverb is an observation, not advice or counsel. This is one characteristic that distinguishes the leader from the follower. The leader has access to wide ranging information, and it is within his/her control as to whether to or when to disseminate the information. Corporate department heads are privy to employee personnel evaluations, pay scales, future hiring/downsizing plans, and future budget numbers. Teachers know the test scores, IQ ratings, and confidential psychologist reports of their students. Pastors who counsel know the marital woes, undisclosed medical diagnoses, and financial giving profiles of their congregants. All these leaders have an overall picture that our peers do not. This opens up new dimensions for future planning; they surely are in a better position to chart directions for their organization.

We humans on earth do not even know what God knows that we don't. There may exist whole other dimensions to the universe that we cannot fathom. When we shake our fist at God in frustration, exasperated because he appears not to answer our prayers, demands, and pleadings, we must never forget that our frame of reference is earth dimensional while his is universal. When we fly, it is amazing to look down on our puny towns from above and catch a glimpse of the bird's-eye or God's-eye view of earth. Drone photography has made this view more prevalent. But the most important knowledge that God has that humans do not is the inner dimension: the thoughts and motives of individuals. We judge people externally; God has a 360° inner view of our hearts. Knowing this, we must defer to God with awe and respect.

# July 16

## Proverbs on Authority—Prudence

"My son, watch your step before the Lord and the king, and don't associate with radicals. For you will go down with them to sudden disaster, and who knows where it all will end?" (24:21).

Thoughtful persons realize that all our actions are being observed—surely by God but likely by others in high places. We live in a highly populated world. Technology allows constant surveillance by video cameras on every city corner, review of our texts, e-mails, Facebook posts, and phone conversations. Even without technology, however, when we're in a crowd and certain that no one's eyes would choose to be on anonymous us, there is sure to be someone looking our way. Much like small children who can't figure out how parents can have "eyes in the back of their heads," someone is taking note of our speech and actions.

I have a habit of drawing an eye in the margin of all the verses in the Bible reminding us that God watches all; it is amazing how frequently this theme reverberates through scripture. Some believe that the great cloud of witnesses who have gone on before have the ability to watch our life on earth. When we speak ill of someone, there is nearly always someone loyal to the person within hearing. We may not be aware that Sam of whom we speak happens to be the neighbor, brother-in-law, or boss of the person with whom we are conversing.

Our mere association with "radicals" can bring judgment on us by God and our peers. It is so easy to accede to a request for their aid rather than take a firm stand declining the request. "Go along to get along" is the course of least resistance, but the consequences, "sudden disaster," are ominous.

# JULY 17

## Proverbs on Authority—God-Ordained

"By me kings reign, and princes decree justice" (8:15).

Sometimes, we forget that it is God who permits our presidents and world leaders to be in place. Oftentimes, we simply cannot understand why an individual won an election or appointment when we are certain they are highly unqualified or even corrupt. God's thoughts are not our thoughts, however, and he sees ahead. Psalms mentions in more than one place that time is incidental to God: a thousand years is as to a day with God. I picture God's view much like we now use direct video recorders: God can "run time" forward to backward, glimpsing the future and reviewing past events. Therefore, our "point in time" assessments of a rotten ruler may be frustrating to us. Why were Hitler, Stalin, or Mao Zedong ever permitted to consolidate power on earth, portending the death and suffering of innumerable people? When we reach heaven, maybe we'll have an inkling of God's timing and purposes.

While we may work diligently for or against the election of a candidate, when the opposing candidate wins, we should not lose heart. God has ultimate control. We should do all we can to bring about the kingdom of God on earth—a kingdom full of justice, compassion, and abundance—our knowledge and understanding is strictly limited: God's is not. We should not forego to support a candidate, thinking, what's the use—it's all designed by God anyway. However, we should pray earnestly before we undertake support of anyone, seeking guidance in light of his much broader perspective. We should continue to work for legislation to bring about justice for all and make our views known. Once a leader is elected, we must acknowledge that God permitted them to take office for his ultimate purposes. "By me, kings reign."

# July 18

## Proverbs on Authority—Just Rule

"It is an abomination to kings to commit wickedness; for the throne is established by righteousness" (16:12).

While attaining a position of leadership may be ultimately ordained by God, the course and length of that administration is very much determined by the actions of that leader. Rulers by definition have the power to influence hundreds, thousands, or even millions of citizens for good or evil. I believe this verse recognizes the exponential nature of rulers' conduct. Good decisions redound to the benefit of many; awful decisions do the same. A single person's action influences many, but if that person is not in a high position of power, the effect generally is limited. Every single action by a ruler necessarily affects many constituents. The verse emphasizes this fact of life. It is designed to impress upon those in power the supreme importance of everything they do. They must weigh and consider their influential reach.

As Christian leaders, we must never lose sight of our God-given ability to positively influence others, especially young people. My heart breaks when thinking of the thousands of children who grew up and left the Catholic Church after suffering abuse at the hands of priests, the church's very shepherds of the flock. Any youth leader or teacher is being watched and listened to intently; an errant remark has the potential to turn away a soul forever. What awesome responsibility!

If you are pleased with a position you hold, the way to extend your term is to consistently act with righteousness. This is a sure formula for establishment of long-term success in leadership. There are many forms of wickedness—greed for personal gain, ignoring corruption under our authority or uncovered in surrounding areas of responsibility, laziness in performing one's duty, but one form of righteousness—acting in accordance with God's will in undertaking elected responsibility.

# July 19

## Proverbs on Authority—King Pleaser

"Righteous lips are the delight of kings; and they love him that speaks right" (16:13).

How do we bring delight to a leader in any position? Tell the truth with love. Leaders don't solely want "yes men." They do not wish to be surrounded by cowards who fear to reveal bad news in a timely fashion. They wish to remain fully informed of developments in their area of responsibility—good or bad. If we must bring bad news to the attention of our boss, however, we should not gloat over another's failure or missteps; we should factually and truthfully disclose the information.

When one enters the workforce or a volunteer position, this observation should be foremost in our minds. Keep the boss in the loop; we will catch more displeasure in failing to reveal information than in revealing unpleasant information. Bosses don't want to be blindsided ever! Why didn't you tell me this earlier? A good employee sees to it that his/her superior is kept abreast of pertinent news needed to rule their piece of the world.

Of course, working diligently is another way to please superiors, but the importance of righteous speech must never be overlooked. We are being paid to have attentive eyes and ears in addition to working hands. We may overhear important tidbits of information at the coffee machine which would be suppressed if the boss were around. "Intelligence" of what is going on in the workplace and the wider world is how a prudent CEO stays ahead of the competition. In a free-market economy, knowledge of future expectations in the market, trends, and upcoming changes is how the war is won. A military leader depends to a huge extent on the reports of those in the field. Let our lips be righteous so as to delight our "kings."

# July 20

## Proverbs on Authority—Favor

"In the light of the king's countenance is life; and his favor is as a cloud of the latter rain" (16:15).

"The king's wrath is as the roaring of a lion; but his favor is as dew upon the grass." (19:12)

These verses are very similar. All thinking people should be calculating how to gain the favor of those in higher places. This can be done cynically, in a calculating manner solely to reap benefits that come from bestowal of such favor. Or we can be calculating how to gain such favor for beneficent reasons. If our goal in life is to bloom where we are planted, we should be taking steps to positively influence all those around us. But influencing those in higher places is likely more effective since rulers have a further reach than our peers. The metaphors of a cloud of the latter rain or dew upon the grass may be analyzed in terms of their widespread nature. Dew touches every blade of grass in the field; clouds yield rain to all: the just and the unjust.

The king's approval is life giving and worth striving for so long as we don't have to compromise our ethics to obtain such approval. Just as a student's goal should be to listen carefully to determine what would "please the teacher," an employee's aim should be to pay close attention to the expectations of the boss and meet those expectations to gain favor. When entering a college class for the first time, the most important day may be the first when the syllabus is covered, laying out expectations for the full term. If we are writing an important paper in grad school or otherwise, reviewing carefully the requirements and guidelines must be a priority before we get swamped in the details of the paper's content. Study laid-out expectations and strive to meet those expectations to obtain life giving favor.

# JULY 21

## Proverbs on Authority—That Look

"A king that sits on the throne of judgment scatters away all evil with his eyes" (20:8).

When a police car is parked beside a highway, the knowledge that the law enforcement officer is watching traffic operates as a tremendous deterrent to speeders or those about to throw a road rage tantrum. The knowledge that a parent is within earshot deters even toddlers from screaming at their siblings or pets. A teacher writing on a blackboard is attentive to what goes on behind her, and her students know her mere presence squelches potential wrongdoers. Anyone in authority draws out better behavior simply by being there.

Again, this is not advice or counsel—it is the fact of life, an observation of how things work. When a child gets squirmy in church, the "look" from the nearby parent generally keeps the child in line. When we know our coach lives on our block, we are ever vigilant about our neighborhood behavior. When prison inmates know they are under surveillance, they refrain from bullying other inmates. The proximity of anyone in authority over us tends to keep us on the straight and narrow.

Therefore, if you want to be an effective manager, unannounced spot checks of the factory floor or assembly line operate as spurs to rule following. Organizations routinely conduct annual audits as a way of ensuring good behavior and correct accounting. When people know someone is watching, they stay in line. Are you a camp counselor? To be a good one, stroll the cabin perimeter at unexpected intervals to deter errant behavior. Bank burglars first study the regularity of guard visits and then plan their break-ins between rotations. Mix it up! Kidnappers observe the routes driven by their intended victims to devise an ideal time for abduction. If we are the leader, this knowledge of the deterrent effect of watching should be put to good use.

# July 22

## Proverbs on Authority—Sovereignty

"The king's heart is in the hand of Jehovah as the watercourses: He turns it however he will" (21:1).

CEOs, rulers, parents, teachers, law enforcement, mob bosses, and kings—they may think they have complete authority over running their lives, but they are wrong. This verse reminds us that God is the ultimate authority—he is sovereign. He has the power to implant thoughts in our minds that cause us to change directions. He has the sovereignty to bring facts to our attention and information we may not have considered or outside influences to bear. God has power to use any number of methods to bring a change of circumstances or a change of action. Yes, we have free will, but God knows our thoughts and motives so he can know what it will take to bring about a change on our part.

Just as in Exodus, God hardened Pharaoh's heart during the visitation of the plagues to bring about his desired miracles to be exhibited for his glory before the Hebrews were let go, he can soften or harden hearts to accomplish his will.

Watercourses are changed by dams, channels, canals, or pumps. Nearly anything firm can change the course of a stream. This metaphor is meant to demonstrate how easy it is for God to change a ruler's heart. A small rip rap dam is used by the Corps of Engineers to alter the Mighty Mississippi to prevent erosion even though the force of a current seems strong. Similarly, God is a master at fathoming what knowledge, event, or influence will cause a ruler to alter an opinion. God is the Creator; we are the creature. He formed us inside and out and understands more about us than we do ourselves. It is not difficult for God to accomplish his purposes on earth.

# JULY 23

## Proverbs on Authority—Diplomacy

"He that loves pureness of heart, for the grace of his lips the king will be his friend" (22:11).

This is another verse demonstrating that powerful executives or leaders covet righteous advisors who are tactful and diplomatic. They may be visionary; they may have big goals. But without effective persuasive advisors to help them carry out their plans, they may not accomplish those goals. The best leaders know how to survey the big picture, take note of the important developments coming down the pike, and formulate a plan. However, those leaders operate best to delegate tasks of implementation and detailed operations to well-suited subordinates. The most valued subordinates have "grace of lips." Perhaps that involves sweet-talking needed resources out of loyal college alumni, sweet-talking scarce resources out of valued suppliers with special incentives, or negotiating the most favorable union contract.

Math skills are essential in business, but speaking skills are paramount in any endeavor in life. Those in authority are constantly evaluating the articulation and knowledge of their subordinates, promoting those who excel in the right word at the right time. Yes, people do rise to prominence due to artistic or practical skills, but the most versatile skill needed in all walks of life is a well-polished tongue that reflects a pure heart. If you wish to improve your speaking skills, listen to recognized orators, read, and observe. Turn off junk reality TV, and listen to great preachers, great lecturers, and professors. God wants Christians to be persons of positive influence in their "garden patch" on earth, and we can take steps to improve those speaking skills likely to further that influence. We can pray for the help of the Holy Spirit to purify our lips, our thoughts, and our hearts, for out of the abundance of the heart, the mouth speaks.

# JULY 24
## Proverbs on Authority—Fickleness

"My son, fear God and the king; and keep company not with them that are given to change" (24:21).

One of the most comforting characteristics of God is his unchanging eternal nature. Despite the abundance of change in our own lives and the lives of those with whom we live, we can always count on God to display his characteristics of love, mercy, and compassion for his people. He is the same today and tomorrow.

Likewise, we may comfortably remain loyal to leaders who are consistent, not fearing utter arbitrariness. Children are deathly afraid of alcoholic parents. Why? Because they never know when the parent walks in the door, whether drunkenness will have turned their normally patient parent into a raging angry tyrant. Inconsistent friends who blow hot one day and cold the next are a trial to relate to. Teachers and professors who change course in the middle of the semester wreak havoc on diligent students. We like to be able to count on another's personality. We want to get to know them so we can predictably relate to them.

Knowing this, we should cultivate in ourselves consistency, faithfulness, loyalty, and steadfastness. Others will be more comfortable in counting on us if they see those patterns continue.

We are firmly warned away from those who are entirely fickle and given to change. We probably all can bring to mind a person in our past who was unpredictably scary—passionate about a cause one day and thoroughly disillusioned the next. We have likely all been burned by the irrationality of a friend's reaction to something we felt certain they'd appreciate. Rejection instead of acceptance is especially shocking when wholly unanticipated. Let's examine ourselves: do we exhibit signs of extreme changeability? Of course, consistency has been termed the hobgoblin of little minds, but change without good reason does not a good companion make.

# July 25

## Proverbs on Authority—Diligence

"See you a man diligent in his business? He shall stand before kings; he shall not stand before mean men" (22:29).

Do you wish to be recognized by your CEO? Your mayor? Your governor? Then get to work, put your nose to the grindstone, and work diligently. Those who achieve the highest sales figures, invent a revolutionary manufacturing process, or find a way to incent the best teamwork are likely to be recognized and stand before those in high places. Slackers have no such expectation. If we become especially skilled in a specialty area, a unique focus, we are more likely to be honored in such a way. However, even ordinary tasks, performed in an extraordinary way, naturally lead to honor.

Examples come to mind. The White House Christmas tree is hung with a uniquely crafted ornament from each state of the union. The president's State of the Union address calls out high achievers who single mindedly pursued a noble cause—"points of light." The Kennedy Center Performing Arts Center holiday gala invites singers and musicians at the top of their field.

Even students in school observe this at end of year recognition programs. Good attendance, high grades, exemplary citizenship, and those lettering in sports are called to the podium for kudos and scholarship awards. Colleges honor academicians but also those excelling in service fraternities, devoting large quantities of community service. Summer library reading programs bestow tokens and rewards on diligent regular readers. Rotary and Lions Club civic organizations honor those donating gifts in kind for community betterment. Keys to the city are bestowed upon those doing noble work for the benefit of the city residents. Merit counts. While visionaries break the ice and lead the way, loyal volunteers in hospitals, GED adult literacy programs, or children's after-school classes receive honor. Let this knowledge incent us to do our best in our endeavors.

# JULY 26

## Proverbs on Authority—Bribery

"The king by justice establishes the land; but he that exacts gifts overthrows it" (29:4).

Is bribery rampant in the seat of government? Does the prime minister or president turn a blind eye? Are other forms of payment made for access to government officials or government services? Some believe that political campaign donations by PACs or individuals has reached bribery proportions in America, so campaign reform seems to be perennially discussed. If only the rich get access, get a hearing on their issues, or get their request moved to the top of the pile, this reeks of bribery, which leads to overthrow, via election or revolution.

If a leader desires longevity in a position, justice and equal access to officials is required. Openness and transparency go a long way toward ensuring an administration has stamina. Cover-up of bribes or informal access payments leads to a 'stink" in high offices, detectable by the people. Government is to be by the people and for the people, not only for the millionaires and billionaires. Constituents in both high and low places should feel assured their issue will be considered by their elected official and handled justly. While kowtowing members of the public tend to inflate an official's ego, the official must be reminded from time to time that flattery is not a sign of acceptance: equal justice for all is the characteristic that tends towards longevity in office.

If a leader wishes to leave an honorable legacy, he or she must keep careful watch on the transactions of his/her underlings directly and indirectly. A gigantic scandal can emerge from a small misstep, magnified in the public eye, on the front page of the newspaper or the lead story on the nightly news. Whatever you call the payment or preference, it will eventually "out."

# July 27
## Proverbs on Authorities—Counsel

"Designs are brought to nothing when there is no counsel, but where there are many counselors, they are established" (15:22).

The best rulers choose their closest advisors carefully. After a presidential election, for example, the populace follows closely the vetting and selection of cabinet members and other key administration aides. Evaluation of the president begins even before inauguration day since a major indicator of success in office is the right choice of intimates. If a leader has too much pride and believes "no one can tell him anything," beware! Part and parcel of being an effective leader is recognizing the gaps in one's own knowledge and working diligently to ferret out wise persons with experience in those gap areas.

But turning from presidential staffing, ordinary parents, teachers, church lay leaders, and business executives operate best by recognizing this same principle as applied to their sphere of responsibility. None of us has a monopoly on experience or knowledge, and the wisdom of governance calls for leaders to surround themselves not with "yes men" but with straight shooters who will objectively and responsibly offer sound advice. Aides must be self-confident enough to risk offending their principal with adverse opinions for the good of the organization. Ego stroking is not the primary task of a counselor; rather, offering researched hard evidence and considered opinions is. "Yes men" are a dime a dozen, but sincere courageous persons who can take a stand and support their view logically are more difficult to uncover.

When we are called to counsel another, the greater the position of responsibility, the greater the burden to give sound, objective advice—not biased to benefit ourselves but unbiased to benefit the greater good of the governed. The strength of our church, our company, our family, or even our nation may depend on it.

# July 28

## Proverbs on Authorities—Teachable

"A wise man shall hear and shall be wiser; he that understands shall possess governments" (1:5).

The other side of the "coin" on the necessity for retaining good counselors is to be receptive to listen to counsel given, with an open mind and accepting spirit. For the very reason that counselors are experts in areas in which the "king" is not, the one being advised must listen intently to the words given but more so, to the motives and underlying background behind the proffered advice. Does the advisor have an ax to grind? An ox to gore? An oar in the fight? A wise "king" maintains upright antenna to detect bias as well as the soundness of advice brought. A wise "king" is a strong observer of character in his/her inner circle so that when a critical decision is pending, the ruler can rapidly discount advice given from a position of "interest."

In short, it is equally as important to attempt to understand the reasons for the advice given as it is to analyze the advice itself. Opinions should be quickly discarded if they come from a non-neutral advisor. Are politics taking precedence over the good of the institution? Is vengeance being sought for past wrongs inflicted? There is a clean slate every day in leading—paybacks and "get even" actions are petty and short term. The long view must be taken by leaders; a vision of the future should seek the best for all governed. Nobility of character demands nothing less.

Generally, a leader's ability to wade through a plethora of information and hone in on the core of an issue is one reason a person has been promoted to a position of leadership. This skill cannot be abandoned when a leader reaches the top. Observation and careful sifting of facts and motives with an open mind remains essential to any leader.

# July 29

## Proverbs on Authorities—Merit

"A wise servant shall rule over foolish sons and shall share in the inheritance" (17:2).

In Bible times and beyond, the rule of primogeniture was paramount. The eldest son inherited the majority of an estate; younger sons were lucky to get any inheritance and servants perhaps merely a lump sum bequest as opposed to a percentage of the estate at large. In modern times, however, a testator can pick and choose whom to leave an estate to. Inconsiderate lazy children may be cut out of a will in favor of faithful loyal servants or employees. The relationship to the owner of the estate is the decisive factor.

This Proverb carries a lesson both to children and retainers. Children cannot automatically assume that they can mistreat a parent or grandparent and expect to inherit or receive favors or promotions based on relation status alone. Their actions, feelings, and motives will be noticed, and estate disposition can turn on these factors. Similarly, faithful loyal employees should not be surprised to be included in an inheritance or to receive favors or promotions. This follows the biblical admonition to "work as for the Lord," whether or not anyone is observing you. Diligence and intelligent management of home or company is what God expects of us. We are stewards not only of his natural world but the sphere of responsibility we manage. We are charged to use our gifts, talents, and skills to better our little corner of the universe and leave it a better place than how we found it.

In short, in God's economy, merit is noticed and takes precedence over familial ties. This parallels the inclusion of Gentiles into God's family as well as his original chosen nation of Israel. When the Israelites rejected God in favor of pagan idols, they lost their inheritance for a time while God fearing Gentiles were honored.

# July 30

## Proverbs on Authorities—Cover-Ups

"He that perverts his ways shall be found out" (10:9).

Those in high places may begin to believe they are invulnerable to "take down." This thinking stems from the old saw about "power corrupting." When a leader takes for granted that underlings kowtow to him/her, the leader starts to imagine that their entrenched power is not subject to disruption. A golden halo floats around their head giving invisible protection from whistleblowers.

However, a clear thinking leader realizes that the higher one ascends in any organization, the more people and processes intersect their sphere. There are more opportunities for the myriad of underlings to observe, detect, and reveal corrupt practices. A hermit living in isolation may have privacy and be secure, but a leader has hundreds, perhaps thousands, of supporting staff who are aware of or can find out the whys and wherefores of daily decisions. With today's social media and universal cell phone cameras, corrupt law enforcement officers are vulnerable to recording and instant posting of mistreatment. Presidential candidates and government officials have gotten into hot water due to a left-on mike following a public event.

Whether in King Solomon's court three thousand years ago or current times, dishonest leaders "shall be found out" according to this Proverb. That is the way of the world and this Proverb reflects "the way things work." Thus, savvy persons are well advised to take care not to pervert their responsibilities, knowing this principle. Likely, this Proverb is meant as a deterrent for those considering a less than honest transaction. A wise person knows and recognizes that this principle applies to all who cut corners or shave the truth. It is not just the other guy, but us it applies to. Read it and weep or, better yet, read it and avoid weeping by acting with integrity.

# July 31
## Proverbs on Authorities—Disunity

"Cast out the scoffer and contention shall go out with him and quarrels and contention shall cease" (22:10).

This hard-hitting Proverb gives cogent advice for those in positions of authority. If your organization has a squeaky wheel in it who disrupts its smooth-running efficiency, boot him! Although this advice may be difficult to implement, it is for the best in the long run to face some short-term discomfort to reap long term unity and organizational stability. Nothing undermines a person in authority more than a single employee or subordinate who is backstabbing, sowing disunity due to gossip, second-guessing, or challenging authority in an unmerited manner.

A "scoffer" is someone who scoffs at authority or rules. Synonyms are rebel, disgruntled challenger, or troublemaker. Let's call a spade a spade. Troublemakers may be one single person in a large group, but they disproportionately consume a manager's time, productive meeting time with complaints, or the law department's efforts in addressing complaints or claims.

Managers should always keep their nose to the ground and their ears attuned to a pattern and practice of troublemaking. While a single negative remark does not qualify someone at the level of a "scoffer," an observable repetition of complaints in many situations is cause for further consideration. Many resentments can be nipped in the bud by removing a scoffer in a timely manner. While those in the group should logically resent the scoffer, they often come to place the blame on the group manager for failing to step up to the hard task of dismissing the scoffer. Sometimes, others can see the group dynamics better than the manager, so listen carefully to suggestions by a trusted employee to save the group morale by removing a scoffer. While a scoffer may put on a good face in front of the manager, peers of the scoffer can likely catch a clear view of the negative impact of retention.

# August 1

## Proverbs Parallels—Speech

"The more words you speak, the less they mean" (Eccl. 6:11).

"In the multitude of words sin is not lacking, but he who restrains his lips is wise." (Prov. 10:19)

A fascinating paradox is that the fewer words spoken, the more they are attended to by our listeners. There is a "time to keep silence and a time to speak" (Eccl. 3:7). Don't tell all you know: "A fool utters all his mind, but a wise man keeps it in till afterwards" (Prov. 29:11); "A man of understanding holds his peace" (Prov. 11:12); and "Restrains his/her mouth as with a muzzle while the wicked are before him" (Ps. 39:1).

As parents, a single word or short disciplinary phrase is an attention getter—no! But a long windy explanation begins to draw glassy-eyed looks from children. As friends, the long involved explanation can be tolerated only by the most patient of friends. A short factual explanation, followed by a polite inquiry into the other's life is more welcomed by our companions. As patients, boiling down our current symptoms into a brief description to the doctor gains more respect and attention than recounting years of history and ups and downs. Around a meeting table, the team member who limits his/her contribution to important issues affecting all the team is welcomed. Long running details about issues not faced by others and not bearing on their scopes of work are barely tolerated. In reading this, you probably have had a person pop into mind who everyone dreads being around, not because they are unpleasant but because their habitual never ending dialog tries the patience of all acquaintances. As teachers, we must first hold the attention of our students: brevity is key in the schoolhouse, our family, and our workplace.

# AUGUST 2

## Proverbs Parallels—Powerful Tongue

"The power of life and death are in the tongue" (Prov. 18:21).

"The tongue is a little member, but it can kindle a forest fire!" (Jas. 3:5)

Just think how much of our lives is "lived" through our tongues or, in this day and age, our fingers (e-mails, texts). Nearly all our relationships in life are sustained by our tongues—what proceeds out of our mouths. We can devastate someone or brighten their day all with our tiny tongue. Once a word is spoken, it is in the hearer's memory forever. How many of us can still hear in our heads a precious loving word of a dear grandmother that made our spirits soar? In the same way, how many of us can hear in our heads the exact words and tone of a harsh unfair scolding we received from a parent, teacher, or person in authority? There is no rewind button on the tongue. Word processors can erase and make disappear written words, but brains cannot erase spoken words.

It's inspiring watching excellent parents, teachers, or mentors bring to life burned out kids with the power of life-giving affirmations. "A word fitly spoken is like apples of gold in settings of silver" (Prov. 25:10). "The mouth of the righteous is a well of life" (Prov. 10:11). That is, it refreshes, sustains, and feeds the listener. Our lips, not just those of our pastor, shall be used to bless and teach others: "The lips of the righteous feed many" (Prov. 10:11). "Wisdom is found on the lips of him who has understanding" (Prov. 10:13).

Let us strive to use our powerful tongues as blessings to others whenever possible. "Pleasant words are as a honeycomb, sweet to the soul and health to the bones" (Prov. 16:24).

# August 3

## Proverbs Parallels—Life-Preserving Speech

"He that keeps his mouth keeps his life" (Prov. 13:2).

"In order to have long life, keep your tongue from evil and your lips from speaking deceit" (Ps. 34:13).

Do you know people who have self-destructed due to an unruly tongue? Bar fights, divorces, road-rage incidents, school expulsions, and law enforcement stops can escalate in the blink of an eye due to lack of self-control, especially control of the tongue. Acts of vengeance, jealous rage, and arrests all stem from tongues out of control. Correct speaking operates as a fence of protection around the speaker. Out of control talk is a major risk factor in crime, marriage battles, and workplace regrets. Children run away from home due to continual criticism by parents. Our self-esteem is fragile and easily injured by loose lips.

How many nights have you lain awake in bed reliving injurious words in a relationship that day? Words are not merely spoken and disappear into thin air—they are stored in the listener's brain's long-term storage. The harsher the comment, the deeper emotions result, which virtually ensures the words will be retained. The more powerful the emotions arising from a conversation, or a shouting match, the more certain it is that the words will be recalled.

Our own responsibility is to monitor our thoughts, and before they become words on our lips, consider the long-term consequences. Not every thought that pops into our heads should be let out the "door" of our mouths. Censure, censure, censure. Deep breaths and counting under our breath can be helpful tools in this effort. Better yet and more effective long term is to immerse ourselves in Holy Scripture, pondering deeply on God's precepts that will improve our Godly relationship, causing the Holy Spirit to transform our minds so that damaging thoughts are fewer.

# August 4

## Proverbs Parallels—Poison Tongues

"Do you see a man hasty in his words? There is more hope for a fool than for him" (Prov. 29:20).

"The tongue is an unruly evil, full of deadly poison" (Jas. 3:8).

*Unruly* means difficult to keep under control. Isn't that the truth? Our speech can poison our most cherished relationships, and all the offered apologies in the world may not set right the relationship poisoned with venomous words. Criticism has been called the murderer of marriages; likewise, it can be the killer of any number of relationships. Closely associated with uncontrolled or unwarranted criticism is lack of recognition of boundaries. How often have we deigned to criticize something not even within our responsibility? Our zone of influence? Why sour a relationship over something not even legitimately within our purview?

So step 1 in controlling the poison in our tongues is to objectively evaluate whether we should say anything about a situation. Oftentimes, our busybody minds start to formulate a negative remark when it is purely gratuitous, not something we should even be commenting on.

Step 2, if the situation is one in which we have an "oar," we should stop and formulate a remark that is delivered in tone and substance as a constructive criticism, a loving remark such that the hearer is convinced that we have their best interest at heart.

Gossipers are detested by everyone for their poisonous tongues. The definition of gossip is a fact or observation, true or not, that is not necessary to pass on. Is it loving? Is it kind? Is it necessary to repeat? What good will come of our repetition of the fact? Engagements have been destroyed due to one out of line remark. Job offers have been revoked; employments have ended due to a poison tongue. Hasty poison tongues must be banned from our mouths.

# AUGUST 5

## Proverbs Parallels—Lips of Knowledge

"The lips of knowledge are a precious jewel" (Prov. 20:15).

"A good man out of the good treasure of his heart brings forth that which is good" (Luke 6:45).

Let's think on the characteristics of a jewel: precious, rare, valuable, easily carried, colorful, long-lasting, and beautiful. Each of these characteristics, by analogy, can likewise apply to profound helpful words we speak. Similarly, "treasures" of our heart are made manifest through our speech and actions. Treasures of our heart most likely equate to the fruit of the Spirit listed in Galatians: the virtues of patience, self-control, kindness, goodness, wisdom, etc. Our lips will naturally reflect these qualities if they are growing in our spirits. There is a direct "line" between the qualities of our heart and the words that are spoken by our lips. Of course, it is up to us to improve the quality of our hearts by close attention to the spiritual disciplines of worship, prayer, Bible study, holy conversation, praise, and meditation.

Being conscientious about self-transformation goes hand in hand with the Spirit's renewal of our hearts and minds. We want our hearts to become full of good treasure of Christlikeness so that our mouths will reflect this treasure. We are in a special position to influence the next generation with the truths of the gospel and secrets of wise living. This should be one of our life's goals: to increase the value of the treasure in our heart by adding to our store of godly virtues and by filling our minds with scriptural precepts. We can be a better resource for others, a better witness, and a better representative of Christ on earth. Although each of us is a precious child of God, loved uniquely by him, we can be of more value to others by improving our store of godly knowledge.

# AUGUST 6

## Proverbs Parallels—Soft Words

"A soft answer turns away wrath" (Prov. 15:1).

"The words of wise men are heard in quiet more than the cry of him that rules among fools." (Eccl. 9:17)

Softly spoken words are natural attention grabbers. Experienced teachers know not to attempt to outshout their students but to drop their voices so that they will quiet down to make out what was spoken. Relationship counselors routinely urge consistent use of this principle in defusing angry blowups—the harsher, louder, and more out of control the comment, the softer, and more deliberate should be the response. At least, a near whisper will catch the loudmouth off guard, causing him/her to self-examine.

We know from experience that the reverse is true as well. "The cry of him that rules among fools" brings to mind the carnival barker or midway tout who we soon tune out. Constant barrages cause our minds to zone out and disregard the message. The louder, more repetitious, and more raucous the "patter," the sooner we disengage. We can scarcely wait to get away from the loudspeaker, walking quickly in the opposite direction.

We have examined many verses about the substance of our words, but these verses address the volume and tone. Just like body posture can reveal more than our actual words so can volume and tone. Human nature and human reactions to loud, aggressive speech remain the same after three thosand years. While psychologists today have invented new terms for the offenses of loud insensitive remarks, our reactions are consistent over the years.

Let us think about any meetings, dialogues, and relationships we can improve with the application of this timeless wisdom. Simmering an agitated child down with soft whispers might just catch them off guard, leading to a new "level set" in their mood.

# AUGUST 7

## Proverbs Parallels—Idle Words

"A fool utters all his mind, but a wise man keeps it in till afterwards" (Prov. 29:11).

"Every idle word that men speak, they shall give account in the day of judgment." (Matt. 12:34)

Do you know someone whose mouth just runs on and on to fill the white noise space? Are you one of those persons? Just because a thought springs to mind again doesn't mean it must get past our lips. If our mouths run faster than our brains, we must readjust our brain speed to evaluate a comment before we speak it. Idle words may not even be harmful words. Perhaps they are just unnecessary, killing trees (paper use), wasting bandwidth (e-mail, text), or using up political capital with our long-suffering friends. Do you have Facebook friends that post not once a day but twenty times a day? These people may have low self-esteem issues and simply feel a need to put themselves in the public light over and over.

Why do people utter idle words? Boredom? Need for attention? Need to impress? If these are our motives, they will likely backfire. If we appear to be needy, people naturally withdraw from that personality type. Instead of impressing, we likely will reveal our desperation for respect, unintentionally lowering our level of respect received from our hearers.

If we are bored and simply filling up time, we have wasted an opportunity to say something edifying, helpful, uplifting, or encouraging. We are put here on earth not just to make noise but to be of benefit to each other, especially those of the house of God.

In picturing judgment day, how mortified will we be to hear each idle word replayed before God and the angels, perhaps even in the company of the saints? Picturing this scene can be a real deterrent to idle words.

# August 8

## Proverbs Parallels—Muzzling

"A man of understanding holds his peace" (Prov. 11:12).

"Rebels speak evil of things they know not." (Jude 8:10)

Ecclesiastes speaks famously of a time to speak and a time to refrain from speaking. Wisdom is knowing when each of those times is. *Rebel* is a word used often in Proverbs and elsewhere as a contrast to the righteous man, the wise man, and the good man. A rebel equates with a fool or a man of no understanding. A person is a rebel because he/she rebels against godly precepts, believing they have no need of instruction from the Bible or godly pastors or counselors. Worse than an idle word is a negative word about situations they are unfamiliar with. It is the height of foolishness to denigrate a person or thing without knowing the facts; not only does the speaker alienate those who know the truth, but also they risk further bad reputation for speaking out of turn and drawing a false conclusion.

We should refrain from comment about an incident or person until we fully investigate. We harm ourselves by hastily jumping to conclusions. Others will be less inclined to give us credibility in the future when we have misspoken in this instance.

Some persons feel compelled to editorialize about every news story, every local development, or every tidbit of gossip. Their peers and friends will tend to withdraw if their editorials are untrustworthy or have jumped the gun. Have you noticed that oftentimes the person who knows the most in a room says the least? The old saw about having two ears and only one mouth reflecting the relative use of the two organs has truth. Another old saw reminds us that we are never learning anything new when we are talking—only when we are listening. Let's hold our peace.

# AUGUST 9

## Proverbs Parallels—Humility before Honor

"For the Lord says, 'Because he loves me, I will rescue him; I will make him great because he trusts in my name'" (Ps. 91:14).

"Humility goes before glory." (Prov. 15:33)

This principle is clear cut in scripture: we must be of a humble mind, dependent upon God before he will honor us. If we "try too hard" to put ourselves in the spotlight, toot our own horn, or publicize our good deeds, this quickly turns into pride, and God hates the prideful. This is parallel with the beatitudes in Matthew 5: Blessed are the meek, for they shall inherit the earth.

*Meek* does not mean timid, cowardly, or shy but one who acknowledges that God is God and that we are not. The meek recognize that in and of themselves, they are powerless, sin-ridden, and destined to fail, but if they give credit where credit is due: to their Creator, sustainer, enabler, and source, they will be honored by God and men. God promises to raise up those who consciously humble themselves. Of course, God knows our motives, and if we are merely acting humble in order to be honored, our impure motive will be seen by God, and this likely cancels the cause/effect between humility and honor.

In thinking of our public figures who exhibited great humility, George Washington and Abraham Lincoln are considered by most historians and Americans as our greatest presidents; what endeared them greatly to the people was their basic ingrained humility. George Washington firmly declined all offers of kingship, trappings of royalty and high-flown titles, inaugurating the simple title Mr. President. Abraham Lincoln had great self-deprecating humor and identified with the common man, having risen from a humble log cabin, log splitter background. People are instinctively turned off by those "on a high horse;" so is God.

# AUGUST 10

## Proverbs Parallels—Long Life

"For those who reverence your name, You will give me added years of life, as rich and full as those of many generations all packed into one" (Ps. 61:5–6).

"The fear of the Lord is a fountain of life to decline from the ruin of death" (Prov. 14:27).

This is one of the most exciting and beneficial cause-effect relationships: between righteousness and long abundant life. Science and medicine are confirming in more ways each day that when we are in the groove, living in the order and pattern designed by God for our bodies and souls, our bodies and souls thrive and are less likely to be physically or psychologically ill. God designed the Ten Commandments and the myriad of other godly principles for our benefit, knowing us inside out. Our Creator wrote the manufacturer's handbook so that our lives would go more smoothly, more blessedly, and more abundantly. Christ said that he came so that we might have life, life more abundantly.

I know many godly saints in our church and community in their nineties who are happy, optimistic, and living for Jesus. Yes, they have aches and pains of aging, but their faces beam with love and joy. If we sow time and effort in developing our righteousness, we reap long life. The correlation is mentioned in more than just these two verses. When we think carefully about this correlation and the fact that long life is bestowed as a reward, as a blessing, this is further evidence that life itself is a gift. This should make us treasure each and every day with gratitude to our Creator. If length of life itself were random or burdensome, it would not make logical sense that scripture would deem it a blessing. Persons committing suicide spit in the face of God, rejecting his holy gift. Sad indeed.

# August 11

## Proverbs Parallels—Peace

"May all good men flourish in his reign, with abundance of peace to the end of time" (Ps. 72:7).

"All of the paths of wisdom are peaceable" (Prov. 3:17).

In the 1970s, the split finger peace sign and the symbol of peace were everywhere. Again in our current time—with arbitrary violence rampant and class, religious, and race warfare seemingly on the rise—we yearn for peace. Do we gain peace by loving our brother? Yes, but more basic than that is the characteristic that we become good and wise. Wisdom leads to righteousness and goodness and justice for all men, which multiplies peace in our world. Analyzing further, what comes before wisdom? Study of God's Word, listening to God, asking God for wisdom per the book of James that sets out a request to God as the starting place for gaining wisdom. A focus on Proverbs and James, the Old and New Testament books of wisdom is a good starting place. As we are observing in this month's readings, the wisdom of Proverbs is echoed in many parts of scripture but especially in Ecclesiastes, Psalms, and James. The overlap between Proverbs and Ecclesiastes is easily understood since King Solomon was reputed to have authored both books.

When our spirits align with the will of God, our bodies are naturally free from guilt, worry, doubt, and fear that we are contravening God's desires. This naturally leads to peace. We can rest easier at night and sail through our days with the knowledge that God supports us and is "for us" in our daily endeavors. Having assurance that our sins are covered, our lives are lived with God's blessing and that we are more apt to have peace with our fellow man increases our joy and optimism. Peace be with you!

# AUGUST 12

## Proverbs Parallels—Guidance

"Feed the hungry! Help those in trouble! Then your light will shine out from the darkness and the darkness around you shall be as bright as day. And the Lord will guide you continually and satisfy you with all good things and keep you healthy too" (Is. 58:10–11).

"In all your ways think on God and he will direct your steps." (Prov. 3:6)

Both of these promises for guidance have conditions: doing the will of God. The Isaiah passage is more explicit about the good works we are expected to do: more detailed in the type of good deeds; feeding the hungry, helping those in trouble, while the Proverbs verse is more general; thinking on God and patterning our lives after his will. Summed up, the single word description of the condition is righteousness. If growing in righteousness is our chief concern, God's guidance is promised.

Conversely, how could we expect to rely on God's guidance if we care nothing about his laws or will for our lives? If we are ignoring God in the everyday aspects of our daily walk, how can we realistically expect to receive guidance for deciding between the big forks in the road? We are urged to seek first the kingdom of God and all these things shall be added unto you. Seeking first the kingdom of God means asking the question: what would Jesus do? How can we best bring closer the kingdom of God, the invisible state of being where his saints act in a way to bring about God's kingdom on earth? All Christ's parables in the gospels concerning the kingdom of God highlight its pervasiveness and invisibility: yeast spreading throughout dough, hidden treasure, pearls, tiny mustard seed's growth.

Growing in wisdom is a sure way to receive God's guidance.

# August 13

## Proverbs Parallels—Edification

"Let no corrupt communication proceed out of your mouth, but that which is good to the use of building up, that it may minister grace unto the hearer" (Eph. 4:29).

"Pleasant words are as a honeycomb, sweet to the soul and health to the bones." (Prov. 16:24)

We have the potential to minister such powerful good into other people's lives with our comments: encouragement, blessing, praise, and recognition. Especially this is true with regard to those "little souls" around us—children whose egos are so fragile. But all of us hunger for a good word: the nearly worn out pastor, the exhausted nurse, the breakfast diner waitress or the clerk at Walmart. Those in the lowliest positions likely receive the least amount of recognition. It costs us nothing to point out a helpful attribute and will surely make the person's day. The common sense principle of Management 101 is that those conducts which are praised are likely to be repeated. If we send an e-mail of appreciation to our pastor, it is twice as likely that next week's sermon will be even better. If our doctor's less than ideal bedside manner is laudable one day, if we show appreciation ("I sure appreciate your patience and kindness today in taking the time to discuss my symptoms"), he/she will be more likely to take note and consciously try to repeat that behavior.

Mark Twain famously said he could "live for a month" on one good compliment. As elementary children, we could bask all week in our teacher's Monday praise. Children desperately crave the praise of their parents; good parents gratify that desire and heap sincere praises on needy children. Their little egos grow healthy and secure when our sincere positive feedback feeds them. "Ministering grace unto the hearer" would be a wonderful daily resolution.

# August 14
## Proverbs Parallels—Truth

"Speak every man the truth to his neighbor" (Zech. 8:16).

"The lip of truth shall be steadfast forever" (12:19).

Truth is the bedrock indicator of right speech. Our credibility and the strength of our witness for Christ are dependent upon our consistently speaking truth. If we are found to have lied, defrauded someone, or misled them, it will be nearly impossible to regain trust lost with that person. If we hate to speak unpleasantness when asked about a subject, it is better to simply deflect and say we'd rather not discuss the subject than tell a white lie to sugarcoat a bad situation. Sincerity can be kind if we take pains to maintain kindness. Good will can be easily and entirely lost if our word is found to be unreliable.

Zechariah speaks of our "neighbor" since personal relations begin one on one. However, this principle extrapolates to groups, companies, communities, and even national governments. In countries where false propaganda was generated to consistently favor a government and cover up bad deeds (China, USSR, Nazi Germany), citizens are conditioned to place no confidence in a government. Our nation has gotten off track from time to time with severe consequences—Watergate, Vietnam casualty reporting.

Franklin Roosevelt was so highly revered because he was not afraid to, in his fireside radio chats, give it "straight" to the people, calling on all their help to overcome the Great Depression, World War II enemies, and bank and employment crises.

God rewards truth tellers by sustaining and upholding them: "be steadfast forever" is a valuable promise. We must never forget that we are ambassadors of Christ. Just as our diplomatic ambassadors represent our countries abroad and the reputation of the United States rises and falls based on their reports, so we can sabotage Christ's good name if our truthfulness is lost.

# AUGUST 15
## Proverbs Parallels—Humility

"If we are living now by the Holy Spirit's power, let us follow the Holy Spirit's leading in every part of our lives. Then we won't need to look for honors and popularity, which lead to jealousy and hard feelings" (Gal. 5:25–26).

"It is better to be humbled with the meek than to divide spoils with the proud" (Prov. 16:19).

We know that God despises the proud, but it is fascinating to analyze the fallout from pride: jealousy and hard feelings. Our culture is enraptured with competition: in sports, in academics, in popularity, and in beauty. Even preschoolers get compared and rewarded for achievement! Children are raised to expect and become accustomed to comparisons. But when Peter asked Christ in post Resurrection discussions, "And what about John?" Christ responded angrily, "What is it to you?" This single episode reveals that while God is entitled to judge and make comparisons, we should worry about ourselves and our improvement. Comparisons can be so discouraging, causing some to simply give up and check out, commit suicide, or become depressed. I am convinced that scripture means what it says about not "looking for honors and popularity" since they do lead to jealousy and hard feelings.

Each of us is different; each of us has unique talents and gifts. Elementary educators speak often about the downsides to uniform education: ducks are outstanding in swimming class but not so good in track and field. Rabbits excel in sprints, but swimming is not their forte. By comparing even our own children within families, we can easily discourage them. Trying to compare them with ourselves and push them to follow in our footsteps is devastating. The artist or musician may not be a college football all-star like his dad, but parents must be humble about their own achievements and focus on their child's strengths.

# AUGUST 16

## Proverbs Parallels—Prosperity

"Be kind and good to others; then you will live safely here in the land and prosper, feeding in safety" (Ps. 37:3).

"The fear of the Lord is unto life and he shall abide in abundance without being visited by evil" (Prov. 19:23).

These verses are good news! The righteous person who is kind and good and fears the Lord shall have safety and prosperity. Safety and prosperity are rewards for right living and honoring God. Those of us who are parents are doubly happy with this good news since we know that our beloved families will benefit as well from our right living. We have not only ourselves to worry about but the futures of our dear children and grandchildren. God's eye is on his beloved children. His angels surround and uphold them. Anxieties and insomnia lessen if we focus on God's promises of provision and abundance "in safety."

We don't have to remain glued to the nightly financial news, fear the receipt of bad news from our financial advisor, or worry that we'll outlive our assets. Those who are kind and good to others and who fear the Lord will be provided for. We do not have to fear burglaries or sneak attacks. Yes, we should be prudent, locking our doors and avoiding high crime areas at night, but fear should not paralyze our activities or thwart our doing of good deeds. If God's eye is on the sparrow, how much more will it remain on his beloved children. We know he's "on duty" 24/7 and does not nod off as we would. Darkness is as light to him; he has x-ray vision no matter the weather.

Our gratitude should overflow when we consider these promises of abundance and safety from our good God.

# AUGUST 17

## Proverbs Parallels—Rewards

"Day by day the Lord observes the good deeds done by godly men and gives them eternal rewards" (Ps. 37:18).

"To the just good shall be repaid" (Prov. 13:21).

The law of reaping and sowing is a bedrock principle of how the universe spins. Even New Agers acknowledge this principle in the form of karma. Life can be an upward spiral for the good: good begets good. Conversely, life can be a discouraging downward spiral for the wicked person: evil begets evil. In which spiral do we wish to exist? It is hard to imagine that any deep thinking individuals knowing of these principles would choose evil. Perhaps Satan's job is to distract folks from learning about these principles: one thing leads to another. The entertainments and enticements of the world call, taking our eye off the big picture of retribution. Reward/punishment is Life 101. Even children should be educated in the simplest form about this "fact of life."

I tend to use symbols in the margin of my Bible to denote frequent themes and patterns. I use an eye to note those passages having to do with the all-seeing eye of God watching our lives. This theme appears repeatedly in many scriptural passages. The eye of God should be heeded thoughtfully. The next action we take will be noticed by God: what a deterrent to evil! Just as parents reportedly, "Have eyes in the back of their heads" in the experience of children, our God in fact does have all-seeing eyes. If we consider the consequences of this fact and the further assurance that we will be rewarded/repaid for our actions, our conduct will be more measured and less impulsive. While forgiveness is always available to the repentant, right action in the first instance is our aim since it brings rewards on earth and in heaven.

# AUGUST 18
## Proverbs Parallels—Stability

"The godly shall be firmly planted in the land and live there forever" (Ps. 37:29).

"The house of the just shall stand firm" (Prov. 12:7).

Notice the reference to geography in both of these verses. Land and houses were considered blessings. Righteous families often live for generations on the same ranch, land, summer lake house, estate, or community. Think through why this is. Godly people pay their taxes, their debts, and their mortgages and avoid foreclosure. Their houses more frequently get paid off "free and clear," are passed to the next generation(s), and are protected among family assets. Their finances are stable, being blessed by God if they are tithers. Godly people generally are wiser in their relationships, tending to cause more stable employment, promotions, and advancement. Persons of integrity are valued by employers, even those employers who themselves are not godly. Godly characteristics, in general, promote stability in most areas of life: marriage, obedient children, extended family relationships, respect in their communities.

Those whose lives reflect God's characteristics: kindness, goodness, respect for others as children of God, respect for the country's laws, avoid arrest, forfeiture of assets, prison terms, and fines. Persons of integrity tend to have fewer accidents since moderation governs. Drunkenness, hair trigger tempers, addictions, treachery, and evil of such ilk leads to instability in life and wasting of a family's resources. The protection of God and his angels tends toward stability of people and assets.

These principles are clear cut and oft repeated in scripture, for those who study and notice their patterns. Our every decision puts us on the path to greater stability and righteousness or ignoring God's laws, making us a candidate for negative consequences of a secular and religious nature.

We must ask ourselves: even if not for myself but merely for the sake of my progeny, shouldn't I act in ways that promote stability?

# AUGUST 19

## Proverbs Parallels—Optimism

"For the good man, the blameless, the upright, the man of peace—he has a wonderful future ahead of him. For him, there is a happy ending" (Ps. 37:37).

"The tabernacles of the just shall flourish" (Prov. 14:11).

Are you a glass-half-full kind of person? Or half empty? I have recently read a joke that says the answer should be: "Who cares? We can always refill the glass!" If we are a Christian striving for righteousness, we have a wonderful future ahead of us, both on this earth and in heaven. We and our house (tabernacles) shall flourish. Even when bad things happen, we know that bad events are not the ending—the hope of heaven and earthly blessings are what we may expect.

If you catch yourself commiserating with grumblers, complainers and naysayers, catch yourself and remind yourself that your future has a happy ending. We must take care to set a good example, for our optimism, cheerfulness, and even joy are what draw other people to God. Who wants to go to church with sad sacks? Church should be a bright spot in all of our lives, filled with smiling, welcoming faces. This attitude is what attracts newcomers to the faith.

Even when we are discouraged, we can change our own attitude by focusing on these good news promises. Tape them to our dashboard, our bathroom mirror, our iPhone Notes app for rereading, when we are in line or have a downtime moment. With a good, loving, consistent, faithful God on our side, that is our bedrock reason for cheerfulness. A good night's rest and a good review of our good news promises goes a long way to setting right our attitudes. Do you have a notebook of your favorite scriptural promises? If not, start one.

# AUGUST 20

## Proverbs Parallels—Poor

"God blesses those who are kind to the poor" (Ps. 41:1).

"He that despises the poor reproaches his Maker" (Prov. 17:5).

These verses are written from opposite perspectives but arrive at the same conclusion. It is God's will that we help and are kind to the poor, dispensing justice when possible. God thoroughly disapproves those who despise the poor and rewards those who are kind to the poor. Are you involved in local church missions to the needy? Do you knit blankets? Donate canned goods to the food pantry? Purchase Thanksgiving baskets in November? Gather Christmas gifts in December? For those uncomfortable handing out cash to panhandlers on street corners, some keep McDonald's gift meal certificates under their seat for handing out at intersections, or even packaged cheese and crackers.

Children whose hearts remain tender often lead the way in showing concern for the down and out. We, adults, tend to harden our hearts, turning our faces away and ignoring hardship. Even if we cannot bring ourselves to interact with the poor one on one, we can donate our giveaways to our local needs organization or donate out of our abundance to formal programs for bettering the unemployed, undertrained, or unskilled. There are a myriad ways to show kindness to the poor; one likely lines up with our preferences. We can begin small, with a church local day mission project, hopefully progressing up to weeklong mission trip and fundraisers for those willing to do hands on work. All of us can pray for the poor. Even though Christ observes that the poor will always be with us, it is still our responsibility to better their condition in whatever ways we are able.

This dichotomy is stark: in an effort to avoid reproach by our Maker and receive instead his blessing, let us consider how we can improve justice to the poor.

# August 21

## Proverbs Parallels—Happiness

"Happy are those who are strong in the Lord, who want above all else to follow your steps" (Ps. 84:5).

"Blessed is the man who hears me and who watches daily at my gates" (Prov. 8:34).

Joy is contagious—how better to "catch" new believers than our smiling faces. As we know from the Beatitudes and modern translations, "blessed" equates to "happy." What a wonderful thing to look forward to—knowing that as our walk with God becomes closer and our character more reflective of his, we will become happier. Psychologists say than when we deliberately pursue happiness, it is more likely to elude us. However, when we serve others as God delights for us to do, happiness is the natural result.

Notice the priority embodied in the Psalms passage. Those who "want above all else to follow your steps" describes those who have their priorities aright. This is parallel to the admonition to seek first the kingdom of God, and then all other blessings and desires of our hearts will be added. "Strong in the Lord" surely describes those who have strong faith, as a result of a spiritually disciplined life of scripture reading, prayer, and seeking God's faith. New Christians can be great examples to others, but the best examples are those who over long years have honed their faith through consistent worship, good deeds, and righteous living.

If you are more often upset than happy, reexamine your daily practices. Are you filling your mind with secular TV, reality shows reflecting dog-eat-dog and trashy books? Or are you filling your spirit with worship music, daily devotions and good preaching, and Bible studies? Garbage in, garbage out. Nutritious food in, mental and spiritual development. We can take an active part in our state of happiness by "watching daily at his gate."

# August 22

## Proverbs Parallels—Resilience

"The godly shall flourish like palm trees, and grow tall as the cedars of Lebanon" (Ps. 92:11).

"The just shall spring up as a green leaf" (Prov. 11:28).

While both of these verses have the obvious similarity of speaking of vegetation, what does the metaphor of green growing things denote? The word "thriving" comes to mind, and even perhaps, flexibility and an ability to spring back when bad times come.

Palm trees are tall, as are the cedars of Lebanon. To grow tall, a tree must receive nourishment and be strong. Green leaves sound healthy as well. To be healthy and grow strong, God's people must receive a steady diet of food, being fed on the Word of God and godly meditations. Palm trees have the flexibility to withstand hurricane force winds and even to continue growing when blown down. Tall trees are firmly rooted; Christians must take care to be firmly rooted in God's teachings, letting wisdom grow deeply into their minds to be available when crises come.

"Spring up" seems to speak of exuberant growth in the first instance—receiving water of life and nourishment, and also springing back if stepped on or crushed. We can prepare ourselves to be able to spring back, by taking deep into our spirits the promises of God, a firm foundation for all occasions.

Tall trees stand out; people take notice of them and admire them. Righteous folk will be noticed similarly by their character and their equanimity in times of trouble.

Even the color of tall trees and green leaves is remarkable. In a deep forest, the forest floor is often brown with a carpet of leaves, downed logs, and fungi. A green leaf, perhaps a luxurious fern, stands out on the forest floor. Let us take hope in these images of growth, resiliency, and stability.

# August 23

## Proverbs Parallels—Perfect Peace

"He will keep in perfect peace all those who trust in him, whose thoughts turn often to the Lord" (Is. 26;3).

"He that fears the commandment dwells in peace" (Prov. 13:13).

Peace seems like our primary goal in these troubled times—both in our private minds, our homes, our communities, and of course, our world. Note, however, the three important conditions: We must trust in him, turn our thoughts often to the Lord, and fear the commandment. We must know and heed the law, meditate on the law and its meaning and maker. The most peaceful persons of our times seem to do just that, bearing out these conditions: Mother Teresa, Dallas Willard, and other theologians and spiritual leaders who remind us to pray ceaselessly.

How do we gain in achieving these conditions? We may use mnemonic devices, external cues at first, or any means to establish a habit in our lives: the striking of the quarter hour on the grandfather clock, alarms on our mobile devices, post-it notes on our mirrors. Any earthly means to improve our heavenly thoughts are laudable. Making our devotions and prayers habitual, just like we develop routines for taking our exercise, our medications, or our meals. My mother kept a small attractive ceramic pot on her breakfast table, filled with notecards of scriptures, reading and meditating on one while eating. We may sign up for verse of the day, spiritual nugget, or other devotional services appearing each morning in our email accounts. Why not harness the technology of today to improve our spiritual state of mind, much like folks utilize fit bits, or other exercise/health aids to boost their commitment to consistent exercise, or weight watchers utilize calorie counters to keep their diets on track?

Human inventions can and should be utilized to boost our spiritual mindsets, leading to peace.

# AUGUST 24

## Proverbs Parallels—Smooth Road

"But for good men, the path is not uphill and rough! God does not give them a rough and treacherous path, but smooths the road before them" (Is. 26:7).

"The path of the just departs from evils" (16:17).

These are lovely promises for the righteous. Similar to Christ's promises of abundant life in general, our life is often viewed as a path, a road, or even a highway. All humans suffer troubles from time to time, but the road of the righteous, as a whole, will be smoother with fewer potholes. Of course, the path of fools is littered with obstacles, many of which have been created or brought about by the fool's actions himself. We can certainly self-sabotage our results by negative comments, laziness, procrastination, and ingratitude. More so, can we destroy our relationships with others by insensitive remarks, constant criticism, self-absorption, and hatred. All of these "manmade" obstacles can be bypassed by the righteous walker of the path of life. Simply eliminating all self-generated barriers sweeps the way clean.

But I believe God causes blessings to come into the lives of righteous persons. Not only will the road be clear of thorn bushes and potholes, but it may be paved with smoothness by our God, swept clean of thistles, with water fountains and beautiful landscaping added! Picturing ourselves striding down the way of life, our gratitude in, and of itself, attracts further blessings into our lives. New Agers call this karma—good deeds bring good into our lives; kindness extended multiplies into kindnesses received. But people of faith believe it is God who actively notices our good deeds and thoughts and rewards us with special graces.

Psychologists speak in terms of visualizing good things which "brings" them into our lives. Others speak of concentrating one's focus on desired goals/objects, and the "universe" aligns to bring them our way.

Let us thank God daily for our smooth path and the removal of obstacles.

# AUGUST 25

## Proverbs Parallels—Direction

"If you leave God's paths and go astray, you will hear a Voice behind you say, 'No this is the way; walk here'" (Is. 30:21).

"In all your ways think on God and he will direct your steps" (Prov. 3:6).

In our heart of hearts, we know that our lives would spin out immeasurably better if we were in God's will, heeding his direction. We can increase our chances of being in God's perfect will if we "think on God in all our ways." Much of God's will is simply learning, internalizing, and following God's law as clearly set out in black and white in the Bible. Of course, the Ten Commandments are a starting place, but Jesus's Sermon on the Mount and the parables are bedrock sources of guides for living. But in areas where the Bible doesn't at first glance appear to directly bear on a pending decision, praying for guidance, deliberating on the issue shortly before bedtime, and asking for guidance is effective. Our minds work, especially with the help of the Holy Spirit, even while our bodies are resting. Perhaps our minds are overfilled and disorganized after a full day; in the morning, after our minds have "defragged" and organized bits of information into categories, often, a fresh solution will come to mind. Whether this is a miracle or simply our amazing minds working optimally, God's will is often clearer upon awakening.

Have you ever experienced a voice behind you verbalizing instructions/directions? Are we listening for such a voice? If we heard such a voice, would we discount it or listen up? If we make a conscious effort to turn off our external stimuli (radios, ipods, DVD players) when we are in the midst of a serious fork in the road, "thinking on God" instead, perhaps this would open the way to hearing God's direction for our lives.

# AUGUST 26

## Proverbs Parallels—Generosity

"But good men will be generous to others and will be blessed of God for all they do" (Is. 32:8).

"He that shows mercy to the poor shall be blessed. He that believes in the Lord loves mercy" (Prov. 14:21).

The cause and effect between generosity, mercy, and kindness to others, and the blessings that redound back to the giver is clearly set out in many places in scripture. It is simply God's law of the universe. Givers are blessed. Sowing brings harvest. Kindness is repaid. Of course, the act of generosity is good for the soul of the giver; in the first instance, a person feels better about him/herself, knowing they have been able to help another. We were designed by our Creator to give, to live kindly, to be merciful. Our spirits are warmed; our souls are "made fat." If you are in a funk, the quickest way to improve your attitude is to find someone else who needs a hand. The mere act of helping another lifts our spirits, for we are then "in the groove" of God's will for our lives. It is always the will of God to be helpful to others, to earnestly look for ways to spread abundance and blessing into the lives of others, especially those of God's own house.

Random acts of kindness are now a fad in our culture—but a good fad. It simply thrills our souls when someone retells how the person ahead of them in the drive through line at a fast food restaurant paid for their meal before they arrived at the pay window! When a child presents us with a hand-colored drawing, the child beams, because they know they have done a small act to cheer another. Their faces have not yet learned to "mask" their emotions, so their joy is patent. Let us do the same!

# August 27

## Proverbs Parallels—Sowing/Reaping

"All who are honest and fair, who reject making profit by fraud, who hold back their hands from taking bribes, who refuse to listen to those who plot murder, who shut their eyes to all enticement to do wrong. Such as these shall dwell on high. The rocks of the mountains will be their fortress of safety; food will be supplied to them, and they will have all the water they need" (Is. 33: 15–16).

"The fear of the Lord is unto life, and he shall abide in abundance without being visited by evil" (Prov. 19:23).

If we do good, act justly due to fear of the Lord, we shall reap his blessings and abundance. Fear of the Lord would be better described as respect and awe for the Lord. Knowing and respecting his rules, both from love/respect for God and fear/knowledge of the negative consequences of disobedience, is a proper perspective. Abundance refers to both provision of what we need in our bodies to live: food, drink, clothing, social relationships and joy, and gratitude in our souls. Fortress of safety indicates not only protection from evil persons in our world but self-confidence, deliverance from excessive worry, sweet sleep at night, rest without fear.

Even if we chose, out of pure logical analysis, to follow Christ due to the rewards promised, not for love of Christ, this would set us on the right path, and blessings would naturally result. Coldhearted weighing and balancing of the pluses/minuses of following Christ's way would lead, in most cases, to the conclusion that the reaping of benefits following our sowing of obedience in our lives, is the rational, intelligent choice to make. Some commentators interpret "abundance" as blessings beyond mere sustenance level—granting of desires, and wishes above what is needed to survive.

# August 28

## Proverbs Parallels—Multiplication

"All your people shall be good. The smallest family shall multiply into a clan; the tiny group shall be a mighty nation. I, the Lord, will bring it all to pass when it is time" (Is. 60:21–22).

"When the wicked perish, the just shall be multiplied" (Prov. 18:28).

If we accept as truth that righteousness and Godliness leads to larger families, we could just accept that promise and stop there. However, our inquiring minds try to fathom the reasons for this. Evil folks often have difficulty getting along with others—letting grudges build up, unforgiveness, bitterness, and its fruits. This tendency estranges relatives, divides clans, and sabotages family relationships. Division in families leads to fewer children, fewer marriages, and discontinuity among generations. Family unity and love attracts others, perhaps enlarging the group via adoptions, remarriages and love relationships. Love attracts; disunity and quarreling repel.

In Bible times, large families were viewed extremely favorably. Lots of little helpers could help with shepherding, gathering the harvest and producing spinning/weaving/textiles from goat/sheep hair.

While today a large brood is first thought of in terms of expense (tuition, food, clothing, medical expenses), we know that spiritually, a large family brings comfort, a sense of belonging and many smiles when gathered together. How joyous our family gatherings at the holidays; conversely, how bleak a holiday without a family to welcome us home with open arms. God created us as social beings. Medical studies have shown that high-risk health factors are associated with loneliness and self-centeredness.

Having children particularly enlarges our hearts since we are forced by the necessities of caring for an infant/toddler to tamp down our selfish desires to put their needs primary. From my observations of childless individuals, a layer of compassion and altruism seems to be missing when compared with parents. Let the multiplication continue!

# August 29

## Proverbs Parallels—Appearance

"Wisdom lights up a man's face, softening its hardness" (Eccl. 8:1).

"Wisdom shines in the face of the wise" (17:24).

These verses are remarkably similar. "Lighting up" and "shining" evokes thoughts of the glory of God shining out from a person's soul. Notice the verses are not limited to the appearance of just the eyes, but of the entire countenance. Kindliness and compassion sometimes seem to literally emanate from a saintly face. Have you noticed how children and pets seem to have a special "radar" for detecting such kindly souls? On the other hand, if children and pets are repelled by a person, beware! I fear adults have masked over their feelings and emotions so thoroughly that we have blocked this Holy Spirit-given discernment.

The hardness of a face exhibits itself around the mouth of a person, which finds it difficult to smile, and in the eyes of a person which do not beam or twinkle. Does a face perpetually seem "on guard"—defensive due to guilt, perhaps or, fear of condemnation for past bad deeds? Or is the face relaxed, open, with a ready smile and inviting countenance? If you take time to observe, often, it is very easy to fathom the basic disposition of a person. Cynical? Hardhearted? Grasping? Or tenderhearted, sweet, and generous? Salesmen are sent to training to "read" people's faces, to know how best to make their pitch. What attributes are foremost in a person, which should be used as an entree to make a sale?

Ordinary persons can heighten their observation powers when dealing with a new person in life. We display our feelings and general character on our faces more than we know. Have you ever gone to a movie and seen a main character not smile the entire movie, until a happy ending? When a smile first appears, it is so eye-catching, so noticeable. Let us draw near to those with soft faces.

# AUGUST 30

## Proverbs Parallels—Long Life

"I know very well that those who fear God will be better off, unlike the wicked, who will not live long, good lives—their days shall pass away as quickly as shadows because they don't fear God" (Eccl. 8:13).

"A joyful mind makes age flourishing" (Prov. 17:22).

Why do righteous people live longer, as a general rule? I believe it is primarily because they are following God's design. All of God's rules for living are for our best interest—body and soul. When we are abiding by the manufacturer's specifications for living, we naturally "run better," causing less wear and tear on our "engines." Fewer pinch points, areas of irritation, worries over guilt, defensiveness, and justification gum up the works. We have only a ground level human's eye view of the world and its workings. God, our Creator, has a million feet high view of the universe and a microscope view of our internal organs and spirit. Of course, he can be depended on to understand us inside and out and develop ways of living which are ideal for us.

"Joyful minds" are lit up with gratitude, blessings, and awareness of God. Glimpses of the Holy Spirit surely lubricate "the works" in a healing, curative, beneficial manner. Bitter minds darken, become closed, and block out the wonder working light of God and his spirit. Commentators and theologians refer often to the Deuteronomic principle: i.e. the dichotomy frequently set out in the book of Deuteronomy. Those who are obedient to God's commands are blessed with abundant crops, fresh water, large families, prolific herds, and peaceful relations. Those who are disobedient may fairly expect God's curses, in the form of drought, miscarriages among families and herds, strife, ill health, and crop failure. Deuteronomy often speaks in more poetic descriptions of these necessities of life: the finest of wheat, the flowing of wine, the overflow of silos, but the principle is exactly the same as these verses.

# August 31
## Proverbs Parallels—Foolish Speech

"It is pleasant to listen to wise words, but a fool's speech brings him to ruin" (Eccl. 10:12).

"The tongue of the perverse shall perish" (Prov. 10:31).

How do our words get us into trouble? When we lie, it is so easy to forget what we earlier said, thus tangling us up when we speak later, making our dishonesty evident to all. When we gossip, others are reluctant to associate with us, knowing that as we are slandering or passing on information about our mutual friend, we will straight away be speaking of them when we are apart. When we criticize, the spirits of our spouse or children or employees wilt before our eyes. When we brag, we drive away potential friends who see right through us. When we continually rehash the past, we shoot ourselves in the foot by failing to focus on the here and now and the tasks that daily await us. When we blather on with too many words, we are tuned out by our hearers. When we push ourselves forward into the limelight at work team meetings, our coworkers roll their eyes and resentment increases.

There are a myriad detailed ways that our speech can self-sabotage our families, our careers, and our reputations. Our honor is somewhat dependent on our deeds, but in today's culture of social media and instant messaging, our fingers sometimes fly faster than our brains, causing deep regrets. Once the horse is out of the barn, out in the world of the Internet, comments cannot effectively be retracted. An accusation on page 1 of the newspaper is little affected by a "found not guilty" verdict reported two years later on page 25. Since potential employers and dates nowadays often peruse social media accounts, our hasty ill-planned words can haunt us forever. Beware our lips!

# September 1

## Proverbs Parallels—Anger

"The anger of a fool is heavier than stones or sand" (27:3).

"A spirit that is easily angered: who can bear?" (18:14).

Sometimes, we coast along enjoying the day, but then we run afoul of someone having a temper tantrum. The power and passion of an angry person has such a major impact on those observing the scene. It is difficult to get the negativity out of our minds. If the anger is directed against us, it is doubly difficult to refocus back to our tasks at hand or the positive blessings surrounding it.

If we happen to live with a person prone to angry outbursts, it is like walking on pins and needles to avoid ruffling their feathers. We must anticipate what events will "set them off" and take pains to tiptoe around these potholes. Even literally, "heaviness" weighs on our spirits, removing our eyes from our own agendas. Serious anger has the power to take over our mood, infecting those around with sad mouths.

Even if an employee is brilliant with flashes of genius, if the person also has an angry bent, the unity and effectiveness of the work group can be sabotaged by one unruly personality. The heaviness can bring down productivity, but even more so, the morale of the group. We spend so many hours a day at work that this potential time bomb is deadly to our even-keeled functioning.

Visualize carrying a wheelbarrow load of stones or sand. Now that is heavy! It does not take too many stones or too much sand to reach carrying capacity, even with the leverage of wheelbarrow handles. A bucket of stones or sand is even worse. This analogy is apt for demonstrating the burden to our spirits when a relative, neighbor, or coworker harbors an angry spirit. Beware!

# September 2

## Proverbs Parallels—Good Children

"A wise son makes a father glad; a foolish son is the sorrow of a mother" (10:1).

"Instruct your children and they shall give delight to your soul" (29:17).

Parents' well-being is inextricably bound up with the conduct of their children. We are naturally invested in our children's success. Our pride is dented if they act foolishly. Our pride is inflated when they achieve great things. Despite our pouring our hearts and souls into raising them the best way we know how, they have the individual power of choice. Smothering parents often find their children rebelling solely to escape the blanket of helicopter parenting.

I recall my children singing in the church children's chorus when very young. My cheeks virtually ached due to my continual beaming pride. At our daughter's first dance rehearsal, I could not take my eyes off of her to watch the others. Whether in time or off step, her prancing around was, of course, darling to her dear parents. Teachers' report card comments can make or break your day. Even when we know they are private between teaching staff and us, they assume supreme importance in our estimation.

Parents of addicts, suicides, or criminals can barely hold their heads up in polite company. They are affected in a powerful way and generally need support groups to get past the trauma of such severe bad conduct.

In contrast, how wonderful it is to be a part of a godly extended family where family reunions allow us to catch up on the growth and development of our great nieces, nephews, and the like, where parents are loving and consistent in their parenting, raising well-adjusted, well-loved, secure little personalities. What greater delight than to see a darling young child on the right path!

# SEPTEMBER 3

## Proverbs Parallels—Disciplining Children

"Chastise your son, despair not but don't kill him" (19:18).

"Don't withhold correction from a child; if you beat him, he won't die or go to hell" (12:13).

"The rod and reproof give wisdom but the child that is left to his own will brings his mother to shame" (12:15).

"Folly is bound up in the heart of a child; the rod of correction shall drive it away" (22:15).

"He that spares the rod hates his son" (13:24).

The sum and substance of all these similar verses is that consistent discipline is a necessary part of child-rearing. If we are inconsistent, the child is quick to pick up on this and sabotage our efforts of teaching right and wrong. If we are tired, lazy, even exhausted from a day's work, we nevertheless need to make the extra effort to summon the last bit of energy to maintain our consistency in rules of the household. If we slip or allow rules violation even once, our past diligence may be easily undermined.

Today's culture objects to child "beating" but a wooden spoon on the backside given with purposeful intent to a toddler, *not* out of anger, can set them on the right path. They will know we are serious about our admonition. Many a mother has carried a wooden spoon in the diaper bag with merely a reference to it letting the child know mom has reached her limit.

Older than toddlers, however, other forms of punishment are preferred: time-outs, toy time-outs, deprivation of privileges for upcoming parties, sleepovers, or treats are likely more effective. Beware using food or sweets, however, as incentives, as this has been shown to potentially lead to eating disorders: anorexia, bulimia, overeating. Never send a child to bed without supper; that is essential for growth and development. Proverbs advocates consistent discipline, so should we.

# September 4

## Proverbs Parallels—Confidence

"Keep the law and counsel and you shall walk confidently and your foot shall not stumble" (3:23).

"He that walks sincerely walks confidently" (10:9).

"In the fear of the Lord is confidence of strength and there shall be hope for his children" (14:26).

Confidence puts a spring in our step and a smile on our face. It lessens fear, raises self-esteem, and promotes overall psychological health. These verses show that when we are on the right path, following God's law, we flourish and set a good example for other Christians. Our Christian walk is not only for our benefit but also for those around us, especially children, students, youth, and others looking to us as a role model. Walking "sincerely" means non-hypocritically. We are the same inside as we display outside. We don't have double standards for Sunday versus the work week. We don't have to put on a mask when we walk outside our house.

All good parents care deeply for our children, so "hope for our children" is a strong incentive to cultivate confidence. Note carefully the steps necessary for cultivating confidence: keeping the law and counsel. Learning and following God's precepts and listening to sermons and teaching sessions, devotional books, and the advice and counsel of more mature spiritual leaders are practical ways of increasing our confidence. It is a powerful thing to ward off insecurity, doubts, and fears that may affect our health, our sleep, and our mental stability with the realization that we are in God's will, known to the best of our ability.

Others are attracted to those exuding confidence. We can have more impact as teachers, pastors, counselors, youth leaders, and authors. Keeping our foot away from evil, on the straight and narrow, is the import of "not stumbling." These are wonderful promises we can take to heart and implement.

# September 5

## Proverbs Parallels—Counsel

"Hear counsel and receive instruction that you may be wise at your end" (19:20).

"Plans are strengthened by counsel" (20:18).

"There shall be safety where there are many counsels" (24:6).

Repetition in different chapters of Proverbs shows their importance to King Solomon or his advisors who gathered these bits of practical wisdom. "Wise at your end" denotes the fact that we are always learning in our lives. If we are diligent about seeking knowledge and wisdom, we will grow in wisdom daily and be much further along in our spiritual path than when we were green and immature youngsters.

Are you facing a major life event dilemma? Whom to marry? Where to work? What major to pursue? Where to retire? Seek the advice of "many counsels." Some you can easily disregard, but most Christians will be happy to give advice in your best interest. We should take most seriously those who have stood in our shoes, facing the same dilemma. When we are young, we are often air headed with unrealistic ideas about different choices before us. But those who have been battered and bruised in the past by poor choices or simply naïve choices have learned valuable lessons and are happy to impart them to save you those same bruises. We should swallow our pride, humble ourselves, and be willing and eager to listen to detailed counsel given by those experts in the field or who have passed the way we are contemplating.

Of course, we must be discerning enough to fathom whether a person has "an ax to grind" or something to sell or gain in the choice we are contemplating. We want to select counselors who are objective and have our best interest at heart and especially our parents and those who love us dearly. Thank God if there are such individuals in our lives.

# SEPTEMBER 6

## Proverbs Parallels—Covetousness

"The ways of every covetous man destroy the soul" (1:19).

"Fools covet things which are hurtful to them" (1:22).

"A covetous man shall destroy the land" (29:4).

Coveting makes the Ten Commandments because of the great potential to destroy our souls and our relationships with others. Why? Because coveting reeks of materialism and the "best things in life are invisible and free." We've heard the latter phrase all our lives, but we know, from careful self-examination, that it is true: love, joy, peace, delight, gratitude, a sense of well-being, a gorgeous sunset or lake view.

How many families have been destroyed by workaholism—running after money to buy fancier houses, cars, boats, second home, vacations? As Rabbi Harold Kushner writes in *When Everything You've Always Wanted Isn't Enough*, he never heard one person, on their deathbed, wish he had spent more time at the office. Rather, most people have regrets that they did not spend tender years with their younger children. They grow up so fast. Poring over catalogs, recreational shopping strolling the aisles at the mall or big box store, making a list of desires after visiting another's more elaborate home are soul killing. There is no ultimate satisfaction in stuff—only temporary fleeting pride.

Food for the soul is found in the Word of God, serving others and meditating on God's blessings. Nourishment for our souls comes from contemplating a mountain view, a deep forest, a shining lake, or other creations of God. Associating with young joyful children and watching them at play is good for the soul. Buying the fanciest new car or watch causes us to worry about protecting them from theft or damage. The writer of the book of Ecclesiastes has much to say about the futility and deep dissatisfaction found from coveting luxuries and wine, women, and song.

# SEPTEMBER 7
## Proverbs Parallels—Criticism

"Remove from you a negative mouth and let detracting lips be far from you" (4:24).

"All fools are meddling with reproaches" (20:3).

Synthesized, these verses indicate that we are foolish if we habitually downgrade others or "meddle" by criticizing situations in which we have no direct stake. I believe criticism is a learned habit which can be unlearned with care and effort and the help of the Holy Spirit in transforming our minds and mouths.

Sometimes, we catch ourselves beginning to form critical thoughts, but we can train our brains to visualize a big red stop sign before the words emerge. Especially if our children are the objects of the criticism or our spouse, we must carefully couch comments in constructive ways so as not to damage these relationships. Even if we are in charge of an employee at work, this is a long-term relationship so care and thought should be used before issuing the remark. Ongoing criticism is purely toxic. The first principle in considering whether to criticize is to consider that people are the most precious thing on earth since they are created by God. Therefore, it is our duty to treat them with kid gloves, suppressing casual criticism ready to emerge from our mouths.

Using the "What would Jesus do" test is a good instrument to evaluate a potential remark. Can you imagine a scriptural passage where Christ uttered the remark we are about to make? If not, we should simply swallow it. Our role should instead be "catching them doing something right" as school teachers say, which reinforces the good conduct and implicitly suppresses the bad conduct. If we are considering a critical remark, are we the designated person "in the world" in the best position to utter it? Is this our child? Our ward? Our responsibility? Our duty? We may be a fool if not.

# September 8

## Proverbs Parallels—Daily Communion

"Blessed is the man that hears me and that watches daily at my gates" (8:34).

"My delight is to be with my children" (8:32).

What is the most effective way to improve our fitness? Daily exercise, aerobic workouts, and strength training. What is the most effective way to slim down? Daily vigilance about what we eat, drink, and how much we move. What is the best way to maintain good dental health? Daily flossing, brushing, and antibacterial mouthwash.

Similarly, what is the most effective way to improve our spiritual walk? Regularity, good habits, and spiritual discipline of "watching daily" at God's gates. Just as in other areas of life we, with disciplined repetition, become habitual about an activity, so must we become habitual about daily Bible reading, devotion, prayer, and meditation (otherwise known as listening to God for answers to our prayers). It is the "dailyness" of our efforts that reaps spiritual growth and understanding. Whatever mnenomic devices we can adopt to regularize turning our attention to God will be of benefit. Orthodox Jews attached prayer boxes to their doorposts to remind them upon entry and exit to pray the Shema prayer. Even in Jesus's time, religious persons attached blue and white tassels to their robes and prayer shawls as devices to remind them to pray.

Today, some people hang crosses or crucifixes on their rearview mirrors, letting the swinging motion catch their eye as a prayer reminder. Others use landmarks on their daily drive to work as a means of bringing to mind coworkers to pray for, family members to intercede for or going to God in prayer.

Why should we regularize our communion with God? God delights to be with his children. Much like we delight in our children's "talk time" at the breakfast table, during car rides or bath time, we look forward to intimate conversations with them; so does God delight in our attention turned to him.

# September 9

## Proverbs Parallels—Self-Improvement

"The path of the just as a shining light goes forward and increases to perfect day" (4:18).

"The wise servant shall prosper in his dealings and his way shall be made straight" (14:15).

Onward and upward! Do you optimistically expect your future to get better? Do you anticipate a closer walk with God as you age? Are you hoping your way forward will be made plain? As our righteousness and wisdom increases due to disciplined Bible study and attention to the ways of God, these verses give us a firm basis to maintain those expectations. Our path as a shining light and our way being straight indicate that we will have certainty in the next steps in our life. We won't be wishy-washy or fickle, changing our mind as does a teenager about what career to choose, which partner to choose for a spouse and which church to attend.

Rather, as mature Christians, we can count on stability in our relationships, our church fellowship, and our faith. Our doubts should lessen and our faith increase. It is much more satisfying treading down a well-lit and straight road than one that is dark and windy. As we study and learn scripture, it will remain in our mind to be brought forward when it is applicable to a pending dilemma. The new Christian may be pulled to and fro by competing doctrine and input from others; the mature wise Christian has landed on one church community and remains loyal and committed.

John Wesley and other early church leaders believed that holiness and perfection were attainable in large degree if we remained focused and committed, not wavering with each passing religious fad. Note the added hope of prospering in our dealings. What a goal to set our minds on: a straight well-lit path to God and to heaven.

# September 10

## Proverbs Parallels—Devising Evil

"He that devises evil shall be called a fool" (24:8).

"The soul of the wicked desires evil; he will not have pity on his neighbor" (21:10).

How do you spend your free time? Thinking about how to "pay back" a coworker? Dreaming of ways to "show up" our rival? Daydreaming about the downfall of one who criticized us recently? If we spend time envisioning negativity for others, we must seriously evaluate our motives in life. All these and similar activities are engaged in by fools.

On the other hand, do you wake up with a hymn on replay in your mind? Do you look forward to a scheduled lunch with a dear one? Are you preparing loving feedback for your child at breakfast? Take note of what is most frequently traversing your mental "channels" as a measure of your spiritual health. Good or ill? As a man thinks in his heart, so he is. As we think, so we are. Are we a fool-devising evil? This verse reflects a hard analysis of ourselves we must undertake. We may think we're a basically good person, but if we are exhibiting frequent road rage or brooding over unfairness by our neighbor, we are simply foolish. Christians are called to forgive, letting go of grudges so that our spirits will soar and be lighter than air. Holding onto images of criticism from the past or vowing to "remember" an evil done to us drags us down to sin and misery.

What are you looking forward to? A family vacation with your loved ones? Or an occasion to "make it even" for an evil deed done to us? What we are envisioning for the future clearly reveals whether we are in danger of "devising evil."

# September 11

## Proverbs Parallels—Double Dealing

"Practice not evil against your friend when he has confidence in you" (3:29).

"He that covers hatred deceitfully, his malice shall be laid open publicly" (26:26).

*Treachery* is another word for *double-dealing*. Being two-faced is another. Being of a "divided heart" is a term used in scripture. If we call ourselves a friend, we are called to loyalty and faithfulness and having the best interests of the other as a priority. There is no worse feeling than thinking a person is your friend and finding out otherwise, finding out that they have put their own self-interest about ours.

The second verse warns that double-dealing will be found out. We may think we have successfully backstabbed our friend, but the truth will "out." In the meantime, we will suffer guilt feelings and fear the time of such revelation. Notice that not only will our friend find out, but also others will learn of our betrayal, which will deep six our reputation as a trustworthy individual.

If you find that you cannot remain a friend, then be open and compassionately break off the friendship. It is perilous to attempt to toe the path between loyalty and betrayal. This is the sort of dilemma that weighs on our minds and keeps us from sleeping soundly.

Middle school and high school are common hotbeds for double dealing against friends, as allegiances and cliques shift and boyfriends come and go. Hopefully as we mature and head to college and the working world, we have learned the pain of treachery against us and will take pains to maintain loyalty in our relationships. If we are torn between two friendships that seem to be mutually exclusive, it is sometimes doable to compartmentalize our lives. Certain friends whose politics are 180° from ours, we can pleasantly discuss everything but the election. Or we can avoid altogether discussing mutual acquaintances loved by one but despised by the other. Sustained friendship and loyalty are the hallmarks of the faithful person.

# September 12

## Proverbs Parallels—Envy

"Envy is the rottenness of the bones" (14:30).

"Don't envy sinners" (12:17).

Envy makes us truly miserable. Comparisons in general tend to make us miserable, and envy is an especially harsh form of comparison. Our lives should be so geared to self-improvement and being of service to others that we scarcely notice attributes about others or possessions of others that cause us envy. Every moment spent wishing we had as nice of a car, as well-behaved children, as toned of a body, as bouncy hair, or as handsome of a husband undermines our self-esteem and takes our eyes off the "ball": becoming the best we can be, with the help of God and the Holy Spirit.

Notice the specific prohibition against envying sinners. This perhaps implies that perhaps there would be benefit in envying other "saints"—closely observing them as examples and role models. There surely would be benefit in selecting wise and righteous church members or companions and patterning our speech and actions after them. The best example is Christ, as revealed in the gospels. Close study of his parables, responses to questions and interactions with those around him would be beneficial. Some Christians are inspired by lives of the saints and study biographies of worthies through the ages.

It is sometimes disheartening to pore through catalogs on a recreational basis when we don't really need anything. Paging through websites of the latest clothes, shoes, designer purses, or technology devices can discourage us and make us feel less than loved. Spare time shopping just to see if anything catches our eye can be disheartening as well, seeing racks of stylish clothes on model thin mannequins. These activities are major opportunities to magnify envy unnecessarily and are best avoided. Envy is a self-prescribed downer best avoided.

# SEPTEMBER 13

## Proverbs Parallels—Faithfulness

"A faithful man shall be much praised" (28:20).

"Many men are called merciful but who shall find a faithful man?" (20:6).

This rhetorical question implies that faithful persons are few and far between and, when found, are deserving of accolades. Whether in the corporate world, churches, or volunteer organizations, anyone who has been a scheduler of personnel knows this to be true. Some workers are brilliant but have poor attendance; some workers show up but take all too frequent breaks. Some workers assume responsibility for the short term but don't stick with it. It is so disappointing to work pleasantly side by side with someone, only to have them drop out within a short time.

Knowing how hurtful and discouraging this is, let us strive to set a great example to others with our faithfulness. The song says, "They'll know we are Christians by our love." But faithfulness is another chief characteristic of the devoted Christian. Being rare in the world, it is noticed by others in the workplace or volunteer organization and is a natural attractor. If we decide to undertake a task, let us evaluate carefully whether we can remain dedicated to it for a reasonable period and do our best to remain responsible and diligent in our tasks. Some persons seem to be naturally fickle, changing their mind about what they wish to be involved in. We should pray for the Holy Spirit to increase our faithfulness as we mature as Christians. This will put us head and shoulders above the rest of humanity and operate as an effective witness for Christ. Let us not be impulsive in our stepping up to a task but think through carefully the time and skills it will require. After prayerful evaluation, once undertaken, let us be a shining light in our faithfulness to the task.

# September 14
## Proverbs Parallels—Friendship

"Like iron sharpening iron, so a man sharpens a friend" (27:17).

"The good counsels of a friend are sweet to the soul" (27:9).

These verses speak to accountability and keeping one another in line. Good friends give us good news and bad news about our conduct and actions. But when they must give us bad news for our own good, friends should do it reluctantly and with kindness. When they give us compliments, they are extra sweet when we judge them sincere, coming from a trusted friend. Sincere compliments go down smoother than compliments which may be insincere flattery given with a view to butter us up for a furtive motive. Can they be trusted we wonder? Were they given for short or long term gain by the giver? When their source is a loyal friend, we may dispense with this analysis.

As friends, we must consider carefully before we open our mouth with constructive criticism. Does the friend already know about their deficiency? If so, why pile it on with another comment? They are likely beating themselves up already and need a supporting shoulder more than an added remark. Only if the friend seems blind to the problem, it is self-sabotaging them, and we believe they will actually listen and take to heart our advice should we then consider how to deliver the news in the kindest possible way. Timing is important too. We must be extra sensitive to what is going on in our friend's life and whether some upcoming vacation, wedding, or special occasion will be marred by our remarks. After the fact observations are only helpful if the scenario is likely to reoccur and our advice is apt to save them from future pitfalls. Marriage counselors advise to keep a ratio in mind: give ten compliments to one criticism. This ratio would be well applied to friends as well.

# September 15

## Proverbs Parallels—Rewards of Generosity

"A man's gift enlarges his way and makes room before princes" (18:16).

"He that makes presents shall purchase victory and honor" (22:9).

Leaders notice those making significant contributions to their charity, church, or political campaign. Teachers especially notice students bringing them an extra nice Christmas gift. Whatever the giver's intentions (bribery, gaining access, or true belief in the charity or cause?), those in charge pay attention to generous gift givers. This is reflective of human nature and is just the way the world works.

In religious institutions, large gifts generally equate to generous hearts and advanced maturity in the spiritual realm. Some pastors relate that generous giving usually indicates a "large heart." Stingy, frugal, penny pinching individuals rarely can loosen their restrictions enough to write a substantial check even if they have ample funds. Generosity closely parallels a giving heart.

Of course, honor is "purchased" by listings in the charitable program for members of the public to see: gold level donors, etc. But respect is generally gained by others serving on the charitable board as well. Hospital boards, children's charities, or service organizations naturally honor big donors: naming clinic wings after them, college buildings, or charity balls.

This verse seems neutral. It is merely an observation about how the world turns since money talks in nearly any organization. But other verses reveal that God especially honors those who help the poor and have a charitable mind-set. "Love thy neighbor" calls for acts of service but, if means permit, a financial leg up if the neighbor has suffered job layoff, unexpected medical bills, or natural disasters such as tornado or flood damage. Volunteer organizations regularly honor major donors, and one's name becomes locally known for consistent faithful organizational support. If you desire to receive honor on earth, this is one practical way to obtain honor.

# September 16
## Proverbs Parallels—Guarantor

"He shall be afflicted with evil who is surety for a stranger" (11:15).

"You might as well surrender your coat as be surety for a stranger" (27:13).

There are few flat prohibitions in Proverbs beyond those reflected in the Ten Commandments. However, this is one. A stranger surely includes those with whom we are recently acquainted but for whom we have no past history or know no track record. These verses flatly caution that we will be sorry, and we are likely to suffer negative consequences. We are most likely to regret undertaking the guarantee. Unless we are truly willing to lose the insured amount, it is a bad idea and could negatively affect our financial situation and credit rating. The stranger has little compunction in failing to uphold their initial obligation since they have no relationship with the guarantor which is subject to damage. The stranger won't have to look us in the eye and feel regret or guilt.

On the other hand, a stranger is be contrasted with a son, daughter, or extended family member with whom we have history and an ongoing relationship. The child or relative knows that the long term relationship is at stake, so they will be more likely to do their best to fulfill the primary financial obligation. Especially with young adults just entering the job market with little credit history, they may not be able to obtain a new car or house loan without parental guarantee. I believe this special case is recognized and implicit within the plain meaning of "stranger." For extended family who have fallen on hard times, if we have the means to help them, it would be laudable to act as surety if our own family's needs are secure. Let us keep in mind this clear distinction between strangers and family members or those of long acquaintance.

# September 17

## Proverbs Parallels—Advice for a Fool

"A parable is irritating to a fool" (26:9).

"A fool that repeats his folly is disgusting" (26:11).

"He that trusts in his own heart is a fool" (28:26).

"If a wise man contends with a fool, whether he be angry or laugh, he shall find no rest" (29:9).

The sum of these verses is that you can't tell a fool anything! She/he will not listen to parables, advice, or teaching. The ego and pride of a fool are such that she/he will not stoop to seeking advice from others or listening to any advice given. Even worse, the fool will not learn from experience: the fool repeats his error and is back at the beginning, not having matured or improved his lot. The fool, a know-it-all, believes that no one knows her/his business and that she/he alone is the best judge of a looming dilemma. Even if the fool is young and mature elders are around, she/he is not interested in inquiring about how past similar situations have been handled. Instead, the fool trusts solely in his own heart. The fool does not inquire of God, consult scripture or experts in the field.

If a wise man sees a fool about to step off a dangerous cliff or commit an avoidable misstep, it is better not even to try to attempt to dissuade the fool. The last verse observes that the fool is likely to laugh off the advice or be offended that someone tried to interfere. The fool discounts all tendered advice as unnecessary and insulting. The wise man will endanger the relationship if he persists in attempting to help. Therefore, the clear choice is for the wise man to go his own way, leaving the fool on his own. It is futile to attempt to advise a fool.

# September 18

## Proverbs Parallels—Healing

"He that trusts in the Lord shall be healed" (28:26).

"Soundness of heart is the life of flesh" (14:30).

"Do not be conceited; fear God, depart from evil, for it shall be health to you" (3:7).

What is the best path to receive healing? Trust in the Lord, cultivate a sound heart, and fear God. When we consider those we have known who have experienced early deaths, it is nearly always associated with drunken driving, suicide following depression, criminal behavior, gluttony, drag racing exceeding the speed limit, or drug use. Yes, bad things happen to some good people, but that is the exception, not the rule. When I list those in my immediate family dying "too young," this pattern clearly emerges. Think about your experience with deaths in your neighborhood, church community, or school.

Longevity generally goes hand in hand with good character—"soundness of heart" meaning integrity and mental wholeness. There are more saints, especially sweet little old ladies, populating the centenarian ranks than rascals. There is clearly a direct relationship between goodness and long life. Perhaps this is because folks who "fear God" have taken to heart the scriptures about our bodies being a temple of the Lord and have consistently treated their body with respect, treating it with good food, rest, and life-giving activities. On the other hand, we have known friends from high school, college, and beyond who have taken extreme risks in their lives: smoking, drinking, engaging in risky behavior without regard for the long view of life who have come to tragic ends.

God's precepts for diet, marriage fidelity, being grateful, and living for others are designed for our benefit: both mind and body. His prohibitions are not simply because he is arbitrary but because he created us inside and out and understands what is beneficial. Let us trust in the Lord and be healed.

# SEPTEMBER 19

## Proverbs Parallels—Dishonesty

"No good shall come to the deceitful son" (14:15).

"The deceitfulness of the wicked shall destroy them" (11:3).

"Crooked weights and measures are abominable before God" (20:10).

Scripture is clear. Dishonesty brings self-destruction to the one practicing it. Why are men and women so slow to believe this principle? It is perfectly clear from Proverbs that while there may be short term gain in practicing dishonest business dealings, lying or cheating others, the gains are short lived. In the end, dishonesty will "out" and be utterly self-defeating.

As parents, we must be vigilant with our young children, and if we see dishonesty, we should deal with it firmly, explaining the consequences, on earth and thereafter. It never pays and will only rain down destruction on their head. God loves justice; therefore, it is abominable to God for persons to contravene justice by cheating others. Especially cheating our own family members is a dead end with extreme consequences. Alienating those dearest to us can only bring regret, guilt, and estrangement.

We know that God will judge all our actions one day, but these verses also implicate negative compounded "dividends" on earth as well. Loss of respect, personal regret, prison terms, and payback are anticipated. These verses remind us of mob movies, where retaliation escalates with no winners in sight. One shooting leads to two, three to four, leaving everyone dead! The Hatfields and the McCoys come to mind. There is no way out; bad deeds spiral downward. It is so much better to avoid that first act of deceit than to agonize over an impossible quagmire of sin and regret.

Especially since most deceit is done to gain a financial advantage, it is more prudent to take the long view. None of us can take any assets with us into the next world anyway.

# September 20

## Proverbs Parallels—Humility

"Glory shall uphold the humble of spirit" (29:33).

"Before a man be glorified, his heart is humbled" (18:12).

"Humility goes before glory" (15:33).

These verses are remarkably similar, demonstrating God's upside-down view of humanity. The world takes a wholly opposite viewpoint: strive for glory! Strive for self-importance! Strive to get in the public eye! Brag on oneself!

These Old Testament Proverbs coincide exactly with the Beatitudes spoken by Jesus at the Sermon on the Mount (Matt. 5). They were truly revolutionary at the time. 'Blessed are the meek, for they shall inherit the earth." The meek, lowly, and downtrodden were never respected, so why did this humble teacher say otherwise? An attempt to analyze the "whys" of these sayings may be futile. Because God says so?

I suppose since pride, from Genesis to present, has been mankind's besetting sin, this makes sense. Pride reveals man's tendency to believe that God is not necessary in life: I can do it myself. I know more than God concerning my life. Anytime we are putting along on all six cylinders running smoothly, our natural tendency is to think independently, disregarding any need for God. God desires that we wholly depend on him, humbly submitting ourselves to his will.

In thinking back over our life, our favorite teachers tend to be those with a humble heart for others first, not themselves. The most loved parents likewise put their children first and humbly subordinate their needs. Examples come to mind: the difference between Gen. Dwight D. Eisenhower, admired by nearly all nations versus egotistical Gen. George Patton and Gen. MacArthur, despised by many. Pastors who are in the business for the fame and fortune generally are outshined in the long term by those serving others with no eye for rewards on earth.

# September 21

## Proverbs Parallels—Greed

"He that is greedy of gain troubles his own house" (15:27).

"Better is a little with the fear of the Lord than great treasures without contentment" (15:16).

"He that makes haste to be rich shall not be innocent" (28:20).

These verses warn that if we place too much emphasis on gain as a priority, we are likely to cut corners, conduct transactions under the table, or skirt the law to achieve our goals. Gain becomes more important than toeing the line with integrity. "Troubling our house" reminds us of workaholic parents who are simply too engrossed to be involved in their children's lives, leading to regret and sadness. Troubling our house indicates failed marriages where business deals trump anniversary celebrations. It is simply a matter of priorities. Which comes first? Money in the bank or love on the home front? Stepping atop a coworker and killing the relationship for recognition and promotion?

One way of looking at this comparison goes back to what is precious in God's eyes. People are precious; they are his delight. He cares little for monetary achievement, except that however much we earn, we tithe on that income. In God's economy, his children always rank higher than bank balances. People are his creation; money is our creation.

Contentment with little entails counting our blessings, not simply toting up our paychecks. When we are on our deathbed, we will realize that "all our money can't a single moment buy" (Kansas, "Dust in the Wind"). People have souls that are eternal in nature; money is fleeting and transient. The comparison between the relative worth of people and wealth is no contest, in God's eyes and even in ours if we think carefully about life's rewards. Helen Keller said, "The best things in life are not seen or heard, but are felt in the heart." Amen.

# SEPTEMBER 22

## Proverbs Parallels—Reward of Peace

"All of the paths of wisdom are peaceable" (3:17).

"He that fears the commandment dwells in peace" (13:13).

Peace is a major theme of our culture in these unsettled times of mass shootings and law enforcement struggles. Our nation craves peace at home and abroad. But how do we achieve that peace? If we immerse ourselves in God's precepts of wisdom and are obedient to his commandments, peace is the natural result. Hope in God alleviates our desperate striving for peace; it is a natural outflow. Our sense of continual striving for status, acceptance, public recognition, and purpose in life disappear when our future is vested in God. We have a reason for living, our fears of death are mitigated, and our knowledge that we are children of God obviates the continual need to prove ourselves to others.

Our purpose is to establish the kingdom of God on earth through right treatment of people, reordering our priorities and thinking in "ultimate terms." Our hunger for possessions to impress others is dampened, and our feelings of self-worth go up as we are generous and helpful to others in acts of service. Helping others boomerangs and increases naturally our self-esteem. We no longer have to go, go, go but can be, be, be. The Christian walk is an upward spiral of self-knowledge, self-acceptance, and improvement in our dealings with others in our lives. We all know from personal experience that personal relationships are the source of our largest stressors, but done right, the source of our greatest satisfactions. Studying the Proverbs, James, and the Beatitudes particularly help us increase in wisdom. Read over and over, Proverbs can be a daily reminder of how to rightly order our lives in the service of God which rewards us with peace.

# September 23

## Proverbs Parallels—Compassion for the Poor

"He that despises the poor reproaches his Maker. He that rejoices in another man's ruin shall not be unpunished" (17:5).

"Do no violence to the poor because he is poor. Do not oppress the needy at the gate because the Lord will judge his cause and will afflict them that afflicted him" (22:22).

Sometimes, it is difficult to feel compassion for the poor. We tend to naturally despise the unwashed homeless beggar under the bridge. Our mind naturally thinks, *Why can't she/he just get a job?* We fear we are enabling a person by giving them a handout, so instead, we store granola bars under our car seat or McDonald's gift certificates so that we can be helpful without doling out hard cash which may go straight to the liquor store or drug dealer. We should not condemn ourselves for thinking through the best way to help in the long term to teach them to fish instead of handing out fish. It is okay to have handy a list of appropriate helping agencies for referral.

But it is our attitude that these verses speak to. While we are helping or even if we decide not to help, we must pray to maintain a kind, empathetic attitude for the poor. We simply have no idea what setbacks or hurdles the person has faced in life: mental illness? Burdensome medical bills? Abuse? Job layoffs? Post-traumatic stress syndrome? If we had faced the mountainous circumstances they had, we may be under the bridge as well. We must discipline ourselves to put out of our minds loathing for the person, and if we cannot do it in our own strength, pray for spiritual power to not harden our hearts but to maintain a sweet attitude. Oftentimes, the person craves simple recognition and a smile as much as a handout.

# September 24

## Proverbs Parallels—Pride

"The Lord will destroy the house of the proud and will strengthen the borders of the widow" (15:25).

"Every proud man is an abomination to the Lord" (16:5).

Pride comes so naturally to us all. It creeps in stealthily, and we must continually bat it down. The chief pointer to pride is hurt feelings. If we find ourselves pouting because we were not given adequate recognition for the major mission project we led, our role in bringing about an improved situation at church or a civic organization of which we are a part, let that be a red light—stop—pride at work. We all suffer these feelings as pride raises its ugly head in all our strivings. We must refocus our minds from the ill feelings about lack of recognition to the certainty that God sees our behind the scenes work and will reward us at the proper time. Our job is to *do* kingdom work, not to be recognized for it. The feedback from our fellow man is nice but should not be expected or anticipated.

In God's upside down kingdom, humility is the paramount virtue for which to strive, not recognition. We are reminded of Christ's foot washing in the Upper Room, which was a total shocker to the disciples. It was the traditional role of slaves or servants whom dinner guests rarely even acknowledged. We must continually remind ourselves that we are performing acts of service *not* for their rewards on earth but because we are being obedient to biblical exhortations.

Disgruntled congregants leave the church most often because feelings were hurt. Their financial support was not publicly acknowledged—their efforts did not redound to their benefit. When those resentments begin to bubble up, that symptom reveals the diagnosis: unbiblical pride.

# September 25

## Proverbs Parallels—Boasting about Tomorrow

"One who boasts but does not fulfill his promises is like thunderstorms without rain" (25:14).

"Boast not for tomorrow, for you don't know what tomorrow will bring" (27:1).

When we have a marvelous vacation upcoming or our family is coming to town or we have tickets to an exciting cultural event and are tempted to brag about them, stick a sock in it! While we can tell those with a "need to know" for logistical purposes, we should refrain from sharing our excitement with others until the event is imminent. Illness or death may strike, changing our plans. We may have to exercise our travel insurance claim rights. Some disaster may intervene before the event arrives.

We must analyze why we want to boast about these things? Pride, again, pure and simple. Likely, we want to increase our status in the eyes of the hearer, a goal that is unworthy.

The first verse focuses more on the ill-thought-out pledge for a building fund, a charitable cause, or a community fundraiser. How disappointed the recipient will be when we don't follow through. It serves no purpose except to feed our own pride to tell someone in advance—just hand in the check. Fear of disappointing others is a good reason for this verse, but I suspect at bottom, humility is the greater purpose in this observation. Just do it! Don't tell the world about it. Anonymity results in more "points" in God's book than earthly recognition. But giving anonymously is a good check on our pride which naturally grows and expands like a bad weed. It does not need any help to blow up like a balloon. Pride threatens to overwhelm up and take over our life if we don't consciously tamp it down.

# September 26

## Proverbs Parallels—Example of Punishment

"The wicked man, being beaten, the fool shall be wiser. If you rebuke a wise man, he will understand discipline" (19:25).

"When a bad man is punished, the little one will be wiser" (21:11).

These verses, although about punishment, are good news! We do not have to experience an arrest, a severe punishment, or a personal disaster to learn a concept. Wise persons continually and closely observe others and learn from their mistakes. If our neighbor's home gets confiscated by federal agents for growing marijuana in the basement, we should make sure our children know about this punishment so they can avoid it. The "little one(s)" are impacted more strongly than the adult, for they are young and impressionable and may be as yet unaware of the harsh cause and effect that comes to lawbreakers. Similarly when an acquaintance gets laid off the job for drinking, both we and our children should be let in on the information—not in an attitude of gloating or ridicule, but as a clear example of the dangers of excess.

One of the chief differences between a fool and a wise man is the observation of human behavior and the world around us to learn from others and avoid pitfalls. Fools take the attitude that they are invincible and no one can "touch them." They falsely believe that it'll be the other guy who gets caught. Wise persons following the righteous way take laws and authority seriously and strive to stay on the straight and narrow. Do not ever forget: little eyes are watching every move we make. Do we lie about their ages to get a lower price at the amusement park or movie? Integrity is revealed in every transaction we're involved in with our family. Pay close attention and avoid the problem.

# September 27

## Proverbs Parallels—Promises to the Righteous

"The fear of the Lord is unto life and [the righteous person] shall abide in abundance without being visited by evil" (19:23).

"The path of the just departs from evils" (16:17).

These verses bring to mind Psalm 23: "Yeah though I walk through the valley of the shadow of death, you shall fear no evil, for I am with you." Obedience to God brings many rewards, but these promises of avoidance of evil are high on my list. We know that opening the daily newspaper brings a litany of murders, DUIs, shootings, and family tragedies. We know that the eye of God rests particularly on those he loves. I note in the margin of my Bible a drawing of an eye to denote this theme, and it's surprising how often it appears. Psalms is rife with this promise. Other verses promise that heavenly angels surround the righteous person, giving aid, and preventing disasters. Have you experienced an instance of angelic protection in your life? Many testify to the saving grace of angels in the midst of car accidents, travelling mix-ups, and breakdowns.

While bad things do happen to good people, even in those bad things, God is with us to prevent the worse thing. Unexpected helpers appear to rescue us, and the fervent prayer of the righteous person brings aid.

Aligning our lives and efforts with God's precepts simply greases the wheels of our lives and makes them run more smoothly than were we chafing continually at God's commands, throwing grit into those wheels and slowing down the efficient turning of our life's course. Don't overlook the promise of abundance in the first verse. Avoiding evil is important, but an abundant life is over the top. What gratitude we should continually show to the God who promises avoidance of evil and abundance!

# September 28

## Proverbs Parallels—Good Self-Interest

"He that keeps the commandment keeps his own soul" (18:17). "The blessing of the Lord is upon the just" (10:6).

If one just introduced to Christianity were contemplating whether it was the "way to go" evaluating the cost as Christ said we all should do when undertaking an enterprise such as building a tower, it would be helpful to read the "good news" about the benefits resulting from a walk of faith in Christ.

Newbies might fear giving up activities: "wine, women, and song?" Newbies might obsess over what sacrifices in life would be called for. Those considering adopting the faith naturally would evaluate any costs flowing from the decision to become a dedicated Christian.

However, it is also good to remind ourselves about the good things flowing from the decision to follow Christ and his commandments. Verse 18:17 observes that our "own souls" benefit from this commitment. This means that it *is* in our own good self-interest to follow wise living and blessings of the Lord result. What blessings are those? Other verses speak of receiving "the desires of our heart," abundance in heart, soul, and even material blessings. The Lord knows our hearts and our passions and desires to bless us in achieving those desires. Are we impassioned about art? Study? Theater? Sports? Music? Travel? We can count on God to open doors to bring those things about when they are in his will and our lives are aligned with his precepts. Our health both physically and psychologically will improve as guilt feelings fade away and a sense of energy and peace result.

"Godincidences" (coincidences orchestrated by God) will bring just the right opportunities, people, facilitators, and resources into our lives to enable us to be of service to others and our souls to prosper. New Agers call this karma; scripture calls this soul keeping.

# September 29

## Proverbs Parallels—Deliverance/Escape

"The just is delivered out of distress; the just shall be delivered by knowledge" (11:8–9).

"The path of the just departs from evils" (16:17).

Should Christians encounter troubles, we should pray for deliverance, citing these verses. The Lord loves for us to have knowledge of and to pray "back to him" his promises for deliverance and care. The Lord's watch care goes before us to prepare the way so that we "depart from evil."

Notice the fact that knowledge can go a long way toward delivering us. I believe that this especially refers to the wisdom for living found in Proverbs and the New Testament wisdom book—James. We must care how God desires for us to live, study his Word, and adopt those principles for our habits of daily living. Such knowledge will go a long way toward structuring a sound, stable, and pleasant life. God does not play "hide the ball"—he sets out the best way to live and desires for us to study and internalize those precepts. Observing mistakes by others and seeking to learn from those experiences and avoiding them is another scriptural way to "depart from evil."

Knowing the right way to raise our children, speak to others, hold our temper, receive righteous counsel for big life decisions, and continually digest and review Proverbs will greatly increase the chances that our life will run more smoothly. We all want to set good examples for our children and leave a righteous legacy. In order to achieve this, we need to be "biblically educated" and inspired by the Holy Spirit to listen for the will of God and look for his leading in our lives. It is worth a major investment in our time to daily study how God desires for us to live so that when the heat is on, we will be delivered by such knowledge.

# September 30

## Proverbs Parallels—Multiplication

"When just men increase, the people shall rejoice" (29:2).

"When the wicked perish, the just shall be multiplied" (18:28).

How do just men "increase" or "multiply?" What comes readily to mind is increase of influence in an organization, church, civic group, or government. Increase of power shortly follows. When a national government is filled with leaders whose interest is the advancement of the nation's people—their pocketbooks, their security, and their freedoms—people do rejoice. People living in democracies certainly rejoice when the good of the people is paramount.

If a government is full of corruption, leaders whose self-interest has overtaken their public duty, the people's desire is for those leaders to perish so that good men can take over and be multiplied. These are not promises as much as observations of how the world truly works. Citizens living under cruel dictatorships naturally desire the downfall of their leaders so that good men will emerge. Good men excuse themselves from public service when they cannot admire or honor those in power. But when dishonorable leaders are voted out or ousted by military coup or other powers, the righteous qualified people hiding in the wings step forward to contribute their gifts and skills to the making of a clean new administration.

In repressive governments, where fear of retaliation causes righteous folks to cower at home, reluctant to advocate for freedoms, little hope remains. But when repressive leaders are removed, honest and capable rulers rise to the top, bringing with them other reputable persons known to them to appoint to positions of leadership. Evil men and righteous men are at natural enmity with each other, and neither cares to associate with the other. Evil men attract other evil persons to surround them, saying "yes, sir" to evil requests. Just men attract and seek other just men to round out a government.

# October 1

## Proverbs on Self-Governance—Self-Control

"He that rules his spirit is better than he that conquers cities" (16:32).

Picture someone whose life is out of control—facing overwhelming bills, broken family relationships, addictive behaviors, long-term unemployment, obesity, or a host of other ills. Most of the deep potholes in life in which we find ourselves are brought about by not "ruling our spirit." Personal responsibility is the watchword in our schools today, and the younger children learn this biblical principle, the better. While we have government welfare programs designed to undergird hurting people, most of those programs would be unnecessary if we learned to control ourselves. This one verse, if learned and taken to heart, sets us on the straight path to success in life. Success is the opposite of "out of control": financially responsible, in happy families, moderate in food, drink, having job satisfaction, a healthy body, and sense of purpose.

If we try and fail to conquer our spirits, we should earnestly pray for strength and help in this endeavor. A steady diet of Proverbs, reinforcing in our minds how God wants us to live and how the wisest of men through the ages have set down for our benefit based on personal experience, should keep in the forefront of our decision making the optimal way. Teachers and parents are fond of characterizing life as a series of individual choices, and they are right. Life is lived one choice at a time; we need not be overwhelmed with ten thousand choices for they only "come at us" one choice at a time. If we are uncertain which choice to make, we must seek good counsel. But let's face it, most times we know the right choice, we are simply unable to discipline ourselves to take it. Self-control is the ticket to good life!

# October 2

## Proverbs on Self-Governance—Loose Lips

"A man who can't mind his speech is like a city without walls" (25:28).

We can rapidly get into trouble with fast driving, shady business transactions, or thumbing our nose at the IRS filing requirements, but most of the time, we seem to get ourselves into deep water through loose lips. Yes, loose lips sink ships in wartime, but they more frequently sink our relationships, our respect, our employment, and our children's love by intemperate speech, which we quickly regret. Whether through oral speech, ill-considered Facebook posts, e-mails, or angry memos, once "let out of the barn," the horse can never truly be retrieved. We can likely all remember a discouraging word from a teacher, parent, or peer early in life. We can not only remember the exact words but also the tone of voice and accompanying "look."

If we wish to have a successful work and family life, we must "mind our speech." If we have trouble in this area, we must consciously slow down, letting our brain process the implications before the mouth engages. Whether we count to ten or simply respond, "Let me think about that and get back with you," it's all about deliberation. We must pray for self-control and a governor on our mouth if we are inclined otherwise. Serious regrets arise if we are impulsive. Friends shun us if we cruelly gossip about mutual friends since they envision us gossiping about them in their absence. Employers are looking for diplomatic, tactful, mature employees to represent them. Teachers are in the spotlight all day long. Even when their self-control is frayed by unruly children, they must set a special example since "little ears and eyes" are observing. The book of James discusses how teachers and pastoral leaders are held to a higher standard in the public eye.

# October 3

## Proverbs on Self-Governance—Financial

"Better is the poor man walking in his simplicity than the rich in crooked ways" (28:6).

Is status important to you? Do you wish to be known for your impressive house and flashy car? Your sparkly jewels and impressive wardrobe? Your globetrotting vacations and large charitable gifts? Look out. Since pride is the root of our overwhelming desire to impress others, we know that we are out of God's will if that is our top priority. A priority to impress is generally dependent on over-spending—living beyond our reasonable means. This verse warns against this pitfall.

Marketing organizations categorize consumers into well-known demographic groups: frugals and status seekers are the two main categories. The clear indicator of a frugal is someone who pays off their credit card each month. If you do not do this, examine your ways and evaluate whether your overspending is to impress others or because you lack self-control. Dave Ramsay and other Christian financial counselors have excellent radio programs, books, and DVD courses to help us get on track with moderation and frugal expenditures.

In addition to expressing overweening pride, the desire to impress is risky because it tempts us to adopt "crooked ways" to achieve our goal of attaining that extra money to afford the new car, house, or trip.

If I just had X, we think we will be satisfied. But the older we get, the more we realize that materialism is an upward spiral—enough is never enough. As a matter of fact, studies have shown that the more stuff we have, the less we appreciate that stuff and the more we crave additional stuff. Stuff takes so much time and attention to maintain, organize, search through, clean, and pay taxes on. Simplicity is the key—it is "better" in all ways.

# October 4

## Proverbs on Self-Governance—Self-Correcting

"He that is righteous corrects his way" (21:29).

When we are toddlers, a spanking or timeout is required to correct our way. When we are teens, grounding or confiscation of car keys is often used to correct our way. When we are in college, a D or F operates to get our attention so that we will correct our way in more dedicated studying. When we enter the workforce, a poor annual evaluation or failure to get a pay raise may be required for us to rededicate our work ethic or improve our skills. Once we're married, a threat by a spouse to leave because they "cannot tolerate that behavior" sometimes causes us to seriously rethink our treatment of another. If we have a problem with drinking or drugs, a family's threat to intervene and throw us in the dry out institution may wake us up. If we are skirting the edge of the law, an arrest and overnight jail detention may save us from the penitentiary.

But true maturity calls for us to self-correct. That is, the just man is aware of correct behavior and does not require anyone to shape up or ship out. We know when we are sliding off the narrow way and change our ways in a timely manner before serious consequences ensue. How does the righteous person learn the correct way? She/he diligently studies Proverbs and other books of wisdom and observes negative consequences suffered by others in an attempt to avoid copying that behavior.

Perhaps we recall self-correcting typewriters from the 1980s, which contained a roll of whiteout tape to easily backspace and cover typos before moving on. This implies that even if we have messed up—made a mistake—we do not compound that mistake by continuing in the same vein, but we stop, change course, make amends or restitution, apologize and move on before someone else calls us to task.

# OCTOBER 5

## Proverbs on Self-Governance—Hardening

"The wicked man impudently hardens his face" (21:29).

What is our reaction when someone criticizes us? Do we "blow it off" as based on jealousy, spite, or ill will? Do we have the personal impression that we cannot have done anything wrong so we fail to even seriously evaluate the criticism? Do we believe we are infallible? If so, we are not governing ourselves in a realistic manner. We all make mistakes, so even a hint of criticism should be closely considered in all soberness.

The chief characteristic of a fool as described in Proverbs is someone who fails to heed advice, fails to entertain notions of a better way, and turns his back on suggested improvements. Instead, he "hardens his face," becoming entrenched in his "know-it-all" view from the "top" of the mountain. Do we catch ourselves deeply resenting any hint of advice from others? In such case, pride has taken over and our reasonable minds have been tainted by pride.

Oftentimes, the hardening of the face is evident in the set of the jaw and the tightening of the mouth. We can picture the bitter person whose heart has hardened past help. Look in the mirror. After receiving a bad report, are you hardening your face? It may require prayer to soften our spirits enough to enable advice to truly soak in and be deliberated over. Pride and "hardening" are inseparable. If we seriously cannot fathom how we could ever be wrong, we are "over the hill" to hardness and had better take another look at ourselves.

If our enemy gives us a "blow," we are to turn the other cheek according to the gospels. I believe this encompasses preparing ourselves for additional criticism by peeling off the hard cover to let sincere advice soak in, especially if it comes from a loved one.

# October 6

## Proverbs on Self-Governance—Watched

"The eyes of the Lord in every place behold the good and the evil" (15:3).

If we are having difficulty self-governing appropriately, we can remind ourselves that one reason it is important to self-govern is that God is watching everything we do. Not only will we be judged at the end of our days but even now, this very instant, God is watching. We can remind our tender children, in a factual but nonthreatening way, that God is watching everything they do so they should try to please him in every way. Just like kids tend to go wild in the classroom when the teacher steps out, our attitude and "reins on ourselves" might be different if we thought God was way up in heaven not heeding or caring about our conduct. But we are assured that he is watching both the good and the evil.

When we are faced with a temptation and think no one will find out our suboptimal choice, this verse assures us differently. If we are having trouble keeping this concept in mind, consider posting a picture of an eyeball on our bathroom mirror, our car rearview mirror, or our gym locker. Greeks have a culture of wearing a blue stone pendant called an "eye of God" around their necks. Wherever and whatever it takes to keep this principle forefront in our minds can be helpful in keeping us on the narrow path.

While people fear more and more that Big Brother is watching our every move with cell phone tracking, urban cameras, credit card transactions, and toll road receptors, these are less important than the fact that God the Almighty is watching not only our external actions and words but also the motives of our hearts and our thoughts.

# OCTOBER 7

## Proverbs on Self-Governance—Preparation

"It is the part of man to prepare the soul" (16:1).

How do we prepare ourselves to live correctly and govern our actions appropriately, living obediently to God's commandments? It is our duty to prepare our soul. We must feed it with knowledge of God's precepts, review regularly those precepts, and think deeply about how to apply them in our daily lives. Regular study of Proverbs is helpful. Some follow the way of wisdom, reading the chapter of Proverbs corresponding to the day of the month. Listening to sermons, live or on the radio, attending Bible studies, DVD ministry series, and delving deeply into scriptures with prayer and meditation time is key to consciously turning our attention to God. We must listen for his leading and pray often "Thy will be done." This helps us to align our souls toward God and our conduct to be pleasing to him.

How else may we prepare our souls to live correctly? Taking "captive" our thoughts as described in the Epistles is crucial. Just because a sinful thought enters our mind does not mean we must follow through and dwell on it. If we know it is displeasing to God, we should promptly refocus our mind on something uplifting, edifying, or inspirational. If we find ourselves having difficulty keeping the thought banished, we should implore the Holy Spirit for strength and aid. Our mind and soul are closely related, so keeping our thoughts pure is our responsibility. We should turn our mind to others in need and think about what acts of service we may do in furtherance of God's kingdom. Focusing on others replaces our self-absorption and is pleasing to God.

Preparing the soul is our duty according to the verse. Let us use our imagination to find resources and opportunities to rightly prepare our soul.

# October 8

## Proverbs on Self-Governance—Honesty

"A good man is guided by his honesty; the evil man is destroyed by his dishonesty" (11:3).

Honesty is the best policy we have heard since we were children. That is about the simplest restatement of this verse. In corporate America, the "headline test" is sometimes used in employee training as a shorthand way for individuals assessing the potential impact of an action or decision about to be made. That is, how would the headline read in describing the business decision, if revealed to the world? For example, "Corporation X hides impact of Y drug to detriment of millions!"

Thinking about the consequences of a decision being made public or even found out by our closest friends and associates has a way of crystallizing our thinking. What about the legacy we want to leave for our children? How would we want our obituary to read? One clear sign of maturity is "spinning out the reel" of our lives and thinking ahead, picturing how an action of ours would impact others and be seen in hindsight.

Greed is at the root of most dishonest decisions, but if we focus instead on God's numerous promises to abundantly provide, perhaps this would lessen our striving which causes us to skate close to the edge of honesty. This verse concentrates on the self-guidance we achieve by abiding by simple rules of honesty. When we are mature Christians, an honest decision shouldn't have to be made after agonizing at long length over alternatives or seeking counsel from many. Maturity springs from repeated right actions which pave the way for automatic choice of ultimate right actions. Obedience to God's desires for integrity and honesty in our life springs from guidance of the Holy Spirit, well understood principles revealed in the scriptures and our God-improved conscience.

# OCTOBER 9

## Proverbs on Self-Governance—Commitment

"Commit your work to the Lord, then it will succeed" (16:3).

We best govern our lives and bring about success by starting at the outset with a solid relationship with God. Committing our work carries with it a settled decision to align ourselves and our purposes with the purposes of God. Committing our work has the sense of several precursors. Knowing the Lord, understanding his purposes for the kingdom of God on earth and resolutely deciding that our work, our purposes will be in obedience to Christ's stated purpose: expanding and making pervasive the kingdom of God throughout the world. While many parables and gospel passages describe the kingdom of God in fascinating ways, this theme can be best summed up as invisibility: yeast pervading a large batch of dough, hidden pearl, buried treasure, life-giving force that turns a tiny mustard seed into a large tree.

We cannot see the kingdom of God directly—only its fruit brought about by faithful disciples spreading the Word and acting upon the Word. Committing our work to the Lord is the cause; the effect is success in our efforts. God desires to bless our work dedicated to him. We know his eye is on the righteous and their activities; his watchful eye follows them in their work on earth and is thrilled to multiply their efforts with supernatural working power and by coordinating various efforts of his saints for exponential results.

So then step one is up to us—consciously thinking of and involving the Lord in our upcoming plans and pursuits. If we live our lives without reference to God, our efforts will be on an earthly scale, but if we dedicate, commit our work to the Lord, he sees to it that success results.

# October 10
## Proverbs on Self-Governance—Plans

"We should make plans—counting on God to direct us" (16:9).

Have you known passive individuals diligently praying and praying for direction from God before they take a single step? Sometimes, inertia guarantees that nothing then will begin. Whether we are beginner Christians just learning about the gospels and how we are directed by God or long time followers, we have some knowledge of the world, our capabilities, and the things of God. I believe this verse calls us to exert some effort to think through plans, envision our stated goal, and the individual steps needed to accomplish that goal and begin. Once we step out in faith with the first step, we may hear a nudging from God: not that way, this way. Not here, there. Not him, her. When we begin a task, momentum carries us along and by any of the means God directs us. Sight, hearing, roadblocks, obstacles, closed doors, and diversions—we are shunted along God's preferred course.

Just as a stalled car cannot be easily reoriented until folks push it together and it is in motion, getting started with that first push is a barrier. The law of physics that says that an object at rest stays at rest until moved by a force applies here. But the key point is that this verse is telling us that we must not wait for an external force pushing us; we must use our internal force or will to start the ball rolling, and at that point, God will guide us through nudges, Holy Spirit leadings, or even "bumpers" as at the bowling alley lanes. Paul began a journey to Asia to preach the gospel, but through a dream of a man in Macedonia beckoning them there, their way was redirected. Let us plan and begin and expect God's direction.

# October 11

## Proverbs on Self-Governance—The Path

"The path of the Godly leads away from evil; he who follows that path is safe" (16:17).

A path is a well-worn way, something visible on the ground or through the forest that beckons one onward. It is visible and those following it know where to place their foot for the next step. Even though the walker may not be able to see around the bend or over the next hill, the next step is, by definition, evident. Other notable biblical references to the path are in Psalms, e.g., "Thy Word is a lamp for my feet and a light for my path." A path has been created, in early America, by animal migration, habitual animal movements to water holes or other attractions or native Americans. Nowadays, a path in the wilderness has been created by others going our same way. We know that saints have preceded us in this life, showing us the way to godliness through books of devotion, legacy of godly children and grandchildren, diaries, or testimonies in biographies.

If one is on the Appalachian Trail, the Pacific Coast Trail, the Katy Trail, or other well-known American trails, one must look for signposts to ensure they stay on the path. Signage displays mileage distances, forks in the path, interesting natural features, and other helpful information for hikers. Likewise, those on the path of the godly should be alert to markers of changes in direction, unusual obstacles, and barriers. The goal of a righteous person is to continually remain alert to potential pitfalls—physical potholes or spiritual detours. Scripture itself heightens our sensitivity to errors committed by our predecessors, subtleties of sin, and shades of gray/black. Reading the lives of the apostles and other not so savory characters gives us a leg up on remaining on the godly path of life that leads to heaven.

# OCTOBER 12

## Proverbs on Self-Governance—Wide Road

"Before every man there lies a wide and pleasant road he thinks is right, but it ends in death" (16:25).

This verse takes some thought and analysis. Perhaps the road is wide because many people have previously chosen it and enlarged it from a path to a road. Many of our peers have gone that route, but that doesn't make it the correct or righteous road. Sometimes, if "everybody is doing it," that itself may be a warning to more deeply analyze our choice. This verse reminds one of the well-known Robert Frost poem, "The Road Not Taken": "Two paths converged in a yellow wood and that has made all the difference." The little-trod path deviates from popular opinion since throughout history, the majority of folks seem to waltz through life without thinking deeply about the consequences of their choices. The few, the proud, the Marines? No! The few, the humble, and the righteous.

How do we discern whether the pleasant road is the right one? What criteria do we use? We have examined other verses urging us to seek the counsel of godly advisors since there is "much safety" in the advice of many counselors. A more direct route is to compare our intended path to examples in scripture, especially the gospels. If we are young and immature, our parents likely have travelled the path before us and have helpful experience. Reading "all good books" can vicariously teach life experiences, both good and bad, without our having to suffer through them ourselves.

Perhaps the beckoning road ahead is "pleasant" because it has appealing signs, coming attractions and glistening enticements. The more glitzy the entrance, the more wary we must be to peer behind the entrance to the true nature of the road. It may be a trap for the unwary to end in death.

# OCTOBER 13

## Proverbs on Self-Governance—Hunger

"Hunger is good—if it makes you work to satisfy it!" (16:26).

God created us with appetite for food for a purpose—to get us moving on the path to foraging or these days working to fill our hunger. God created us with hunger, and Genesis also tells us that all things God created were good. Today, we have state and national social welfare programs to help those who cannot feed themselves, along with many local food banks and charities. These make sense for orphans, disabled, the short-term unemployed, and aged folks who are unable to work to earn their living. However, these backfire when able bodied persons able to work are able to apply and receive such benefits. This creates a sense of entitlement. Why would anyone work if they could receive a long-term handout? When developing policies about aid to the poor, this verse should not be lost sight of. It appears to be God's plan that we hunger to incent us to get off the couch, beat the streets or Internet, and apply for jobs for which we are qualified.

More than just food, if we hunger for an education or for an improved life, let that hunger act as a motivator to get going, get busy, make contacts, apply for scholarships, and search out opportunities. What do we deeply desire? If we day dream about opening a gallery filled with original artwork, what are we doing to achieve the dream? If we envision an Olympic gold medal, are we exerting the daily discipline of diet, training, and coaching to systematically work toward that goal? If we hope to see our name in lights, are we seeking out the best voice and dance coaches and rehearsing on a habitual basis? Self-examination about our aims and desires in life is a good thing if it gets us moving.

# OCTOBER 14

## Proverbs on Self-Governance—Pursuit

"Wisdom is the main pursuit of sensible men, but a fool's goals are at the ends of the earth!" (17:24).

What are we pursuing in life? Youth? Beauty? Fame? Fortune? If we are sensible, we have learned that those goals are ephemeral and fleeting. "Nothing but vanity" is the term Ecclesiastes gives to these pursuits. A look at our check register, library checkout record, and calendar quickly reveals our primary pursuits in life. If books of wisdom, teaching DVDs, and seminars/lectures are not appearing in those places, perhaps we should consider whether our priorities are in disarray. What are we recording on TV—entertaining fluff? Or serious programming that explains the science of the universe, history, and the lives of exemplary persons through the ages?

The main goal of wisdom is to make us more self-aware and God aware. How best should we relate to persons, our chief job in life? How best should we become a better disciple of Christ? Are we spending more than one hour in Sunday school each week learning about the Bible and studying its commentaries?

If we want to be a sensible man or woman, not to impress others, but for ourselves and our true success in life, we should rethink how our time is mostly spent. Of course, while we are young parents, the majority of our time may be consumed with little people's needs, but after that phase of life passes, so as to avoid deep regrets later in life on a misspent life, we should brainstorm practical ways to pursue wisdom in life. If you have not viewed any *Great Courses* series, check them out for the world's best educators' lectures on religion, philosophy, history, science, biographies, and the arts (in DVD, CD, and written formats). Many libraries carry them. Getting wisdom—the main pursuit for sensible people.

# OCTOBER 15

## Proverbs on Self-Governance—Vengeance

"If you repay evil for good, a curse is upon your home" (17:13).

Some biblical admonitions are soft and relative, but the mandate to forgive and forego taking vengeance on another is absolute both in Proverbs and the gospels. When I think of extended family unpleasantness, nearly all of it springs from violation of this rule. Most divorces and broken homes result from someone's failure to forgive and grudge holding creating long-term bitterness. Most church schisms, many corporate takeovers and brokenness in our world would cease if this single verse were heeded. While we cannot control the world, we have total responsibility for our position on forgiving others, wiping the slate clean and not repaying evil for evil. The oft repeated saying about our minds being capable of creating heaven or hell on earth springs chiefly from this single principle: "To forgive or not to forgive—that is the question." We must take to heart that there is only one correct biblical answer to that dilemma.

So much energy is wasted on daydreaming about how to get back at "that person" from junior high school to nursing home. If we come to believe that God has created the rules for living with our best interest in mind, we can bank with confidence on the truth that forgiving and "just moving on" is far and away the better course for our bodies, minds, and spirits. "Vengeance is mine, says the Lord" reserves to God the sole job of imposing any needed punishment upon the wrongdoer.

And don't overlook the consequences of contravening this principle: a curse upon our home! Evil boomerangs right back to us and involves not only us but those in our household! If we have problems accepting this clear cut admonition, let us meditate awhile on this cause/effect relationship.

# October 16

## Proverbs on Self-Governance—Selfishness

"The selfish man quarrels against every sound principle of conduct by demanding his own way" (18:1).

This is another crystal-clear biblical principle for self-governance. Selfishness is contrary to "every sound principle of conduct." Of course, it creates for us a poor reputation. Others tend to shun having lunch with a friend who talks solely about themselves and never inquires into what's going on with the companion's life. Children love their grandparents because they generally have the grandchild's feelings in mind above their own sacrificially. The best loved teachers and doctors in the world are the ones who have their students' and patients' interests in mind above their own. The most respected character in our modern world as shown by periodic polls has been Mother Teresa who unselfishly acted to care for the lowest of the low for her entire life.

In short, we shoot ourselves in the foot by acting selfishly. Even if we do not feel unselfish, if we have the strength of will to act unselfishly, our hearts can change. While "fake it 'til you make it" is not a saying commonly applied to self-governance, I believe it is beneficial for several reasons. When we have acted altruistically, we get a dose of the "feel good endorphins," which reinforces our good deeds, making us predisposed to repeat such actions in the future. Expressions of gratitude and positive feedback from those around us act as further reinforcement. Note that the verse explains that not just one sound principle of conduct is violated when we act selfishly but every sound principle of conduct.

In the workplace, who wants to serve on a team consisting of those only looking out for number one? Teams operate more smoothly when team members do not compete to get credit for the outcome but contribute with an unselfish attitude for the good of all.

# October 17

## Proverbs on Self-Governance—Mouthiness

"A fool gets into constant fights. His mouth is his undoing! His words endanger him" (18:6–7).

Think back to school days. Who ended up in the principal's office—the mouthy kid who disrespected the teacher. Who got thrown off the bus, requiring his/her parents to drive them to school for a month—the loudmouth bully. Who gets ejected from the college baseball game—the mouthy player who cussed out the umpire. Who gets arrested at a traffic stop—the driver who loses his/her temper when being ticketed. Who gets fired—the employee who tells the boss what she/he really thinks of him. Who gets murdered in prison—the provocative inmate.

Our mouths, even before our fists or our middle digits, are prone to landing us in deep water faster than nearly anything in life. While self-governance implicates correct thinking, what is allowed to emerge from our lips comes from our hearts and our brains, so our lips are the last best barrier to self-caused trouble in our lives. "Out of the abundance of the heart, the mouth speaks."

When we have children in the car, our response to rude gestures on the part of another driver is surely branded into their minds, filed away for their driving days. When we are arguing with a store clerk, we can be sure that others behind us are straining to hear every word. If we are a Christian, our mouthiness operates as an extremely poor witness that would be hard to overcome by an inquiring church visitor who recognizes us from a recent unpleasant scenario.

If we have noticed a pattern in our recent life of constant fights, it is clear there is a fool in our life—the other person or maybe us!

# OCTOBER 18

## Proverbs on Self-Governance—Forgetting

"Love forgets mistakes; nagging about them parts the best of friends" (17:9).

Psalms says that God forgets our forgiven sins—he wipes the slate clean, and they are as far as the east is from the west. Likewise, we must discipline our minds, with the help of the Holy Spirit, to turn over a new leaf when we are offended. It is our job as a friend to overlook faults, for we have committed plenty of our own. And we all know the same is true of spouses. Once the mistake has been discussed, apologized for, and put to bed, we must move on, not dredging it up during the next three quarrels to throw in our friend or spouse's face. Resurrecting them is apt to cause permanent damage, parting "the best of friends." In order for any relationship to last, this requirement is essential, for we cannot sail through life expecting no bumps and bruises. We are broken people who intentionally or even unintentionally cause offense. Yes, some persons are thick skinned and just let the offense roll off while others are remarkably sensitive and thin-skinned, but we take our friends as they are. We must realize that personalities and sensitivities differ.

Which do we prefer: to be always right or to be friendless? For we surely will be friendless and perhaps forever single if we do not learn and take to heart this essential requirement for relationships.

Have you known people in your career who have jumped from job to job because they "can't stand" this boss or that coworker? Have you known churches never satisfied with their current pastor? Yes, even pastors make mistakes that we must overlook and put behind us. Children must even forgive parents, whose house they live in for eighteen or more years, because parents come home from work exhausted, hungry, and stressed. Humans are mistake-prone; to live in relationship, we must forget mistakes.

# OCTOBER 19

## Proverbs on Self-Governance—Lazybones

"If you love sleep, you will end in poverty. Stay wake, work hard and there will be plenty to eat!" (20:13).

What task is more basic to self-governance than getting ourselves out of bed in the morning? Do you repeatedly hit the snooze button when the clock radio kicks on? That is a serious indicator of laziness (or needing to go to bed earlier!). Ben Franklin encouraged us with "Early to bed, early to rise makes a man healthy, wealthy, and wise!" Surely, this was the source of that quotation from *Poor Richard's Almanack*. A rhyming verse sticks in our mind better and is more easily taught to kids, but the Bible verse is straight from the source of ultimate wisdom.

While growing teenagers are prone to be lazybones in the morning, when we grow up, we must outgrow this habit if we expect to achieve success in life. Many of the best employees are the ones who arrive before others, assessing that their ability to get a lot done works best before other distractions begin. I have found that to be true in my corporate career—the early bird often gets not the worm but the promotion because it is an indicator of consistent diligence. Conversely, the tardy employee screeching into the parking lot twelve minutes late each morning seems to coincide with the employee who cuts corners and does as little work as possible except when the boss is around.

Let's be honest with ourselves: if we habitually hit the snooze button twice, simply reset the alarm to a realistic time to arise on first alarm. If we truly intend to get up at 6:30 a.m., then get up at 6:30 a.m. We can practice keeping our actions consistent with our intentions and get better and better at it—just like other skills.

# OCTOBER 20

## Proverbs on Self-Governance—Alcohol

"Wine gives false courage; hard liquor leads to brawls; what fools men are to let it master them, making them reel drunkenly down the street!" (20:1).

The word that self-governing people must take careful note of is *master*. If we have a family history of alcoholism, this inherited disposition may make it too risky to even touch one drink. If we have no such history, we should develop, at a young age, a self-imposed drink limit. Perhaps one glass of wine on an empty stomach is enough or two with a full meal. Of course, our weight and other medications enter into the effect that alcohol has. Even on special occasions, our self-limit must apply. If we exceed our limit, we can be sure that regrets and embarrassment are sure to follow, not to mention "brawls" and DUIs. Alcohol is a known poison. If we are simply unable to control our intake and stick with our limit, that is the sure indicator of an alcoholic who needs AA or other therapy to return to self-governance.

Only fools let alcohol master them; the same holds true for other harmful addictions. How many careers, marriages, and political aspirations have been ruined by alcohol? Carrie Nation and other temperance leaders in the 1800s campaigned relentlessly against the evils of alcohol, having experienced the terrible damage it wreaks. During the era of Prohibition, it became clear that government control of alcohol was a sham and totally ineffective. While some counties are "dry," it is all too easy to cross jurisdictional lines to the corner liquor store. While some cities require bars to close down at 2:00 a.m. (or other hour), the "party" can be easily moved to a nearby home. That leaves us where we began: self-governance is the only effective tool for alcohol use.

# OCTOBER 21

## Proverbs on Self-Governance—Commandments

"Keep the commandments and keep your life; despising them means death" (19:16).

We have examined individual verses addressing various aspects of governing our life, but this verse takes five steps back to operate as an overall "governor" of our lives. First note that the endpoints of the choices are the ultimate: life and death. We know that "way leads on to way" and the first step in the wrong direction tends to downward spiral into a plethora of vicious consequences. So the most reliable starting place for a life well lived is the knowledge of the commandments. Read them, memorize them, categorize them, and apply them. While many topical books on Proverbs have been written, I found it satisfying early in my study of Proverbs to create a spiral notebook, collecting all the Proverbs verses on anger, speech, wealth, etc., for easy reference.

If we are faced with a dilemma about children, for example, it is easy to flip to our page of all the verses in Proverbs about children to see if a solution becomes clear upon reading this collected wisdom. While concordances can be helpful with regard to references in the entire sixty-six books of the Bible, an individual topical handmade index of Proverbs is very practical as an aid to living life the best way possible. After all, while others give us advice, we govern ourselves, hopefully with help of the Holy Spirit's leadings. The sign of a mature person is when they stop blaming others for their ills in life and take personal responsibility for all their own decisions.

Ignoring the wisdom of the Bible in our life leads to death; whether early or late, the destination is set. Commandments are life giving, tending to life enhancing rewards and consequences. The dichotomy is clear.

# October 22

## Proverbs on Self-Governance—Reverence

"Reverence for God gives life, happiness and protection from harm" (19:23).

We have been focusing on prohibitive verses. This is a positive verse. If we wish to govern our lives so that happiness and protection from harm result, we must adopt the positive attitude of reverence for God. While New Agers may explain "positive karma" as resulting from positive thoughts being projected into the universe, Proverbs clearly sets out a cause-and-effect relationship between reverence for our Creator. Reverence encompasses "giving credit where credit is due." The first step is a simple acknowledgment that God is the ultimate reason for our existence. He created the world, all that we enjoy and us individually, not randomly but purposefully. The beauty of our world, the best creation of all—love between humans and even between humans and pets—is a gift of God. For those things alone, sensible thinkers will acknowledge and reverence God.

But I believe the second principle built on that first layer of acknowledgement is that adoration and gratitude toward God bring upon us further blessings. God desires for us to acknowledge and thank him, and he rewards our gratitude. Just as we are inclined to brainstorm amazing gifts for friends and children who we feel confident will appreciate them, God is a multiplier of our meager efforts at praise. Psalms assures us of this multiplier principle. Other verses assure us that God's eye is upon the righteous—thus, the benefit of protection from harm. He or his ministering angels take special note of those attentive to his commands and obedient to his laws. His "ear is attuned to their cry."

This verse uses the word *happiness*, but perhaps joy is a more apt promise. Psychologists say happiness is dependent on "happenings" while joy springs from our hope of heaven.

# OCTOBER 23

## Proverbs on Self-Governance—Reproofs

"Punish a mocker and others will learn from his example. Reprove a wise man and he will be the wiser" (19:25).

How do you tolerate criticism? Gratuitous unsolicited advice? Reproofs? That is an effective test of our maturity in wisdom. Do we fly off at the handle, get our back up, and become super defensive? If so, we are likely foolish, a rebel, mocker, and disobedient to God. If our feelings are wounded but we have the wisdom to carefully evaluate the remark for any seeds of truth that we should take to heart, we are on the road to wisdom. This is a clear divergence in reactions to criticism. Wise teachers, bosses, parents, counselors, and pastors instinctively know this to be true. If they are trying to gently correct someone in trouble but the troublemaker will "have none of it," there is little hope for improvement in conduct until the person grows a bit in wisdom. Proverbs uses these terms interchangeably throughout: fool, mocker, rebel. A chief characteristic of a person fitting those descriptions is "blindness" and "deafness" to even constructive criticism. The fool is so certain of their invincibility that they refuse to listen to anyone about a better way. They refuse even to acknowledge that a better way might exist, much less one bearing on their life. Self-absorbed people are virtually impervious to reproofs of nearly any type.

How does the word *mocker* equate to fool and rebel? A mocker "blows off" authority, making fun of righteous persons who follow an external standard for their conduct. Mockers don't believe anyone knows more than they do about "their business." Mockers have no respect for authority in general but advice givers in particular. Mockers' egos are so big they block the view of other perspectives.

Listen to reproofs and thrive!

# October 24

## Proverbs on Self-Governance—Good Sense

"Good sense is far more valuable than gold or precious jewels" (20:15).

Few of us would admit we lack good sense. But from where does good sense derive? Godly parents are surely a prime source. Kindly compassionate teachers, even older siblings and extended family, are a huge boon to attaining good sense if we had the good fortune to have them. Of course, we must give credit to wise Sunday school teachers and pastors, scout leaders, coaches, and other positive influences on our lives. But whether or not we have experienced such relationships, good sense flows from God and his scriptures. The book of James admonishes any who lack wisdom to pray to God for wisdom. When the young King Solomon prayed for wisdom to rule his mighty inherited kingdom, God was so pleased with his plea that he gave him not only great wisdom but also magnificent wealth and power to boot.

Good sense naturally leads to a good satisfying life. Gold and jewels do not naturally lead to a good satisfying life—in fact, they can lead to corruption and misplaced priorities. We know that on the final day of our lives, we will not be bemoaning a lack of another ruby, but we may well be bemoaning that we had not matured enough to care about good sense. Good sense probably is the sum of biblical wisdom plus practical life experience. However, good sense does not naturally equate with old age. Some people (especially those who fail to yield to or heed reproofs) never seem to learn. Good sense about handling money, engaging in relationships, relating to food/alcohol, and setting goals in life goes a long way to establishing a platform for a life successful in all its aspects. Those uninterested in attaining good sense are likely on a slow downhill glide to destruction.

# October 25

## Proverbs on Self-Governance—Planning Ahead

"If you won't plow in the cold, you won't eat at the harvest" (20:4).

Most worthwhile blessings in life require planning and systematic effort. It is so easy to make excuses and procrastinate hard jobs, but time gets away from us, and before you know it, empty pantries result. The wiser we are, the more we recognize that days, weeks, months, and even years of effort are needed to achieve most desirable ends. The more we mature in wisdom, the more regular become our habits of accumulating the necessary calendars, memory joggers, best laid plans, and systems to regularize our life events. Not forgetting a grandchild's birthday, let's face it, is a major motivator to keeping diligent calendars and "dayminders." Thank goodness for smartphone calendars with daily reminders.

Planning ahead requires an investment, not only in time but also in accumulated good habits. Have you been to a workshop about how to efficiently organize your affairs anytime in your life? Professional organizers have developed numerous tips to get us started, but I think this verse speaks more to following through on intentions than it does to adopting technology. First, we must sit down and prepare goals, developing intermediate and direct steps to accomplish those goals. Some people may not have estimated the seed needed for planting, much less ordered the seed, calculated the frost date in their locality and serviced the tractor and planter to enter the field at the right time. Letting things slide catches up with us. Before you know it, the summer drought has hit, and planting season is behind us. Springs rains have passed without our crop benefitting from them, the essential nurturing they need. So many major accomplishments in life consist of an amazingly detailed set of preliminary steps which we must keep on top of. Disregarding them will lead to extreme regret.

# OCTOBER 26

## Proverbs on Self-Governance—Fear of the Lord

"In the fear of the Lord is confidence of strength and there shall be hope for his children" (14:26).

People who maintain the appropriate respect for God, the Creator of us and the universe, are rightly aligned with eternal values and know it. When they firmly believe that God is God and they are not, they are a created being of God; their perspective is correct. Knowledge of this correct perspective pervades the soul, bestowing confidence of strength. This comes from knowing that God is their protector and that death, the ultimate fear of many, is not to be feared but merely acknowledged as a transition from one state of being—life—to another state of being—eternal life in God's presence in heaven.

Christians with confidence of strength do not fear what others can do to them and do not fear the future in life. God's promises of provision take away worries about "will there be enough?" "Will I be able to provide for my family?" Faith in God puts to rest fears of all shapes and sizes. Fear of illness dogs many, but we are promised that God will be with us throughout life—through good and bad, health and sickness. While many unpleasant events can occur in our lives, many are brought about by our misconduct and lack of sense. If we are striving to live by God's commandments, the ultimate fear—of evil and death—is reduced to another event in life. Dread does not loom like a scary monster but a season in life that God will help us through.

And don't overlook the last promise of this verse: a bountiful legacy of hope for our children. While abuse, evil, and sin abound through families for generations, so does righteousness and hope!

# OCTOBER 27

## Proverbs on Self-Governance—Daily Communion

"Blessed is the man who hears me and who watches daily at my gates" (8:34).

Have you established a habit and pattern of daily scripture reading, prayer, and meditation? If you want to be blessed, this is the key. Whether you have a daily devotion sent to your e-mail account, a daily scripture delivered to your smartphone, or have a daily book of devotions next to your bed or easy chair, it is up to us to prepare daily reminders to turn our mind to godly things. We cannot simply hope we'll find a spare moment to spend time with God. We must pave the way for communion to happen with our daily routines of life. Most diligent disciples find that morning is the best time to establish "time alone" with God; otherwise, the day simply gets away from them, and they're too tired at bedtime to pick up scriptures. Much like giving firstfruits of our income, dedicating firstfruits of our time pays off in godly living.

Hanging a religious calendar on our bathroom mirror with daily thoughts and a scripture reading is a help. Having a container of cards with scripture verses on the breakfast table is another way to turn our thoughts to our Creator. Praying while taking our daily walk or run is a laudable habit to develop. Life is daily and there is great virtue in letting the dailiness of life work in our favor as far as religious life goes. Keeping our car radios tuned to religious music helps our minds dwell on praise music. Often, these tunes get "stuck in our heads" (the Germans have a phrase "earworm" to denote this phenomena), so that in the middle of the night when we awake, the song is playing, or the first thing in the morning. There are innumerable ways to further daily communion with God in our lives—be creative!

# October 28

## Proverbs on Self-Governance—Covetousness

"The ways of every covetous man destroy the soul" (1:19).

"Fools covet things which are hurtful to them" (1:22).

Does your mind dwell on getting, getting, getting? If so, perhaps we are spending too much time perusing catalogs, cruising Amazon for deals, and scouring the want ads. We "feed" our habit of coveting by doing such things. Recreational mall cruising certainly pumps up our feelings of covetousness. Whether we are stopping by Armani Exchange or the Goodwill, continually turning our minds to acquiring things can be habitual and not in a good way. Television series like American Pickers and Hoarders reveal how many folks make a hobby and habit of purchasing things. The thrill of the hunt is apparently what motivates "pickers." There are worse habits to cultivate, but there are better ones as well.

What if we made a conscious effort to check our covetousness by turning our minds to the needs of others? Volunteering at our local hospital? Library? Meals on Wheels? Elementary school reading program? God created us to be blessed by helping others in need. We will feel better and be prouder of ourselves if we assess our gifts and talents and find a way to give instead of acquire. Giving of our gifts to prepare tax returns for the elderly at our local senior center or serve meals at our local soup kitchen will pay dividends in our self-worth. If we are handy with a saw and hammer, handyman or woman programs for shut-ins is a gratifying way to use our talents and bless others. If we are crafty, joining a charitable crafters guild for knitters, quilters, or crocheters can benefit the local hospital or nursing home while we bless ourselves. Reading to elementary children or becoming a student mentor can redirect our coveting bent to a self-giving bent. These activities will bless our soul instead of destroying our soul.

# October 29

## Proverbs on Self-Governance—Redirection

"Turn your foot away from evil and He will make your courses straight and bring forward your ways in peace" (4:27).

The choices we make in life originate first in our mind but next in our feet. To where are we walking or driving? The casino? Local bar? Strip club? Evil and bad habits lurk in such places. Even if invited by a good friend, it is up to us to turn our feet away from such places. These days, our fingers may also lead us into evil: porn sites anyone? By exercise of our will, with the help of the Holy Spirit, we can choose wholesome places as our destination. Setting goals to spend time with our families or to increase our time volunteering will "make our courses straight and bring forward our ways in peace."

If the ultimate desire of our hearts is to dwell in a state of peace, this practical verse clarifies our role in attaining that desire. We must redirect our path and steer clear of places where temptations abound. Those decisions are clearly within our purview, peer pressure notwithstanding. If our life is a slough of despond (*The Pilgrim's Progress*), we can return to solid ground by thinking clearly about our desired destination and setting our course in that direction. If we are in the grip of some type of addiction, it is up to us to take that first step to locate a local AA or rehab institute. The path will get swampier and swampier if we allow sin to suck us down. There is solid footing nearby if we can turn ourselves toward it.

How does peace result from a worthwhile solid path? At a deep level, our souls recognize that following God's commands is right. Our guilt level declines and we know we are accepted by God.

# October 30

## Proverbs on Self-Governance—Diligence

"Well does he rise early who seeks good things" (11:27).

First things first. How are we about getting ourselves out of bed in the morning? Do we hit the snooze button three times? Do we cover our head with a pillow to catch forty more winks? If so, we are wasting time—burning daylight as they say. If dragging ourselves out of bed is difficult, we must examine our bedtime to determine whether we would benefit from an earlier bedtime. Our very first act of each day is emerging from the bedclothes and facing the tasks of the day. While some folks are naturally morning persons and others are not, we all can become more productive morning persons by moving up our bedtimes to ensure we get a full complement of sleep.

If we defer getting up and have a deadline to meet, our punctuality at work or at our meeting will be compromised as we scurry about, stressed already, to get ourselves ready and out the door. A more relaxing day begins with sitting up and getting out of that bed when the clock radio clicks on. If we often have "time to burn" between the alarm and exit from our house, then we can either reset our alarm for later or resolve to use that time to pray for those about whom we are concerned. Diligent use of our first moments sets a good tone for the rest of our day. We feel better about ourselves if we rise to the occasion and not procrastinate our first task. Diligence gives us a boost to move forward in achieving the rest of our goals for the day. Our energy level normally is highest at the beginning of the morning and dwindles as the day goes on. We were designed by our Creator to "get to it" in the morning.

# October 31

## Proverbs on Self-Governance—Our Thoughts

"The thoughts of the industrious bring forth abundance" (21:5).

Have you heard the saying, "If you think you can, you can. If you think you can't, you can't." Some psychologists theorize that energy flows from the brain waves in our heads—that our thoughts truly do create our life on earth, be it heaven or hell. While science is still studying this phenomenon and someday may be in a position to objectively verify this theory, this Proverb affirms that the plans and goals of the industrious person get results! Perhaps this is an upward spiral of good plans, good effort, and good results giving us confidence to reach for higher goals in the future.

How do your thoughts run? If they tend to negativity, gloom and doom, examine how they relate to your efforts. Perhaps we need to clean up our act on hard work which will boost our confidence level to breed creative goals. The relationship between diligence and thoughts is fascinating. While popular self-help books tout the benefits of positive thinking, the missing link may be diligence. Our effort figures in to our success; mere positive thinking without effort is lacking. Elbow grease is as important as the right vision. They go hand in hand. A precondition to the effectiveness of positive thinking is hard work and willingness to continue that work when a new creative idea is birthed.

God blesses us with creative ideas, and perhaps he chooses those to bless who have demonstrated in the past that those ideas will not "go to waste" or "die on the vine" due to lack of effort. If you were a grant bestower, a charitable benefactor or philanthropist deciding who to award funds to, we as humans can identify with a desire to reward those who in the past have worked hard to achieve their goal. Maybe God does the same since we are created in his image.

# November 1

## Proverbs on Fools—Know-It-All

"Fools despise wisdom and instruction" (1:7).

It is instructive to familiarize ourselves with the characteristics and attributes of a fool so that we may avoid those pitfalls. Proverbs is rife with descriptions of fools; righteous persons do well to learn and heed those descriptions. We must continually examine ourselves to ensure we are not exhibiting those traits and, if so, correct our path.

The most obvious trait exhibited by a fool is a "know-it-all" attitude. Fools believe they hold a monopoly on knowledge, wisdom, and common sense and "no one can tell them anything." They do not spend time or money on books, lectures, or instruction of any kind. They have no use for wisdom of elders or those experienced in a field. They plow ahead heedless of caution flags from others and secure in the conviction that they and only they are the true experts.

Wise persons, on the other hand, are constantly on the lookout for new knowledge, advice from experts, and books bearing on a pending issue. Their egos are not so inflated that they cannot hear tips from others, especially those who have trod the same path earlier. Humility entails dismissing our egos so that we may listen and pay attention to avoid pitfalls of others who have been that way. It is patently obvious that anyone who has done something before will know more than the newbie. Wise persons can always benefit from learning about the experiences of others.

Travelers pick up a guidebook; travelers on the path of life do well to pick up the universal guidebook—the Bible. Fools consider history books a waste of time; wise persons familiarize themselves with history so as not to repeat it but to improve on it. Let us pause and listen to advice from others and from the ages.

# November 2

## Proverbs on Fools—Criticism

"Go against a foolish man and he knows not the lips of prudence" (14:7).

Fools simply cannot stand anyone telling them what to do. If someone attempts to instruct or help them, they fly off the handle and get incensed. They cannot believe the impudence of another thinking they lack wisdom in how to proceed. In their view, this is a rude insult to imply that they are somehow lacking in knowledge. Even if the speaker is truly trying to be helpful, the fool takes the comment as an insult to their intelligence or preparation. This indicates that pride is an overarching trait of a fool. Lack of self-control is akin to this, for flying off the handle exhibits anger and imprudence.

If an acquaintance of yours puffs up and gets super defensive when you make a comment, beware. This fool is not the kind of friend you want to bring into your fold of close buddies. Anyone who blithely brushes off or, worse, angrily bristles when receiving advice is a candidate for an A-1 fool.

If you are in a large meeting and someone exhibits extreme defensiveness, note carefully that trait and avoid promoting them or assigning them additional responsibility. Wise persons want and need to listen to the views of others; their ego is not slighted by taking time to hear the observations of others, especially those longer in the business. Also, however, managers should not close down comments by the least experienced. Sometimes, they have "fresh eyes" and can think outside of the box in a truly creative way. That is the primary job of a manager: to hear all sides, weigh alternatives, and choose the best option.

If a CEO's ego is such that she/he has only "yes men" around them, that company is in danger since it is led by a fool. Listening to advice and criticism is the sign of a prudent person.

# November 3

## Proverbs on a Fool—Parents

"The fool despises his mother" (15:20).

"A fool laughs at the instruction of his father" (15:5).

Take careful note of how a person speaks of or treats his/her parents. This single indicator tells a great deal about a person. The Ten Commandments instruct us to honor our parents. Rebelliousness begins at home, and failure to honor one's parents indicates that bowing to authority has not yet been learned, and therefore, the person will necessarily experience a rough time in the workplace, in a marriage, and as a member of any church or organization.

While the majority of parents are good-hearted and do the best they can raising children, even abusive or cruel parents must be pitied by their children. An abusive or cruel parent undoubtedly suffered a poor childhood and, for that alone, deserves pity. Grown children of abusive parents do not have to closely associate with their parents in adulthood but nevertheless should do their best to show basic respect for them. No one is perfect and children must acknowledge that their parents spent years in self-sacrifice to raise them despite their flaws.

If a parent gives us instruction, again, nearly all parents have the best interest of the child at heart. The fool, however, "blows off" any attempt of the parent to instruct them. This is a sign of immaturity on the part of the child to ignore or laugh at parental advice. There is likely no one on earth more likely to love us and want the best for us than our parents. For this reason alone, parental advice should be considered and heeded more than that of our peers or others. It is a rare parent who does not dearly love their child and want the best for them; they must be given the benefit of the doubt and, at a minimum, listened to with respect.

# NOVEMBER 4

## Proverbs on Fools—Unreliable

"Don't rely on a fool" (26:6).

"Wisdom is too high for a fool" (24:7).

Why is a fool unreliable? A fool does not carefully study the facts or take advice from others since they believe they alone know it all. A fool is self-centered and prideful so has little regard for the impact his/her decisions make on others. Lack of consideration for others leads one to setting little store by the effect of his/her decisions on those counting on him/her. If an acquaintance proves unreliable more than once, we should reconsider whether we should invest further in the relationship or depend on him/her. In short, unreliability is a primary indicator of a fool. There may be many reasons for such unreliability: failure to study, failure to plan or prepare, lack of regard for the consequences, lack of care about anyone but oneself. All them lead to disappointed persons, burned by unreliability.

This description should prompt us to self-examine. Are we dependable? Faithful? Reliable? Punctual? Do we follow through on our promises and carry out our responsibilities? If not, we should strive to improve our virtue of faithfulness, a rare virtue. The righteous person knows that our example in life is witnessing for Christ. Others take careful note of our follow-through. If we fail to carry out our assumed or assigned responsibilities, we are slandering the goodness of Christ to the world. Our reputation for faithfulness reflects directly on our excellence as a disciple of Christ.

Some may treat punctuality lightly, but wise persons realize that others must waste time waiting on us to show up or complete our portion of a joint task. This is rank inconsiderateness to presume that others' time is less important than ours. Let reliability be our hallmark.

# November 5

## Proverbs on Fools—Pitiless

"The soul of the wicked desires evil; he will not have pity on his neighbor" (21:10).

God is merciful; righteous persons should strive to reflect this endearing characteristic of God. Fools, on the other hand, are wicked and exhibit the opposite of mercy: pitiless. They lack compassion for those in need—the widow, orphan, needy, or sick. The book of Isaiah speaks repeatedly of justice as being closely tied to this characteristic. The prophet exhorts the people of God over and over to love God by displaying mercy to the marginalized in society. The culture of the time had gotten hard-hearted; people looked out for number 1. Isaiah urged repentance of this trait and encouraged the Israelites to stand out in a crowd, differentiating themselves from the culture by their speech and actions in caring for their neighbor.

If you are a single person considering a person as "spouse material," how the candidate treats the least of the least is a powerful indicator of his/her heart. Are they merciful and compassionate or harsh and pitiless? How they treat you one future day after the "glow" has worn off is indicated by their treatment of others. Most marriage counselors observe that the honeymoon phase of a relationship generally runs about eighteen months. Thereafter, the daily grind of life overshadows the giddiness of first romance, and an even-keeled merciful spouse willing to forgive our foibles will "wear" much better than a hard-hearted, impatient spouse who displays pitilessness. Will your fiancé give you the benefit of the doubt or hold you to a standard of unattainable perfection?

Some have defined love as a will determined to seek the best in the other, at all times willing good to the other. The wicked fool, however, cuts no slack for anyone and is pitiless.

# November 6

## Proverbs on Fools—Self-Destructive

"The foolish pulls down with his own hands that which is built" (14:1).

How often we watch the news or read the newspaper and shake our heads at the way a fool has self-destructed! Fools fail to think through the negative consequences of a pending decision to understand how things will end up. Gluttons are digging their grave with their knife and fork; addictives are ruining their health, their relationships, and shortening their lives. But even setting these obvious negative behaviors aside, those habitually criticizing their children or spouses are fools for not taking to heart the serious injury done to their egos and security of their relationship. Those in the habit of backstabbing others at work fail to see that such conduct boomerangs, causing others to distrust them, fearing that they will be the subject of gossip when they are not present. Most all negative behavior is self-defeating, ruining organizations and relationships in the long term.

Do you find yourself engaging in self destructive behavior? If so, analyze closely why this is happening. Laziness? Spite? Failure to think through the ultimate consequences? It is easy to see the log in another's eye when they crash and burn due to foolish choices, but we must periodically self-analyze to ensure we are not following suit. We must "run the video" to its completion to see what fallout will occur if we take a certain path. If there is a ticking time bomb in our mouth ready to be released that, once spoken, can never be retrieved, have we envisioned the look on our child's face when they hear it? Words are irretrievable no matter how sincere the later apology, so they must be carefully considered. They not only destroy others' view of us, but we disgrace ourselves and ruin our reputations.

# NOVEMBER 7

## Proverbs on Fools—Dangerous

"It is better to meet a bear robbed of her cubs than a fool trusting in his own folly" (17:12).

When we analyze the metaphor in this verse, a mama bear, the first characteristic that jumps to mind is dangerous. Since a fool trusting in his own folly cares not to hear what others think and therefore has only a single perspective bearing on the situation, it is risky to proceed. Riskiness equates with danger.

The prudent person invites the input of others, considers alternatives carefully, looks both ways, analyzes long-term fallout, and chooses a path carefully. The fool charges ahead without regard for views of others or long-term consequences. The more riding on a decision, in terms of financial repercussions or relationship impacts, the more deliberately we should tread. Many choices cannot be undone once made. Reparations or apologies don't always put things right. Most often, adultery severely undermines a marriage no matter how many dozen roses are delivered or vows of faithfulness are thereafter given. Once trust is broken in a marriage or a business partnership, repair is rarely possible. Once integrity is breached in an employment relationship, credibility is rarely regained. While it takes years to establish a trustworthy reputation, it can be undone in a split second.

To avoid folly, we must not act impulsively on the spur of the moment, thoughtless of the long term effect, but thoughtfully with a view to the ultimate impact. How many employees have been fired after they mouthed off inappropriately in the heat of the moment? How many engagements have been broken when inappropriate flirting or worse occurs? Life is precious; people and their feelings are precious—too precious to charge ahead without thought. There is safety in many counselors, but a fool trusts in his own folly.

# NOVEMBER 8

## Proverbs on Fools—Wandering

"A man that wanders out of the way of doctrine shall abide with corpses" (21:16).

How does one wander out of the way of doctrine? Little by little. Often, a fool stops going to church, so the fool does not receive the benefit of hearing scripture and teaching. Or the fool stops reading the Bible, and therefore, the biblical law fades into the background and does not come to mind at the appropriate time when needed. Or perhaps the fool attends church on Christmas and Easter but drops out of Bible study and Sunday school, thus hearing no explanations of scriptural admonitions. Maybe the fool lays aside all devotional books and turns to crime novels or romance. The less often we apply our minds to learning and understanding scripture and its application to our everyday lives, the easier it is to simply wander "out of the way of doctrine."

This verse warns of the horrendous consequences of such wandering: death! Again, self-destruction ensues since the conscience has become dulled. Guilt piles up, but the heart is hardened so the fool pays little attention to it. Distractions in life are many: sports, entertainment, fashion, and recreational outings—none of which is harmful in itself. However, if these distractions reach such high priority in our lives that we skip church for the "kickoff," the boat ramp, the Sunday soccer league, we are in danger of wandering out of the way of doctrine.

We must deliberately structure our life activities to make absorbing doctrine a key component of our living. We must continually bring to mind the important things in life according to God so that we can order our lives after such priorities. Even though we may be faithful home Bible readers, our pastors are nearly always in a better position to explain doctrine to us in meaningful ways. Let's stay on track.

# NOVEMBER 9

## Proverbs on Fools—Disgraced

"A fool is born to his own disgrace; even his father shall not rejoice in a fool" (17:21).

No one other than God loves us more than our parents. They were present at our first moment in life and raised us from adorable toddlers to adulthood. But we can lose even our parents' esteem if we adopt a foolish lifestyle. If we have done something shockingly foolish, our friends will noticeably begin to desert us, failing to return our calls or accepting our invitations. Our neighbors will turn their heads when they see us in the driveway. Our business acquaintances will make themselves scarce. If we have engaged in criminal acts or foolishly burned bridges in our relationships, we can repent and change our ways. But sometimes, we can never get past our disgraced reputation. Memories are long and clear.

When we lose the affection of our parents, we are surely at the bottom of the pit. Let us use the gauge of the temperature of our parental affections as a barometer of where we stand in life. Even the best of parents can tolerate being "burned" only so many times in the course of our lives. If we trample on the affections of our parents, they are not superhuman and can tolerate disgrace only so far. In thinking through the consequences of our actions, let the anticipated impact on our parents be a measure of the prudence or foolishness of a decision.

The first part of this verse smacks of Calvinism or predetermination, but I don't believe that is its meaning. It is not inevitable that a person become a fool; personal choices are what lead to that category. We can always correct our way and avoid disgrace, even disgrace severing our parental affection.

# November 10

## Proverbs on Fools—Heedless

"A reproof avails more with a wise man than a hundred stripes with a fool" (17:12).

This verse means that you can beat a fool nearly senseless and she/he will disregard it, make excuses, rationalize conduct, and not heed the punishment. The fool will convince himself that he was wrongfully accused, that the rule did not apply to him, or that there was a misunderstanding. The fool will not take seriously the fact that punishment results from violation of a rule. The fool believes the rule applies to everyone else but him. Therefore, punishment of a fool does not act as a deterrent for other fools or for the same fool on the next occasion. It is simply ineffective to change the course of his/her behavior.

In contrast, the wise person pays attention to and heeds punishment or even threat of punishment. We should not need to be beaten with a hundred stripes to change our conduct. The mere suggestion of negative consequences should cause us to thoughtfully reevaluate our intended course. This distinction is one to be watched for when observing the conduct of another person. Do they take seriously rules and their consequences or set themselves up as "sole judge" of whether the rule is intended to be taken seriously? Those in a position to hire/fire or select personnel for a project can learn much from a person's response to potential punishment. Are they ultra-defensive or contrite? Rebellious or humbled? Do they argue heatedly with a law enforcement officer on a traffic stop or show respect and willingness to comply with the officer's requests?

Pride seems to be at the root of the fool's response to punishment. A fool's ego simply will not acknowledge that she/he could have done wrong or that her/his conduct warrants punishment.

# November 11

## Proverbs on Fools—Futility of Wisdom

"A scorner seeks wisdom and finds it not" (14:6).

"The instruction of fools is foolishness" (16:22).

Even if a fool attempts to apply himself to acquiring wisdom, his/her general state of mind and prideful attitude will not allow him to soften his self- defense barrier enough for it to soak in. *Scorner* is a term used virtually interchangeably with fool, rebel, or wicked one. That term alone sums up the posture of a fool with regard to knowledge acquisition. The fool "scorns" the fact that anyone knows more than she/he, and therefore, an offer of teaching/knowledge is most often brushed off. Why would anyone spend any of their precious time under the feet of a sage if their ego is puffed up sky high? The fool's back is heightened so everyone is below his/her level.

This egotistic position is to be sharply contrasted with the wise person who observes all and is always attentive to increasing accumulated knowledge and experience. This characteristic is often summed up in the term "teachability." Its lack is the overarching flaw of a fool that will cause downfalls. Even in the face of available books, teaching CDs, lectures, seminars, and convenient examples, the fool brushes off any need to improve their store of knowledge. A fool's number 1 priority is pleasure, power, selfish desires, and money. Eternal treasures to be stored up in heaven relate to personal relationships, help for others in our purview, and evangelism. The fool has no use for such things, being bent on self-focus. The contrast between the fool and the righteous person looms large regarding this characteristic, but it is next to impossible to make this point to the fool. Refusal to listen to others, even those with his/her best interest at heart, is a fool's chief attitude.

# November 12

## Proverbs on Fools—Thoughts

"The thought of a fool is sin" (24:9).

What occupies your mind? The mind of a fool is occupied with sin of all kind. Is gaining more of the pie for oneself continually on your mind? Is getting ahead in the world, heedless of all others, your primary focus? Is using another person for your own purposes paramount? When you are daydreaming in the car, in bed at night when sleep eludes you, or waiting for someone, what generally is rolling around in your head?

If your thoughts are "neutral"—that is, the pending "to-do" list, what to cook for supper, what next errand is in need of doing, what activities will be waiting for us when we reach home—then we do not warrant the moniker of fool. But if our minds are habitually dwelling on porn, the addiction that entraps us, or how to pay back someone who has wronged us, all those are sin. Holding grudges and vengeance toward the alleged wrongdoer are dangerous paths to let our minds retread. "Vengeance is mine, says the Lord," so we know that habit is clearly wrong, and by force of will and the Holy Spirit, we must "let it go." Most premeditated murders arise from great bitterness engendered by grudges. If a path is getting worn in our brains from repeated dwelling on reliving a wrong, we are on a downward spiral from which we must take pains to escape.

Coveting is another well-worn downward path. If we obsess about our neighbor's new house, car, young beautiful wife, or boat, this is sin. The more we try, in our own power, to not dwell on a sinful subject, the more our mind may return there. The time tested way to avoid this repetition is to replace the sinful thought with a pure uplifting thought—scripture passage or sermon point.

# November 13

## Proverbs on Fools—Imprudence

"The folly of fools is imprudence" (14:24).

"The childish shall possess folly" (14:18).

Imprudence characterizes the immature, the childish. Imprudence is the opposite of common sense, practical, experienced, or well thought out. Imprudence arises from impulsiveness and failure to consider the consequences of an action. Since fools have no use for instruction or the advice of others, they "blow off" instruction manuals and how-to guides and plunge forward on their own, assuming they are capable of figuring out something new themselves.

The prudent, however, go out of their way to cautiously seek advice from someone they know has recently acquired the new object, travelled in the same foreign country, or just suffered the same surgery and physical therapy for recovery. While not everyone's observations are of equal weight, almost all offered advice has a grain of truth in it that should be considered and compared with other comments. Do you call the first carpet cleaner, surgeon, or car repair joint in the Yellow Pages or contact a few trusted friends for recommendations? Experience goes a long way in winnowing out fly by nights. The more that is at stake money wise, health wise, or impact wise, the more prudence should be exercised.

While attending an un-vetted movie only risks a few dollars and an hour and a half of one's time, other decisions involving much time and money warrant soliciting advice from several other trusted individuals. What decisions do you have upcoming in your life, and how should they be handled? Fools flounder from one human disaster to the next, never thinking through why that might be true. The older a person is, the more she/he has learned from negative experiences and the happier they are to save you from similar pitfalls. The fool, however, has no use for the voice of experience.

# NOVEMBER 14

## Proverbs on Fools—Pride

"In the mouth of a fool is the rod of pride" (14:32).

Pure and simple, the root of the fool's brush-off advice from others, instruction from books, or helpful comments is the fact that the fool's opinion of himself is paramount. She/he is unable to fathom the fact that anyone else is smarter or more experienced. Self-confidence, however, is misplaced when the circumstances are new to the individuals. Refusal to study and adopt God's precepts comes from the underlying attitude that no one, not even a supreme deity, can understand our current dilemma.

Step 1 of a righteous person's analysis of any situation, in contrast, is to acknowledge that God is all knowing, all powerful, and omnipresent. God's heaven-high perspective and timeless grasp of all human endeavors is brushed off by the fool. Since "a thousand years is as a day" to God as described in Psalms, God can see background in another age, the future in ages to come, and the impact of this day's choice on our life and those of others around us. Fools think of this moment alone and overlook future consequences. Setting ourselves up as our own idol and above God is the ultimate rod of pride. Fools disregard any need for God or his myriad great powers and characteristics or simply fail to think about them at all. Again, pure self-focus overrides any consideration of God's greater wisdom or the impact of our pending decision on anyone but ourselves.

Regrets pile up quickly for those who ruin precious relationships or self-sabotage their employment opportunities because they impulsively charge ahead without evaluating pros and cons. Shooting oneself in the foot is easier than pie for fools with blinders of pride blocking important external factors bearing on the road ahead.

# November 15

## Proverbs on Fools—Sacrifices

"The sacrifices of the wicked are abominable because they are offered of wickedness" (21:27).

If a fool (wicked person) faces a desperate situation and suddenly decides to try making a vow, fasting, or giving to the church or charity in a last-ditch attempt to effect a favorable outcome, God rejects these measures as futile. Motives are wrong. The wicked person is not acting in faith but in desperation. God turns his head and refuses to accept their sacrifice. Why? Sin blocks petitions. (See 1 Peter.) Another example of this is the gospel parable about the embittered person at the altar praying. Christ commanded that if we were estranged from our brother, we must leave and seek sincere reconciliation before returning to resume our prayers. When we are knee deep in sin, the only initial prayer acceptable to God is a prayer of repentance.

In Old Testament days, of course, persons seeking God's favor brought doves, goats, oxen, and other animals to sacrifice in the temple. The modern equivalent is perhaps to write a big check to the Building Fund, the Red Cross, or United Way. Or perhaps we vow to abstain from alcohol for a period of time: bargaining with God in exchange for a desired outcome. Such bargains are ineffective or may even backfire. They are offensive to God. *Abominable* is a strong word indicating severe displeasure on the part of God. Perhaps desperate measures not arising out of faith harden God's heart against fools, causing him to turn his head or cover his ears when we next petition. Is our heart pure? Are our motives sincere and in accordance with God's will? Or merely self-seeking?

The student desperately praying for help in final exams cannot expect miraculous answers if they have tuned out God for months on end and dug a deep pit of sinful deeds. God's Word is clear.

# NOVEMBER 16

## Proverbs on Fools—God's Scorn

"He shall scorn the scorner" (3:34).

Again, scorner is used interchangeably with rebel, wicked, and fool throughout Proverbs. The fool estranges himself from God by heightening his ego and concluding she/he needs no help from God or his Word. God is omniscient and sees through our masks and facades to our inner motives. He knows the contents of our heart. Acknowledging the fact that we merit scorn from the Creator of the universe should be a serious deterrent to further sin. Thinking through the effect of totally disregarding God's rules for living should have the realistic person shaking in their boots. But the scorner believes she/he is equal to God and has nothing to fear from anyone.

The arrangement of the universe is simple. God made it and the rules governing it and its occupants. The misplaced view that one can disregard those rules is the height of pride and ego. The comparison would be an ant disregarding the power and weight of an elephant coming its way. We are created beings; God is the Creator. If we bother to consider this relative relationship, it should terrify any clear thinking humans. We simply cannot beat the created system. We can scorn the system, but we will break ourselves doing so. Our best efforts to distract our puny selves from this ultimate truth with entertainment, food, drink, wine, women, and song will be ineffective in the long run and draw scorn from God. His patience only runs so far. Much like the whining ungrateful Israelites in the desert, while God is long suffering, his patience does not extend forever.

God brought punishment in the form of war, exile, and sieges on disobedient Israelites, his chosen nation. He will do no less to scorners who today have the benefit of his printed Word and a multitude of churches.

# November 17

## Proverbs on Fools—Transparency

"The devices of the wicked shall be rooted out" (15:5).

One myth that fools hold dear is that no one will ever find out their transgressions—their sins against God or others. Proverbs promises the reverse. Whether in the short or long term, at some point, every sin will become known to the world. Many times in this lifetime, financial or other frauds collapse of their own weight, and the front page news is awash in headlines that are shocking: Enron, mortgage loan collapse, Watergate, arms conspiracies—the list is endless. I believe this Proverb applies to both earthly and judgment day disclosures.

Schemes on earth are betrayed by disgruntled conspirators, prudent regulators, inside whistleblowers, deathbed confessors, and diligent investigators. IRS non-filers are commonly revealed by fraud units. Even if one generation is unaware of a predecessors' sins, the next finds out due to diaries, e-mails, texts, or unerasable documents found on hard drives. The manner of finding out is inconsequential; what is certain is the fact of ultimate transparency on earth or in heaven. A fool is simply blindfolding himself to count on making it to the "end" without a misstep. This verse promises otherwise.

Even if a fool successfully promulgates a fraud to his old age, his/her reputation and legacy to later generations is crushed when ills pop out. A life of respect can be wiped out in a moment of indiscretion. Fools would do well to heed this promise and act accordingly. Any pyramid scheme or complex fraud is subject to collapse based on its complexity alone. We never can escape the x-ray eyes of God's piercing all knowingness; but disclosures of persons such as investigators, treacherous partners, whistleblowers, detectives, and journalists will oftentimes bring ill deeds to light.

# November 18

## Proverbs on Fools—Calamitous Future

"Sudden calamity shall fall upon those who hate instruction" (1:27).

While most Christians are natural optimists, due to their faith and hope of heaven, fools do not enjoy such a rosy outlook. Whether they are born optimists or pessimists, close examination of Proverbs reveals that fools have no basis for optimism. Their misdeeds will find them out, as we have just seen. This verse alone points to a poor outcome for those whose ego and pride put a block on their willingness to accept or even consider advice from others or from scripture.

This prediction is dire, so if a fool cared enough to study scripture and discover this verse, this would put fear into one's outlook. The irony, however, is that fools likely don't care enough to search scripture for practical advice for living and warnings of their future. The interesting twist is that not only do they have negative futures to anticipate but also that the disastrous future will come suddenly—a calamity. Christians reading Proverbs should be deterred by this prediction and incented to stick to the path of righteousness. It is futile for righteous persons, however, to attempt to warn fools, for by definition, their chief characteristic is to "get their back up" and refuse to listen to advice of others. Fools are utterly convinced that they and only they have a lock on the future and that no one knows more than they do how to conduct their life.

God brings about such destruction in a variety of ways or allows such destruction to fall based on the ignorance and foolishness of the fool. If this verse were to come to the attention of a fool, would she/he heed it and change course? One would hope so since the verse is so specific and direct, but a fool must open his/her mind to serious consideration of God's Word before repentance is likely.

# November 19

## Proverbs on Fools—Speech

"Eloquent words do nor become a fool not lying lips a prince" (17:7).

Unbecoming denotes a disconnect—in this case, between character and speech. Even if a fool is a good speaker, the audience will quickly discern that something is afoul. A fool can take Toastmasters training, speech classes, employ a speech coach, or take other measures to make more attractive their speaking ability, but discerning persons can fathom something amiss. "Out of the abundance of the heart, the mouth speaks" is another verse that explains the reason that "eloquent words do not become a fool." When the words emerging from a fool's mouth do not ring true and do not synch with the poor condition of their heart, it doesn't take long for righteous, wise listeners to take notice. Just as Mark Twain commented that telling the truth was so much easier, since one only had to remember one thing, keeping things straight in a fool's storytelling remains difficult.

Similarly, those in authority such as princes must be especially carefully about speaking with integrity. Their subjects expect powerful people to give them the straight scoop since so many eyes are on them and so many have a vested interest in those who govern. If a ruler, senator, or officeholder leads us astray, we are especially chagrined since elected officials are being watched carefully. In Congress, for example, there are ombudsmen, auditors, and investigative positions whose job it is to monitor official speech to judge its integrity and to ensure it is in accord with laws. If an official misspeaks, that error or fraud is much more likely to be found out than when a private individual speaks.

In short, due to the close connection between the condition of the heart and the short pipeline between the heart and the lips, this observation type verse is nearly self-evident.

# November 20

## Proverbs on Fools—Acquisition of Wisdom

"What does it avail a fool to have riches seeing he cannot buy wisdom?" (17:16).

This verse points up the matter of priorities in life. Wisdom can be pursued in this life through reading books, attending Bible studies, studying commentaries, listening to teaching CDs, attending sermons, lectures, and tuning one's radio to Christian teaching. The wealthy righteous man likely prioritizes the acquisition of wisdom and obtains all the most pertinent resources to increase in wisdom. A wealthy fool could do the same if she/he were so inclined. However, the point of this verse is that: 1) a fool with money would be unlikely to prioritize obtaining wisdom, so she/he would be unlikely to desire to spend resources on such acquisition; 2) even if a fool were to spend resources in an attempt to increase in wisdom, the fool could be expected to ignore or brush off advice from wiser persons due to his/her high level of pride.

Righteous persons tend to be systematic about filling in the gaps of their knowledge, observing closely magazine advertisements, billboards, church bulletin announcements, or Internet invitations to seminars or lectures by learned persons. The fool plows through life heedless of golden opportunities, choosing instead to pursue pleasure or self-aggrandizement. It has been said that one's priorities can be quickly evaluated by studying one's checkbook register and personal calendar. This is a call for each of us to look back over these items to get an overview of where and on what we spend most of our free time. If we are not prioritizing acquisition of godly and other wisdom, this is an important aspect of improving our Christian walk. While we can diligently pursue self-study, it is generally much more effective to hear viewpoints of different persons of wisdom to expand our perspective.

# November 21

## Proverbs on Fools—Comparison with Self

"A fool receives not the words of prudence unless you say those things which are in his heart" (18:2).

This verse speaks to the concept of keeping an open mind. Have you seen those Facebook memes showing a pie chart of those "changing their mind" based on Facebook political rants of others? The irony of the chart is that posts by liberals never change the viewpoint of conservatives and vice versa. The chart shows a big fat zero as the number of people whose minds have been changed by something political they read. We all tend to be entrenched in our view and brush off any information deviating from our held position.

In short, a fool has his/her mind made up, and even the most persuasive position of another is quickly disregarded if it does not perfectly align with the fool's long-held position. We are wasting our time in spending resources or effort to dissuade them from their view. The fool puts himself in the position of the sun around which all competing positions orbit. The sun is immoveable; all other bodies are positioned in relationship to the fixed sun. This is the gist of this verse.

Righteous persons, in contrast, are wise if they listen to and consider other positions in case persuasive arguments have merit. Another famous secular quote, "Consistency is the hobgoblin of little minds," echoes this sentiment. Let us examine ourselves: are we utterly immune to persuasions by others? Do we even read periodicals or editorials competing with our settled position? Or have we simply closed our minds to anything not measuring up to our "rut." Times change, world circumstances change, and new scientific discoveries are made daily. The wise person is not so close minded as to refuse to keep abreast of new developments, in the event they warrant a revision of our view.

# November 22

## Proverbs on Fools—Peers

"A friend of fools shall become like them" (13:20).

Wise parents through the ages firmly caution their children that choosing friends wisely can have a lifelong impact on their character and success in life. While Christians should not lock themselves away in Bible studies, social activities, and church functions in a way that isolates them from the secular world; nevertheless, our chosen close friends should best have Christian values. While we are in the working world or serving in community organizations, we will certainly be in positions to rub shoulders with persons of all views. However, in selecting our intimate friends with whom we share leisure time, Christian friends are those we naturally will have most in common with and who will help in influencing us to maintain our Christian walk and growth.

Children have not yet matured enough to understand the dangers of getting pulled off track—either gradually or suddenly. That is why parents sometimes insert themselves into encouraging friendships with good kids. Bullies, rebels who disrespect teachers, parents, and pastors, and other ne'er-do-wells are dangerous peers and may strongly influence tender immature lives. Maturity and wisdom reveal the risks of such associates. When we are young, we are easily flattered by the attentions of others, and our judgment may be impaired when selecting friends. We may be so thrilled that someone is paying attention to us that we fail to consider the long term dangers of close association and including the person in our inner circle of confidants. This verse from Proverbs is short but direct and serves as a warning to those considering their chosen band of friends.

Living the high life with generous high rollers flashing money is tempting, but a long-term view considers character as important as excitement.

# November 23

## Proverbs on Fools—Polar Opposites

"He that walks in the right way and fears God is despised by him that goes by an infamous way" (14:2).

The more mature we get, the easier it is to spot those who hold Christians in contempt. When considering whether to adopt someone as a friend, observe closely how they talk about and treat Christians. Do they pursue unity and overlook inconsequential differences? Or do they display contempt for Christians trying to walk the narrow path? You can tell much about a person by noticing who their enemy(ies) is.

This Proverb is not a "should" commandment; it is a basic observation about how human nature works. I believe this natural opposition of righteous persons and fools arises most likely from the guilt fools feel when around righteous persons. Fools know deep in their souls that they are on a stray path, but their pride and ego will not admit that they are offtrack. As Christians, we want to ensure that the opposite observation is not true: Christians are called to love even their enemy. We must be firm in our Christian witness to treat others kindly, even those we can see are off track, acting foolishly. Since we are cautioned firmly in the New Testament against judging others, our job is to treat others with respect and kindness, not call them to task for misconduct. We must maintain our good example in the hope that they will notice the difference between our conduct and theirs and desire to emulate Christ. We shoot ourselves in the foot if we treat fools with contempt and turn them off from seeking God. Persons are turned to Christ by the love we display, not by a lecture on immorality.

While natural opposites in viewpoint and conduct, note carefully that this Proverb is "one way" only.

# November 24

## Proverbs on Fools—See-Through Folly

"He that is a fool lays open his folly" (13:16).

This Proverb again is not advice or instruction; it is an accurate observation of how a fool operates. Why does a fool tend to lay open his folly? The fool has convinced himself that there is nothing wrong with the way she/he is living, so why cover up? A fool often is shameless, not even bothering to be discreet about his conduct that does not rise to the level of criminality.

This observation should be considered by persons striving to improve their Christian walk. Do we feel guilt when we stray off the path? That is a healthy sign that our consciences have not yet been seared to insensitivity. If we find ourselves not worrying about what others think or God thinks, we are treading dangerous ground. Callouses may be developing on our tender hearts if we fear not what other good persons think.

How does a fool lay open his folly? Perhaps he brags in the office about the women he has seduced or his winnings at the casino. Perhaps he hurries to advertise to his buddies about the new porn site he discovered. Or perhaps she bothers not to hide flirtations with a married man. Have you been shocked when a person bragged about what they shoplifted? Embezzled from their employer? Stolen from their mom's purse? If this conduct does not shock us, it is time for a self-examination. A callous indifference to the reactions of others to our misconduct is a bad sign that we have no qualms about ignoring God's precepts for living. A fool who lays open his folly is not past hope but has made up his mind that his is the only opinion that matters. The more we sin, the less we care about its consequences.

# November 25

## Proverbs on Fools—Banishment

"The wicked man shall be driven out in his wickedness" (14:32).

This verse could be speaking of the last judgment and eternal punishment, consequences for evil conduct on earth by those in authority, or both. I believe it refers most likely to observations about earthly life. If someone is convicted of a crime or merely indicted, most of the person's circle of friends drops them like a hot potato. No one wants to be tainted by exposed wrongdoing or found to be associating with a disgraced person. The person is suddenly dropped from dinner party invitation lists, charitable solicitation lists for fundraisers, and other social opportunities. While the fool is in the midst of wrongdoing, others may not yet be aware of the risky behavior. But once it is formally acknowledged by the powers that be at work, in the community, or neighborhood, other former associates tend to make themselves scarce.

A wise person is aware of this social risk and lets it operate as a deterrent to wrongdoing. Fools, however, will not listen to cautionary advice and charge ahead heedless of this serious consequence. It is the natural result of others' shock at their behavior and the understandable reluctance to be drawn into the net of suspects. Friends wish to avoid at all costs being painted with the same brush so they steer clear. The fool finds himself at home, isolated, licking his wounds and wondering what hit him.

Some Native American tribes would formally banish adulterers, thieves, or other serious wrongdoers from the village. This sets a harsh but firm example for younger tribal members and hopefully deters them from similar misconduct. Some strict Jewish sects, Mennonite and Puritan communities, would take steps to excommunicate sinners who they deemed fools beyond redemption.

# November 26

## Proverbs on Fools—Dishonorable

"It is futile to give honor to a fool" (26:8).

If a personnel manager has a poor employee and wants to prod the employee into self-improvement, the manager might consider praising the employee for the (few) good things the employee has achieved in an attempt to turn around their behavior. Our education system of late has attempted to recognize even small improvements in low-performing students in order to encourage better conduct. If you are married to a mean spouse and think you can change their behavior by focusing solely on their good habits, this tactic is likely futile. This verse tells us we are wasting our time in attempting these measures, for a fool is oblivious to the need to improve and cannot see that attempts to change him/her are of any consequence.

If we spend a lot of time considering how best to get the attention of a foolish low performer, this verse advises us that we'd be better advised to spend our time elsewhere. Fools tend to wear blinders where their own behavior is concerned. They are so self-absorbed that they fail to realize how their foolish behavior affects anyone else. They exist in their own sphere and give no credence to help offered by others in the form of attempts to reinforce good behaviors. They cannot see that their performance in life is less than ideal. The bubble in which they dwell is transparent like bubbles are, so others can see inside their bubble like a one-way mirror. The reverse is not true, though. Despite the transparency, fools don't bother to look out to those surrounding them and care not what impacts they make.

There are many situations in which we might contemplate giving honor to a fool—for their own benefit in an attempt to get their attention. All are futile.

# November 27

## Proverbs on Fools—Definition

"He that devises evils shall be called a fool" (24:8).

How does a fool reveal himself? His preoccupation in life is devising evils. Can you think of examples? If a fool spends a great deal of time obsessing about a grudge and creating scenarios to get even with the offender, this is devising evils. Unforgiveness in general is the central root of so many evil devices.

Those who oppose abortion are on firm ground to lobby, engage in peaceful protests within prescribed "distance from clinics" rules, write articles and letters to the editor, give speeches, and engage in persuasive acts. But if they find themselves plotting to harm clinicians, they have crossed over the line into devising evil since murder is prohibited by the Ten Commandments. Those protesting pipelines for environmental reasons similarly may legitimately engage in political action of all types, but when they move into the realm of planning vandalism to property or harming pipeline construction workers, they are fools for devising evil. If a person is envious of a rival at the office or one competing for a part on Broadway, when they devise sabotage against the other's career by false accusations or injury (like the infamous women's ice skating scandal), they are clearly foolish. "Mean girls" in junior high who slander the other girl competing for the attentions of the high school athlete have devised evil.

We must guard our thoughts as they may quickly morph into devising evil. Envy, jealousy, resentment, and bitterness are generally the beginning of devising evils, which we must nip in the bud. If we find our thoughts stuck in a rotating track, turning over and over in our mind ways to "do someone in," we are in deep water and on the road to devising evil.

# November 28

## Proverbs on Fools—Laughter

"A fool will laugh at sin" (14:9).

Do we take sin seriously or brush it off? Is sin a life or death matter to us or a laughing matter?

A tenderhearted Christian always has eternal values in mind; adopting the mind of Christ reinforces in us the horror of sin in the eyes of our holy pure high God. Since God is absolutely spotless and Christ has covered our sin with his own precious blood, continuing in sin is a slap in the face of our Redeemer. Our reaction to sin reveals a great deal about our state of mind. On a sliding scale, the lighter we deem sin, the more we offend God. While our culture tends to place less and less emphasis on sin, tending to political correctness of not judging others, it is a fool who has devolved to laughing at sin. Even though we are not in a position of judging others' sins, a fool's reaction to sin is the subject of this verse.

Human nature's tendency over time is to accommodate to sin the more it is repeated. The first time we are confronted with a sin in our life or another's, we may have a strong reaction. Gradually, however, we may take it for granted that sin is commonplace in our world and fail to take a stand publicly in a city council, a PTA meeting, or the office conference room. When we see a slow slide into sin, we must check ourselves or our reactions to others, continually reminding ourselves how God views sin. To pattern our lives after that of Christ, we must maintain his view of sin when we confront it. The plumb line of right conduct has not moved during the ages in God's eyes.

# November 29

## Proverbs on Fools—Subordinate

"The fool shall serve the wise" (10:23).

"A fool shall be filled with his own ways and the good man shall be above him" (14:14).

These verses indicate that in the long run, character prevails. People can easily spot fools who casually sin and care nothing for righteousness. In the workplace, corporate executives carefully watch their peers and subordinates, and pure "yes men" of no substance tend not to get promoted. Anyone with a company's best interest at heart knows the importance of integrity, even when no one is looking, and honorable managers generally win the promotion. By natural selection then, the managers of character generally end up on top, and those of lesser character remain in subordinate roles.

In extended families, the "good big sister" often ends up managing the family's affairs since we all want trustworthy relatives minding the business that affects us all. In local civic organizations, the transparency of fools is manifest and their opposites—those of character—win the confidence of the nominations committee. While there are exceptions to these Proverb observations, they both are generally reflective of how society works. Looking to biblical characters, we see this trend playing out as well. Joseph ended up the second highest ruler in Egypt while his conniving brothers bowed to him. Jacob and Esau, Sarah and Hagar, and other side-by-side characters come to mind. King David towered over his older brothers based on character, not age. Merit predominates in most organizations.

In any organization or group, be it a local church or a sorority, since most members want the best for organizations of which they are a part, they naturally gravitate to selecting leaders they respect. A fool tends to "try too hard" to impress others, but others see through them. The best leaders, like Abraham Lincoln, are respected due to their humility.

# November 30

## Proverbs on Fools—Dense

"Wisdom is enshrined in the hearts of men of common sense, but it must shout loudly before fools will hear it" (14:33).

Wisdom is attainable, but fools have no desire to find it and, therefore, ignore it even when it is nearby. What do you spend your leisure time doing? Selecting and perusing profound books or educational TV programming? Or watching mindless entertainment? We all need downtime; we all need "nonthinking" activities when our minds are in "neutral." But fools care not for improving their minds in godly wisdom. Normal volumes of lectures, newspaper articles, new books, or educational programming do not interest or catch the attention of a fool. It takes a very high "shout" of volume to gain the attention of a fool, whose attention is directed elsewhere. Fools have blinders on their eyes and ears. Fools, in a word, are dense, inattentive, heedless, and distracted by flashy attractions.

Knowing this characteristic of fools, we would all do well to examine our time priorities from time to time to determine whether we are wasting precious hours on earth in worthless pastimes. There are many verses in Proverbs and Psalms cautioning us to carpe diem, seize the day—not put off 'til retirement or old age serious pursuit of godly precepts. Perhaps we think that when we are young, we have a free ticket to live our life how we want it, thinking there'll be plenty of time to get serious as we approach old age and death. If so, this is a sad attitude which will most certainly lead to regrets. When we are in our last decade of life and our mind turns to heavenly issues, we will wish we had diligently studied God's Word, concentrated on other books of wisdom, but it will be too late. Do it now.

# December 1

## Proverbs on Finishing Well—Aging

"Love and keep wisdom and it shall preserve thee" (4:6).

"Old age is a crown of dignity when it is found in the ways of justice" (16:31).

If we heed God's directives as found in Proverbs and elsewhere, aging can be a time of increased satisfaction, a time of contentedness that we've lived right without many regrets. Age can be a truly golden period when we reflect back over our relationships, our accomplishments, and our future in heaven. If we have treated others with justice, we can be proud of our life's work and secure in the knowledge that our legacy will be a good one. Our children and grandchildren can take pride in our life, and our church and community will mourn our loss.

The "preservation" spoken of in chapter 4 can be of two types: preservation of our mental and physical powers and preservation of our very lives. If we have followed a righteous path, our guilt level will be minimal, and our physical health will not have been harmed by focusing on angry feelings, grudge holding, or payback vendettas. When we lay down to sleep at night, our sleep will be sweet, unhindered by visions of "should have beens." When our every step is molded to God's will, God promises to bless our lives, our families, and our endeavors.

Of course, old age brings natural physical aches and pains, but the minimization of mental anguish enhances our manner of existence. Even if we face serious physical diagnoses, reveling in the promises of God to watch over us and walk alongside us lifts our spirits and gives us a sense of peace. Whether our earthly circumstances and family situations are pleasant or involve lacks, redirecting our attention on God and his wisdom for our lives is a mood enhancer.

# DECEMBER 2

## Proverbs on Finishing Well—Long Life

"Forget not God's law and keep his commandments for they shall add to you length of days" (3:2).

"Length of days is in wisdom's right hand" (3:16).

Have you noticed this correlation? Saintly people age gracefully and well; moreover, they live longer as a general rule. Billy Graham and Jimmy Carter come to mind as do many in the church. If you have not observed this pattern, think back over your favorite delightful elders—the sweeter the older. Life seems to make us better or bitter as it progresses—more saintly or more curmudgeonly. Age magnifies our basic tendencies—the passage of time enhances the essence of our personalities and concentrates its attributes for good or ill.

While generalizations remain generalizations, there is truth in these Proverbs, corroborated by our life experience. Those dying young in tragic accidents often do so due to rebellious acts on their part: reckless driving, drinking, drugging, fistfights, disobeying orders of law enforcement officers, or alienating family members. Close observation of sweet elders reveals the opposite: they were good children who obeyed their parents, listened to their teachers and did well at school, obeyed their coaches and excelled in sports, complied with their bosses' directives and were promoted at work, and avoided arrest their entire life! Compliance with rules, God's and the world's, smoothes our way in life and skirts many of the most obvious potholes and risky behaviors. Faithful spouses avoid the rage of jealous "other husbands." Rule followers avoid traffic stops. Honest tax filers escape IRS audits. Character in the workplace skirts Department of Justice investigations.

Summing up, our life on earth and in heaven is blessed by our wise living, wisdom being defined as closely adhering to God's Ten Commandments and will for our lives.

# December 3

## Proverbs on Finishing Well—Gratitude

"Count your blessings and be satisfied with what you produce" (27:27).

Are you in constant turmoil over what you don't have? Or are you at peace and thankful for what you do have? This single self-analysis helps us to correct an unhealthy perspective and focus on the provider of all life's blessings. All worship arises first from an attitude of gratitude, so if we are continually striving for more, focusing on our lack, we will be unable to cultivate a sincere attitude of worship.

The purpose of all our multibillion-dollar advertising industry is to create in its viewers discontent and wanting more, more, and more. Advertising promotes comparisons and envy, which leads us to making ill-advised, unnecessary purchases. Consumerism is largely driven by this false created sense of need/want. We can boost our mental and spiritual health by putting down those slick magazines with rod thin models wearing thousand dollar clothes and jewelry. Alternatively, we can choose to pick up scripture for a dose of well-being and contentedness. Our minds are directly fed by what resources we select to feed them.

If we are in a funk spiraling down to gray depression, we can stop the cycle by pulling out a pad and paper and systematically listing our blessings along with the source of each: our great God. Giving credit where credit is due is a matter of focus. If we are stressing out over an upcoming major decision or occasion, we can remind ourselves that God is sovereign. Turning over the issue to God for handling drops our stress level. Thanking God in advance of his watch care and omnipotent working out of circumstances in accordance with his will is the right course. The sweetest persons on earth are the humblest—who consistently give God credit for all blessings in life.

# DECEMBER 4

## Proverbs on Finishing Well—Parenting

"Train a young man according to his way, even when he is old, he will not depart from it" (22:6).

"If your child is wise, the parent will rejoice" (12:15).

If we want to be busting our buttons at our child's high school graduation with honors, we begin the process when they are toddlers. If we want to be beaming when our beautiful children walk down the aisle to marriage, our work begins at the first tantrum. If we hope to be sobbing wholeheartedly when our child is dropped off on the first day of college, we must develop close rapport when they flash us that first infant's smile. If we want to be bragging to our friends when our grown child gets that first big promotion at work, we want to begin assigning age appropriate chores at age five.

Well-adjusted gracious children do not just spring up; they are carefully and consistently parented in a godly way according to Proverbs and other godly wisdom. Sometimes, we fear that the trials of childhood will never end, but they exit the nest faster than we can turn our heads. Pride in our children is a goal all parents aspire to, but it takes much diligent investment in time and love.

The humorous adage about treating our children well since they will be choosing our nursing home is based on solid wisdom. If we neglect our children or worse, treat them cruelly and unjustly, our golden years will nearly certainly be marred with regrets and bitterness. While we may rather be golfing on Saturday, if our child has a sports or school event, our obligation for a short eighteen years of our life is to put their activities first. Eighteen years out of a normal life span of eighty years is not much in the overall scheme of things.

# December 5

## Proverbs on Finishing Well—Governance

"Mercy and truth preserve the king and his rule is strengthened by clemency" (20:28).

"Take away wickedness from the face of the king and his throne shall be established with justice" (25:5).

Are you in a position of power? If you hope for a well thought of term, character and virtue are essential. A noble legacy, whether local or international, is based on governing in accordance with God's attributes: mercy, justice, fairness, and clemency. Leaders who are harsh, arbitrary, and self-serving may fool the public for a short while, but in the end, they will be found out. Our human natures are quick to smell a rat and injustice will "out." While kings are not the norm in this day, these verses are as true as ever in the midst of modern forms of governance. Today, laws incent whistleblowers to reveal corruption so it is even more difficult to keep rottenness hidden. In the face of instant communications and personal media, one truth teller can blow the cover off of insider misconduct.

During the Orange Revolution in Ukraine, a corrupt rigged election was uncovered by a translator for the deaf in the corner of a TV screen. While the audible reporter claimed that one person had won the election by an overwhelming landslide, the subversive incredibly brave sign language interpreter signed the truth: the challenger had really won by a landslide. The deaf community quickly notified their hearing families and friends that the audible reporting was totally false. Massive protests in the streets ensued, leading to the removal of the "elected" official. Modern citizens expect honesty and integrity from their governing officials, and violators of these principles are vulnerable to public pushback. A single tweet on Twitter can change the course of history when truth is revealed.

# DECEMBER 6

## Proverbs on Finishing Well—Legacy

"In the fear of the Lord is confidence of strength and there shall be hope for his children" (14:26).

Is your confidence level shaky or buoyant? Are your expectations for your children fearful or optimistic? If our endgame is a life well lived and great expectations for our children, step 1 is learning, meditating on, and following respect for God and his precepts. We simply cannot hope to have our life draw to a graceful close if we range "off the farm." God's path is clear; his will is evident; the character he desires is transparent. We must make a habit of consulting God and godly counselors when large life decisions loom, referring to scripture early and often.

Motivation has been said to be getting started on something; habit is about choosing the right path without agonizing over it. Integrity must become automatic in our lives. Our example will shine through loud and clear to our observant children. They are so close to us for so many years, how can we not influence them? If we are wrestling with a fork in the road, one test of correctness is envisioning how our children, when they are grown and knowledgeable about the decision, will view our choice. Our actions come to light: in the form of written records, testimony from our contemporaries and adult understanding of actions they observed in their youth.

There are wonderful and tragic stories of events coming to light during or after funerals. It is so gratifying to have our father's contemporaries recount to us as grown children the generous hidden deeds done by our parent to help others. On the other hand, how miserable we would feel to hear of cheating, double-crossing, or treachery committed by our parent during their life after their death. How do we truthfully anticipate our legacy being left?

# December 7

## Proverbs on Finishing Well—Humility

"The fruit of humility is the fear of the Lord, riches, glory and life" (22:4).

"To the meek the Lord will give grace" (3:24).

While popular culture elevates power, beauty, wealth, and ego, godly wisdom reveals the reverse. Some commentators term this phenomenon "God's upside-down economy." The Beatitudes of course embody this 180° different view of man's endeavors. The last shall be first. The meek, the poor in spirit, the humble will come out on top in God's reward system.

Who will be sitting on thrones in heaven ruling others? Not the kings of the earth who had thousands in obeisance, personal bodyguards, and Learjets—but the Mother Teresas wiping the brow of dying beggars. It is difficult to wrap our culture soaked heads around this topsy-turvy observation. We envision Christ washing the feet of his apostles in the Upper Room with a basin and towel. This one example undoubtedly stuck in the minds of those present for eternity.

The trappings of our rich and famous: perfect bodies, jet-set vacations, designer gowns, giant jewels will fade from view in the end times. On our deathbeds, we will not be reflecting on our investments and the contents of our safe deposit boxes, but our dear mother who held our head when we were throwing up with the flu when we were age five. Acts of love and service remain paramount in our minds. After suffering a death, miscarriage, or illness, it is not the largest bouquet of flowers sent that occupies our mind but the kind words, gracious note, and ordinary handmade casserole that mean the most.

Children are amazingly able to look past pretense of dress and position in life and are strongly drawn to the raggedy person in their midst who beams at them with kindness and takes the time to acknowledge their doll or blankie.

# DECEMBER 8

## Proverbs on Finishing Well—Integrity

"The robberies of the wicked shall be their downfall because they would not do justice" (21:7).

"He that deceives the just in a wicked way shall fall in his own destruction" (28:10).

Crooks prosper in the short term, but they simply fool themselves to think that crime will ultimately pay. Dishonest folk are simply blind to the rules of life as established by God. Scripture makes clear that crime will not pay in the long run. Crime is, simply put, self-destructive. Criminals or scoffers of the law either have not studied Proverbs or choose to ignore clear cut precepts.

Rebels must harden their hearts and minds so that their guilt-ridden consciences do not nag them. Rebels must have a way of dulling their minds to the truth of the natural laws of reaping/sowing. New Agers acknowledge this principle but call it "karma" or the "universe" paying back our actions.

The smallest candy bar shoplifted in junior high can infect our psyche and cause wounds in our soul unless paid back to the store owner. The cruel taunt in grade school has a damaging effect on our self-esteem unless apologized for and set right. This is one reason long term relationships are difficult: marriages, siblings' lives, and business partnerships. There are so many occasions to offend the other that can fester and get blown up unless we call a halt, apologize, make restitution, wipe the slate clean, and begin anew. Our sinful human natures cause us to stumble and fall in our interpersonal dealings, but we must clearheadedly see our failings for what they are and choose to rotate and walk aright.

Another principle we know from living is that one failing commonly leads to another; a small theft leads to a bigger one then to a major embezzlement. We must continually be vigilant to correct our characters daily.

# December 9

## Proverbs on Finishing Well—Health

"In the path of justice is life, but the byway leads to death" (12:28).

"A good name makes the bones fat" (15:30).

"Soundness of heart is the life of flesh" (14:30).

The direct correlation between soundness of mind/spirit and soundness of body is paramount and becomes clearer every year through scientific verification. God's truth in Proverbs revealed this principle thousands of years before medical science observed and confirmed it.

Who is that person with sparkling eyes who looks you directly in the eye, walks tall, and exhibits a bounce in their step? Of course, it is the vibrant person who is living to the best of their ability according to the wisdom of the Bible and knows in his/her soul that their life is flowing easily along the pathway revealed by God. "Thy will be done" is their life's motto, and their actions coincide with their speech.

In contrast, who is the person skulking around with poor posture that will barely raise his/her head to meet your eyes? This is someone who is guilt-ridden and has something to hide and whose conscience is eating them alive at night when they have chronic insomnia. That person surely has no use for God's precepts nor interest in learning or applying them.

Relationship to God is a major determinant in our vibrancy, the clarity of our conscience, and acceptance by righteous persons. We have an inborn knowledge of God, atheists notwithstanding. Our bodies and souls were created by God to operate best in synch with his precepts. Much like a worn-out tire running on a rough road, friction is generated by bumps and bruises caused by disregard of God and his rules. Such friction and tensions wear out vehicles and wears out our bodies more quickly.

# December 10

## Proverbs on Finishing Well—Wealth

"One is as it were rich when he has nothing and another as it were poor, when he has great riches" (13:7).

"Substance got in haste shall be diminished but that which little by little is gathered with the hand shall increase" (13:11).

How does one end life having enough to live comfortably? These verses make clear that "get rich quick" schemes are not the way. Contentment, steady diligent work, and saving are the keys. Do you know those always playing the lottery hoping for the big kill? Frequenting the local casino hoping to rake it up one day? These are surely not the ways to old age security. Loyal skillful toil for an employer, faithful service to a business, and consistency in life's expenditures are the correct path. Even a person "poor" in life will have enough (chapter 13) if the person's perspective is correct: dependence on God and gratitude for blessings we do have. Reliance on God for our "daily bread" is what the Lord's Prayer sets out as a good standard. Our goal should not be to hoard great portfolios to provide for every eventuality but to cultivate our relationship with God and our families so that we will be provided for in our old age.

Another way "substance is got in haste" is taking shortcuts on integrity: stealing a little here or there from our employer or our nearby relative may seem like the thing to do on a given day but is not a good strategy, short or long term. If we set arbitrary standards for our life, have $x accumulated by age twenty, thirty, or forty or make partner by age thirty-five, we usurp God's sovereignty and timing which is always perfect. Slow, honest, and steady win the race.

# December 11

## Proverbs on Finishing Well—Punishment

"Don't reject the correction of the Lord, for whom He loves He chastises as a father to a son that pleases Him" (3:11).

"He that loves correction loves knowledge. He that hates reproof is foolish" (12:1).

Our goal in life should not be to avoid all punishment. Our goal should be to think through any criticism or punishment we get and absorb it in a beneficial way to avoid the same pitfall next time. Life is a series of experiences, and we can either rail against them or analyze and learn from them.

We may not like to think of God punishing us, but we have no qualms about picturing a loving parent disciplining their toddler. Our perspectives must appear like those of a toddler to our heavenly Father. His perspective is universe high and wide, compared to our shortsightedness. If we can look back on a negative experience in life and be thankful for the warning we received which prevented a much worse consequence in future days, we are on the path to gaining wisdom. Hindsight is very helpful to us in considering the beneficial nature of a negative consequence (punishment) only if we are open-minded, observant, and not bitter. Some people rail against all negativity and fail to consider that a setback was for their ultimate benefit. Better to have a small setback early in life than a major disaster later on when dependents and subordinates are relying on us. The further we progress in life, generally, the more impact poor decisions have on us. Persons are inclined to excuse or overlook foibles of youth as "par for the course" but have no such patience with responsible adults in authority. "They should have known better." Life's lessons are best learned as we go if we are smart enough to heed the lessons.

# DECEMBER 12

## Proverbs on Finishing Well—Boasting

"Boast not for tomorrow, for you don't know what tomorrow will bring" (21:1).

"Humiliation follows the proud" (29:23).

"He that makes his house high seeks a downfall" (17:16).

Boasting is so tempting, but Proverbs is clear that it generally backfires and invites disaster. When we plan a knockout vacation, redecorate our living room, and find a killer outfit, we are so tempted to brag to our friends. But this creates envy in others and resentment of us by our friends. Moreover, it is not the life attitude God would have for us. It is unbecoming for a believer.

This is a strong temptation for many of us, but we must continually remind ourselves of the end of these three verses. We actually invite a disaster. We tempt fate and make more likely that we will have to return to that friend with our tail between our legs and report the reverse. If we can discipline ourselves to keep our lip zipped, it is much more likely that our high and mighty plans will come to fruition.

God values the humble; God wants our boasting to be in our faith in him, not new material possessions. Boasting in Christ was written about by Paul more than once in his letters, so every time the temptation to boast pops to mind, let's quickly capture that boast and convert it into a boast about our amazing God. Having something to replace a boast with seems more doable than merely suppressing it altogether. Much like smokers chew gum instead of light up, we can boast in Christ instead of our material success.

Secondly, another replacement strategy is to turn the boast into a prayer of thanks and praise to God for the blessing since God is the source of all our blessings. Let these two strategies help curb our boasting to avoid inviting disaster.

# December 13

## Proverbs on Finishing Well—Peace

"Joy follows those who take counsels of peace" (12:20).

"When the ways of man shall please the Lord, he will convert even his enemies to peace" (16:7).

When we are at peace with our family and friends, we sleep better at night. We are more relaxed and our overall quality of life, our general satisfaction level, is better. At the end of our lives, we yearn to be at peace with our loved ones and have them deeply regret our passing. If we hold grudges and are at odds with our loved ones, they may be glad at our passing. 'Taint no way to live.

What about those confirmed enemies who we can't stand and they can't stand us? Do we desire to reconcile? Do we genuinely want to improve the relationship to bring about peaceful dealings? Of course, we can earnestly pray for a breakthrough. But this verse seems to offer an effortless way to improve relations. We should mind our own conduct and conform, insofar as possible, to the precepts of God. The natural result of righteous living, the follow-on consequence, is a change of heart on the part of our enemies! That cause/effect is near miraculous and a wonderful blessing for his righteous ones.

Then the end result of peace with family, friends, and former enemies is joy. Saintly disciples exude joy in all their "doings" and "beings." Faces exhibit happy smile creases instead of frowny lines. Periodically when we are sitting alone waiting or have downtime, it would be wise to focus on those with whom we have ongoing friction; call them to mind individually, pray for reconciliation and blessings upon them, and see what happens. Our overall quality of life cannot help but be improved when our enemies are at a minimum or even nonexistent! Joy flows from peace.

# DECEMBER 14

## Proverbs on Finishing Well—Abundance

"By instruction the storerooms shall be filled with wealth" (23:4).

Do you desire to die with a large legacy to leave to your children, your church, and your alma mater? This is important to some Christians but unimportant to others. If you envision an ending like this, this verse provides the path to that scenario. Make obtaining wisdom a priority! I believe that "instruction" refers to living obediently to all God's precepts—Ten Commandments on down to Proverbs, Ecclesiastes, and Christ's New Testament Beatitudes and parables. Close study of the Bible leads to just dealings with our business partners, amicable relationships with our families, respect from our fellow church members, generosity to others that leads to paybacks, prudent, not extravagant spending, and full tithing that leads to multiplication of blessings from God (see Malachi 3). All these courses generally lead to an excess in our bank accounts and possessions.

Sometimes, it is easier to understand a point by negatives. If we ignore godly instruction and disregard godly principles, we may end up with multiple divorces and child support payments, layoffs from our jobs due to unethical practices or lack of diligence on our part, vengeance exacted by those we have wronged, prison terms due to criminal activity, empty pockets due to addictions, and the like. In short, we avoid all these pitfalls by walking the right path, the godly course for living. Boiled down, right living leads to abundance; disobedient living leads to disasters for personal relationships and goals of wealth.

Sin is a slippery slope downhill to self-destruction. Faithful living can be viewed as a slight upward path to joy, peace, and wealth. There is direct correlation between how we live our lives daily and the state of our finances. Is our number one goal to impress others? Or to live, as Thomas Yancy terms it, for an audience of one, God our Creator?

# DECEMBER 15

## Proverbs on Finishing Well—Transparency

"If you confess lack of strength, the Lord will render according to your works" (24:12).

"All the ways of a man are open to his eyes, the Lord is the weigher of spirits" (16:2).

God is omniscient; he knows our innermost thoughts. Nevertheless, he desires that we share our lives and thoughts with him in an intimate manner. Just as we are thrilled when our children bring their problems, issues, and fears to us for help, this furthers our relationship with him to intentionally "knock on his door" in a confessional manner. Doing so can be the impetus for action on his part to smooth our way and aid in resolution of our problems. The old hymn encourages us to "Take it to the Lord in prayer." This simple reminder reflects God's desire for us. He created us to be in relationship with him, and one of the practical ways to further that is to confess our troubles, our doubts, our fears, and our weaknesses to him, inviting him to come alongside us to comfort and help us. The key promise in the first verse is "will"—not might, not sometimes, not perhaps.

Similar to a close personal relationship, if we desire to become more of one mind, we should not withhold our thoughts and doubts from our friend/spouse but bring it out in the open for discussion. God can be our best friend if we will open the door and invite him in for conversation.

Conversely, if a friend finds out from another about a major event in our life that we have not shared with them, they will feel slighted. They will likely be offended that we did not take the time to include them in our misery or joy—either one. "Sharing" with God and others leads to heightened relationship and help from God.

# DECEMBER 16

## Proverbs on Finishing Well—Simplicity

"The just who walks in simplicity shall leave blessed children" (20:7).

"The Lord will protect those who walk in simplicity and guard the ways of the saints" (2:7).

These verses provide that two blessings arise from walking in simplicity, leaving behind blessed children, and receiving protection from the Lord. I believe walking in simplicity refers to obediently following the narrow way of righteousness and avoiding straying off the way into the ways of the world which are contrary to God's precepts. Simplicity perhaps also refers to childlike faith, not questioning God's laws for our lives but accepting them as truth applicable to and beneficial for our lives.

The opposite of simplicity may be continual doubting, questioning and searching for truth, ignoring the Bible and its rules for our lives. We can save a lot of grief in our lives, a lot of wasted time, a lot of dead-ends if we resolve once and for all that God's ways are best since he created us and knows us inside and out. His omniscience allows him to see our thoughts, motives, fears, and doubts. His provision for our lives in terms of clear cut direction makes our lives run more smoothly and with less anxiety. Thoroughly studying, understanding, and applying the Ten Commandments, the Proverbs and Jesus's sermons eliminates much late night tossing and turning about decisions in our lives, both large and small. The simple popular test: "What would Jesus do?" is a starting place. Another Christian maxim is: "What is the loving thing to do?" The way of love, the way of Christ, and the way of simplicity all meld into an exalted direction for our lives.

If we live righteously, our children cannot help but observe our actions and loving responses to them and those around us. Hopefully, our lives will be an inspiration and blessing to them as well.

# DECEMBER 17

## Proverbs on Finishing Well—Fat Soul

"The soul that blesses shall be made fat" (11:25).

"A merciful man does good to his own soul" (11:17).

While our culture admires thinness and detests fatness, a fat soul is one which exists in a state of abundance, always grateful for the blessings of God. A fat soul overflows with thankfulness and acknowledges the source of all goodness in our lives. Worship naturally flows out of a fat soul, spilling out on others in the vicinity, spreading goodness, peace, and love to all.

How does one come to a state of soul fatness/abundance? These verses show two paths: blessing others and exhibiting mercy. Both of these actions are other-oriented. They spring from a state of altruism—unselfishness. Outward focus on those around us as opposed to inward navel gazing follows the viewpoint of Christ.

In short, being merciful brings rewards to oneself. In contrast, hardening our hearts, harboring bitterness, and grudge holding damage our souls. Maintaining a state of unforgiveness is like a reservoir of poison in our souls, toxic to our body and spirit. Letting go of a personal injury is like a clean sweep to our inner "houses," allowing a fresh start and love to begin to regrow. "Vengeance is mine, says the Lord." It is not our job to pay back or get even. It is our Christian duty to exhibit mercy and distribute blessings as Christ himself would have done. Judging and comparing others with ourselves leads to spiteful attitudes, a sense of superiority and holier than thou. Humility recognizes that we are all God's children loved by him.

We are to be channels of grace, peace, and love. Much like channels of water flowing through, channels do not "dam up" and hold in but sweep away negativity to continually allow replenishment of our attitude with fresh grace and love—all good for our soul.

# December 18

## Proverbs on Finishing Well—Gaining in Altitude

"The path of life is above for the wise that he may decline from the lowest hell" (15:24).

"He that yields to reproof shall be glorified" (13:18).

The Christian walk leads steadily upward for the person who gains wisdom and listens to and heeds criticism. We must retain soft hearts, open to advice from godly counselors, and open to biblical teaching and wisdom. If we arrive at a place of "know-it-all," thinking we have arrived and have no need of additional wisdom, look out. This attitude hardens our hearts and forecloses additional learning. The Bible is a book of endless enlightenment. No matter how many times we read it, it offers something new and pertinent to our then current stage in life. The effect of Bible study cannot be quantified; it can operate as a balm for our souls, a goad for right living, and a convicting agent when we have gone astray. It is all things to all people.

We should resolve early in life to engage in daily Bible reading and study and never abandon such a goal. John Wesley urged us on to a life of holiness. Charles Asbury stressed the pursuit of perfection, godliness in all areas of our lives, and a continual striving for improvement to the end goal of saintliness. Sanctification is another term for the attempt to eliminate all ungodliness from our lives and to substitute righteous decisions and actions in all things.

Wisdom plus humility is the formula for gaining in altitude—toward heaven and pure holiness. The wiser we become, the more we must keep humility before our eyes as a reminder to not get too high and mighty. Low and mighty—that is the ticket—onward, upward to glory but with a humble heart.

# December 19

## Proverbs on Finishing Well—Straight On

"The wise person makes straight his steps" (15:14).

"Wisdom delivers you from the evil way and from the man that speaks perverse things and from the strange woman" (2:12).

"The prudent man bypasses evil" (27:12).

Proverbs are like signposts on the road of life. They point to right living and heaven and operate as danger signs warning of potholes, lane closures, and dead ends. An ounce of prevention is worth a pound of cure, the old saying goes. Studying, understanding, and adopting the wisdom of Proverbs clears a smooth road ahead. Temptations and sinful distractions can be easily avoided if we saturate our minds and souls with the wisdom of Solomon, whom God blessed with great wisdom following his prayer for wisdom to govern the people of Israel. Experience is a hard teacher; those suffering in that school are knocked around by disappointment, rejection, unwanted negative consequences, and bruises and wounds of all kinds. There is a way to escape most self-imposed punishment: becoming aware of Proverbs pertinent to an upcoming life decision.

Since Proverbs is scattered by topic and not organized into an easy to reference table of contents, it may be difficult to search for godly advice when needed unless one first acquires a topical Proverbs, uses biblegateway.com to look up relevant passages, or creates one's own topical list. It is easy to sort Proverbs into grouped verses by subject: a tabbed binder is an easy tool to accomplish this. Obvious topics are anger, wealth, children, speech, etc. The more we study Proverbs, the more an applicable verse leaps to mind when needed. Reading the chapter of Proverbs daily that corresponds to the day of the month is a repetitive way to ingrain them into our minds. Our goal in life should be to journey straight onward to heaven without painful detours.

# December 20

## Proverbs on Finishing Well—Right Speaking

"To speak a word in due time is like apples of gold on beds of silver" (25:11).

An apt timely word is priceless—that is the import of this verse. It is of great value. Especially later in life, we gain by age, wisdom, and experience the power to influence our children, our grandchildren, and young persons in a special way. Elder saints in our church are treated with great respect, and younger members are anxious to hear the voice of age and years of living. Even at our funeral, our legacy can be impactful and long lasting.

I'm sure each of us can recall an instance when an encouraging word came at just the right time to keep us from deep depression or giving up. A single comment echoes through our head forever. We can likely recall the exact time and place when a priceless comment was made to us. Just when we thought all was lost and no one respected our work or even took notice of our existence, a word of praise or thanks could forever brighten us.

After funerals, grieving relatives receive hundreds of sympathy cards, casseroles, and offers to help but what about six months down the road when the flood of well-wishers has trickled to a halt? Not forgetting the grief-stricken is important and our brief call, card, or visit can do wonders to restore an even keel to those who are leaning toward the deep end, the morass of grief. On the other end of life, when a couple miscarries, many feel too awkward to make a contact, but these and other unacknowledged tragedies in life must be addressed head on with tenderness and sympathy. These potential parents feel sure no one has grieved like they did; they must be reminded that things will improve and sunshine will come again.

# December 21

## Proverbs on Finishing Well—Accumulation

"Substance got in haste shall be diminished but that which little by little is gathered with the hand shall increase" (13:11).

"Some distribute their own goods and grow richer; others take away what is not their own and are always in want" (11:24).

"The blessing of the Lord makes men rich" (10:22).

The natural God-promised result of diligent labor, generosity, and right living is wealth and abundance! Some argue with the so-called prosperity gospel, but there are plenty of verses in Proverbs and elsewhere which support this principle. Get rich quick schemes are ineffective, but loyalty to a company coupled with stable regular effort is the way to prosperity. Likewise, we simply cannot out give God. If we are merciful to the poor, we "lend to the Lord and shall be repaid." Acting with compassion to others brings the blessing of the Lord. Living righteously, obedient to God's laws, keeps us in the center of his will and blessing.

"Mind your pennies and they will mind you" is a wise old saying. If we early on develop habits of saving regularly, tithing regularly, and spending prudently, our pennies will be multiplied into substantial retirement accounts. The years exponentially accumulate our small but regular savings, and while we grow old, our dollars become a comfortable cushion for our golden years. Regularity is key. But if we have come to wisdom later in life, there's no time to waste. Begin now! Study biblical principles of tithing in Malachi chapter 3, a Dave Ramsey Financial Peace University course, or another biblically-based curriculum to get on track. Generosity to others is the natural result of a tender compassionate heart; distribution of "our goods" will cause them to boomerang back into our coffers and "grow richer."

These laws to wealth are clear and well documented by anyone putting them to work for us.

# December 22

## Proverbs on Finishing Well—Greed

"He that makes haste to be rich shall not be innocent" (28:20).

"A man that makes haste to be rich and envies others is ignorant that poverty shall come upon him" (28:22).

"He that is greedy of gain troubles his own house" (15:27).

We have contemplated several verses promising gradual increase in wealth by prudent living, diligence, and tithing. These verses are their counterpoint. Greed carries with it a strong sense of impatience and the implication that we can jump ahead and increase our wealth by skirting the rules. Lying, cheating, treachery, and criminal behavior appeal to the greedy individual who cannot tolerate the patient, gradual accumulation of wealth.

Note also the reference to envy of others. Focusing on others' wealth and continually comparing our circumstances to those of the wealthier is toxic, leading to illegal shortcuts to wealth. Avoidance of envy strengthens our position and causes us to focus on ourselves, our work behavior, and our accomplishment of our duty. That is proper perspective and a healthier way of living.

"Troubling our own house" is serious business. Who wants to make their children virtual orphans by getting sent to the penitentiary? Who wants to endanger their marriage due to the public humiliation of getting "found out" after some IRS audit, corporate embezzlement scheme, or worse? Proper perspective would prioritize our families over accumulation of wealth. Families are irreplaceable; money is fungible. Money is a means to an end: comfortable living, lack of need. Families and the love they engender is what makes the world go 'round. Our homes should be havens of peace, acceptance, and grace. Greedy unethical behavior directly threatens those qualities. Our thinking must be of a long-term nature, not a short-term "get rich quick" mode. The end of comfortable wealth does not justify unethical means.

# December 23

## Proverbs on Finishing Well—Humility

"Before a man be glorified, his heart is humbled" (18:12).

"The fruit of humility is the fear of the Lord, riches, glory and life" (22:4).

"Humility goes before glory" (15:33).

If our end goal is glory in heaven and on earth, these verses show that humility is an essential first step.

There is no way around it. The most admired pastors, presidents, teachers, and politicians are those not too full of themselves. Arrogance and overweening pride put folks off. We simply cannot abide a friend or close associate—someone whose self-importance places them above all peers. While human nature puffs up our pride, God nature deflates it to humble levels. While we may not like the fact that humility precedes glory, it is simply the way the universe is constructed in God's world. We cannot escape this reality. We must understand the relationship between glory and humility and strive to squash our pride to reasonable levels.

One practical way to approach this principle is to never cease to give ultimate credit for the things of which we are proud: our gifts, our appearance, our children, our skills, to God who provides us with all things. He designed us in our mother's womb, and we can take no credit for our genes, our intelligence, our gifted hands, or our brain. While our parents may have increased our intelligence and skills by nurturing us carefully, reading to us early and often and providing us with lessons, again, gratitude should be given to our parents. Let us honor them with the respect they are due. Even those with the gift of making money easily due to business acumen must realistically assess the source of that gift. God multiplies provision to grateful creatures. As Paul wrote, if we must boast, let us boast of God and his goodness and mercy.

# DECEMBER 24

## Proverbs on Finishing Well—Obedience

"Keep the law and counsel and there shall be life to your soul and grace to your mouth" (3:22).

On this Christmas Eve, we think more of beginnings—a birth in a humble stable, an obedient Mary willing to carry a heavenly child, and a life of service to the world ending in obedient suffering on a cross. But each step in Christ's life was gained through obedience to his Father. Similarly, we as children accomplish more in life by obedience to our parents when we are toddlers, obedience to our teachers when we are in school, obedience to our coaches as we play on sports teams, and obedience to our employers when we reach the working world. Infinitely more important than those life situations, however, is lifelong obedience to our heavenly Father in his eternal wisdom.

"Keeping the law" is another way of characterizing obedience to God. Proverbs lays out many observations of human nature but also many precepts for living. Learning them at the knee of our parent or Sunday school teacher, pastor, or scout leader gets us in the correct right path for daily living in an obedient manner. Do we know how to relate to others? How to manage money? How to look ahead to avoid potholes? How to control our speech and anger? If not, we must first apply ourselves to learning the principles and, secondly, work to follow those principles. Obedience to law enforcement requests makes our life run more smoothly. Obedience to civil laws removes risk from our lives. Obedience to revealed biblical truth is like adding smooth pavement to a gravel road: it smoothens our life's way in many respects.

Youth groups are an especially good place to introduce lessons based on Proverbs before teens have gotten off track with worldly bad advice. The Christ child can inspire us to this course through his obedience.

# DECEMBER 25

## Proverbs on Finishing Well—Generosity

"He that makes presents shall purchase victory and honor" (22:9).

"A man's gift enlarges his way and makes room before princes" (18:16).

"Many honor and are friends of him that gives gifts" (19:6).

This is the season for gift giving. Of course, we give gifts to our dear family members, but at only this time of year, we remember the postman, the pastor, the teacher, and others that impact our daily lives. Churches collect gifts for the orphanage, the nursing home, and the refugees. These verses summarize, as a practical matter, the effect of gift giving. We "purchase" victory and honor, we smooth our way before VIPs, and we enlarge our list of friends. While this may sound mercenary, Proverbs in its imminently practical way is simply describing the way human nature works. Of course, we view someone more favorably who has given us a nice gift. We cannot help but think more kindly of someone who goes out of their way to choose, purchase, and wrap a thoughtful token, expensive or not.

While we may tend to deny that a gift biases us toward a person, our human nature recognizes otherwise. So we can use these principles to our advantage or not. They are undeniable. Yes, we can curry favor with our child's teacher, our prickly neighbor, or our unpleasant coworker with well-chosen gifts. Overlooking an appropriate giving opportunity likewise can alienate or exacerbate a tricky relationship. These Proverbs verses are not taking a position about whether this correlation is good or bad—they are similar laying out the way things are.

So in this season of giving, we should think carefully about gift giving and use this opportunity to show gratitude and love but also to further our dealings in the world. Human nature works that way.

# DECEMBER 26

## Proverbs on Finishing Well—Vitality

"The fear of the Lord is a fountain of life to decline from the ruin of death" (14:27).

"The mouth of the just is a vein of life" (10:11).

"Hearken to my words and incline your ear to my sayings; let them not depart from your eyes, keep them in your heart, for they are life to those who find them and health to all flesh" (4:20).

Do you aspire to be a ninety-year-old saintly ball of fire who is a blessing to many and an example to your loved ones? Most of us envision ourselves as a vibrant active senior, but how do we accomplish this? We have more impact on this outcome than we believe according to Proverbs. The term "fountain of youth" probably developed from this phrase "fountain of life." "Fear of the Lord" is an essential step toward life-giving vitality. Fear or awe of the Lord, respect for the Lord, puts us in proper perspective to our Creator. When we are in proper relationship, worship arises from gratitude to God as source of all blessings. We are "in the flow" of how earth and heaven rightly operate.

We must "hearken to his words" to gain the wisdom for righteous living, knowing how best to relate well with his other children, how to exercise self-control over our bodies, mouths, and even thoughts and how to become more Christlike as we age. "Inclining our ear" to his sayings means scheduling time in our busy lives to prioritize Bible study and acquisition of godly wisdom. Knowledge of God's law is life giving to body and soul. Associating with the just and becoming a just person ourselves leads to satisfaction and blessings—a vein of life. God's prescription for youthful countenance and body is in these verses.

# DECEMBER 27

## Proverbs on Finishing Well—Honesty

"The lip of truth shall be steadfast forever" (12:19).

"He that hates bribes shall live" (15:27).

Does dishonesty disgust you? Does a double-crosser make your stomach ache? Does a liar cause you to turn away in distress? The line between honesty and dishonesty is not gray in God's estimation. It is black and white, and blackness is something we should abhor.

If we wish to retain our job, our intact families, our respect in the world, and our sweet sleep at night, we must distinguish clearly between honesty and dishonesty and ban the latter from our thinking. It is simply not an option to "fudge" the facts or skirt the law if we want to remain "steadfast forever." If we want to extend our life, we should carefully toe the line where honesty is concerned. This issue is made light of by our popular culture, but it is extremely important to our integrity and God's view of us.

Dishonesty in the workplace, corruption in government, and little white lies to others is serious business and will shorten our life if we engage in them. To the contrary, if we assiduously maintain good character in these respects, our life will be extended. We will suffer less guilt, be less prone to punishment at all levels, and be able to hold our head high in front of our loved ones. Regret, guilt, and "should have beens" decrease, and we can age gracefully knowing we have dealt in a righteous manner.

"Living for Jesus, a life that is true" is the first line of a simple old hymn reflective of these verses. Setting an example for our children by never lying about their ages to save money on admissions could have a profound impact on generations to come. Honesty is important and has life and death impact.

# DECEMBER 28

## Proverbs on Finishing Well—Exalted

"The just run to the name of the Lord and shall be exalted" (18:10).

If we aspire to be honored on earth or heaven, this verse clarifies the path. We must cling to the name of the Lord in all circumstances. Dependence on God leads to glorification. The closer we align ourselves to God and his will for our lives, it is inevitable that we shall be honored. Learning about Jesus and living like Jesus is the route to a good end to our lives. Funerals of righteous people glorify the deceased and God. When we walk out of the service, we find ourselves inspired to live likewise. Even the grieving loved ones find themselves satisfied with their memories of the saintly one and hopeful for a certain heavenly reunion. Regrets are fewer, good memories are sweeter, and hopes are magnified when a life well lived in Christ is described.

Let's not overlook "the just." This characterizes a righteous person who shows mercy when it is appropriate, fairness in all things, equality of treatment of God's children, and right relations with acquaintances. *Just* is equivalent to *righteous, godly, obedient,* and *holy.*

When bad things happen on earth, the first thought of the godly person is to seek help from God, turning over the problem for handling. While we must work diligently to accomplish actions within our knowledge and purview, if there is uncertainty about how to proceed forward, God is the source of our wisdom and inspiration. It is surprising how often praying just before sleep brings about a clear solution upon awakening. God shows us the way and takes over the "night shift" when we lay down our heads.

Our chief aim in life should be to live obedient to God's precepts, but exaltation is the promised result.

# December 29

## Proverbs on Finishing Well—Flourishing

"The tabernacles of the just shall flourish" (14:11).

"The fear of the Lord is unto life and he shall abide in abundance without being visited by evil" (19:23).

If we hope to have a home bursting with blessings, love, grace, peace, hospitality, and beauty, our conduct in life can bring about that outcome. Do you truly believe that there is a direct relationship between our behavior and conduct and the state of our abode? These verses state so. Safety and abundance prevail where we have due respect for God and his wisdom. Proverbs 1 opens with wisdom, begins with fear of the Lord. This is the bedrock starting place for all blessings in life: acknowledgment of the source of all. While we may rationalize that it was our hard work and self-discipline through the years that steadily built up a bank account so that we may hospitably entertain others with an open hand, God is the one who gave us the power to earn money, the body, and intelligence to succeed at our jobs.

Safety and security are implicit in the phrase "without being visited by evil." We can place confidence in our future, be free from worry, and faithfully hope in finishing well in this life and the next. We do not have to lie awake at night fretting about potential home invasion, fire, storm, or other disaster. If they occur, we can rely on God and the kindness of church members and social organizations to help us get back on our feet. This verse demonstrates the unlikelihood that disasters will occur when we have our life in order.

"Flourishing" is more than mere safety and security. It speaks of abundance, joy, peace, and blessing to all living within. What a wonderful promise to focus on!

# December 30

## Proverbs on Finishing Well—Beloved

"He that follows justice is beloved by the Lord." 15:9

The ultimate blessing is to be beloved by the Lord. Following justice is a necessary condition. Again, justice nearly equates with living righteously and treating our fellow children of God with respect and dignity due them by virtue of that status alone. Justice is spoken of frequently by the Old Testament prophets: Isaiah, Micah, Jeremiah and others. In an age when wars, treachery, assassinating one's enemies and taking advantage of widows and orphans without government safety nets was nearly the norm, justice was held up as a lofty goal to pursue. Over and over, prophets railed against injustice and urged the people of Israel to differentiate themselves from the surrounding peoples by this characteristic. What does the Lord require? To walk humbly with our Lord and treat others with justice.

Since justice is a primary characteristic of God, if we aspire to pattern our lives after Him, we must necessarily adopt this characteristic in our own lives. Even in this day, exhibiting justice will make us stand out from our culture and glorify the name of Christ. God desires for us to be a witness for Him by living a just life and he will love us for doing so. Being beloved by the Lord is a high aspiration—it is difficult to envision a higher goal in life. Teaching our children, grandchildren and students to be fair in all things will pave the way for them to likewise be beloved by God. Even in elementary schools today when the name of God can barely be uttered, values of kindness, fairness and truthfulness are being taught as secular values. Once they are ingrained in little minds, hopefully these values will not depart from them and they will come to ultimately understand the source of those values.

# DECEMBER 31
## Proverbs on Finishing Well—Examples

"The wicked man, being beaten, the fool shall be wiser. If you rebuke a wise man, he will understand discipline" (19:25).

"When a bad man is punished, the little one will be wiser" (21:11).

We do not have to personally suffer all the slings and arrows of life to gain in wisdom. If we are wise, we will be observant in all areas of life and learn from others. Even small children can heed life's lessons early on when they see negative consequences abound to others. Sometimes, events make a greater impression on children than life-hardened adults. We are given eyes and ears to closely observe life's events and avoid falling into the same trap.

When a student sees another being sent to the office, suspended or expelled, she/he doesn't have to experience the negative consequences personally to learn the lesson. The wiser the person, the more closely attuned to the world and its lessons we will be. The powers of observation we are given are great if we will heed them. We do not have to be arrested and thrown into prison to avoid committing crimes; we can read about this cause and effect relationship in the newspaper every day. While cheaters may win in the short term, treachery "outs." The short-term gain is never outweighed by the long-term punishment and damage to reputation. This truth can be clearly seen by the observant.

Whether in grade school, high school, college, or the workplace, the principle of crime doesn't pay is transferable. We reap what we sow is a similar truth embodied in Proverbs and elsewhere in scripture. Even New Agers acknowledge this "principle of the universe" which is more accurately attributed to God our Creator. There's no need to gain firsthand knowledge of this; secondhand knowledge is just as convincing.

# ABOUT THE AUTHOR

Ruth Sears has been fascinated by literature but particularly the book of Proverbs for many years. She graduated from Lathrop, Missouri, high school as valedictorian. She attended Central Methodist University with a Bachelor of Arts degree in English literature and business, graduating summa cum laude. She then obtained a juris doctor in law degree from the University of Missouri. While there, she served as an editor of the Missouri Law Review and had articles published in the Review.

Ruth has written all her life, working first as a law clerk for the Hon. Robert T. Donnelly of the Missouri supreme court. Thereafter, she was employed by Southwestern Bell Legal Department in Topeka, Kansas, St. Louis, Missouri, and Dallas, Texas, retiring from the reorganized AT&T after a thirty-year career of litigation, appellate work, and in-house corporate counseling. Her writing/editorial work consisted primarily of brief writing, drafting of legal memos and contracts, and review of corporate marketing publicity and training materials.

Since her retirement, she volunteers at her local church, leads domestic mission trips annually, teaches GED through the Rockwall Library, travels widely, reads voraciously, attends movies weekly as a tried and true movie buff, walks and swims. She is a delegate to the North Texas United Methodist Church annual conference each summer. Ruth is married to a retired attorney who loves to fly his Cessna. They have two grown children. She and her husband and reside in Texas and Kansas.

She is a perpetual student and has been a voracious long time reader of devotionals, commentaries, religious books, philosophy, quotations, Great Courses, and other wisdom resources. Ruth reads Proverbs daily and commends it to young and old alike.

CPSIA information can be obtained
at www.ICGtesting.com
Printed in the USA
FFHW022039240919
55177884-60925FF